TOURISM ENCOUNTERS AND CONTROVERSIES

New Directions in Tourism Analysis

Series Editor: Dimitri Ioannides, E-TOUR, Mid Sweden University, Sweden

Although tourism is becoming increasingly popular as both a taught subject and an area for empirical investigation, the theoretical underpinnings of many approaches have tended to be eclectic and somewhat underdeveloped. However, recent developments indicate that the field of tourism studies is beginning to develop in a more theoretically informed manner, but this has not yet been matched by current publications.

The aim of this series is to fill this gap with high quality monographs or edited collections that seek to develop tourism analysis at both theoretical and substantive levels using approaches which are broadly derived from allied social science disciplines such as Sociology, Social Anthropology, Human and Social Geography, and Cultural Studies. As tourism studies covers a wide range of activities and sub fields, certain areas such as Hospitality Management and Business, which are already well provided for, would be excluded. The series will therefore fill a gap in the current overall pattern of publication.

Suggested themes to be covered by the series, either singly or in combination, include – consumption; cultural change; development; gender; globalisation; political economy; social theory; sustainability.

Also in the series

Tourism and Violence
Edited by Hazel Andrews
ISBN 978-1-4094-3640-9

Tourism, Performance, and Place
A Geographic Perspective
*Jillian M. Rickly-Boyd, Daniel C. Knudsen, Lisa C. Braverman,
and Michelle M. Metro-Roland*
ISBN 978-1-4094-3613-3

Volunteer Tourism
Popular Humanitarianism in Neoliberal Times
Mary Mostafanezhad
ISBN 978-1-4094-6953-7

Tourism, Recreation and Regional Development
Perspectives from France and Abroad
Edited by Jean-Christophe Dissart, Jeoffrey Dehez and Jean-Bernard Marsat
ISBN 978-1-4724-1622-3

Tourism Encounters and Controversies

Ontological Politics of Tourism Development

Edited by

GUNNAR THÓR JÓHANNESSON
University of Iceland, Iceland

CARINA REN
Aalborg University, Denmark

RENÉ VAN DER DUIM
Wageningen University, Netherlands

Routledge
Taylor & Francis Group

LONDON AND NEW YORK

First published 2015 by Ashgate Publishing

2 Park Square, Milton Park, Abingdon, Oxfordshire OX14 4RN
711 Third Avenue, New York, NY 10017

Routledge is an imprint of the Taylor & Francis Group, an informa business

First issued in paperback 2017

British Library Cataloguing in Publication Data
A catalogue record for this book is available from the British Library

The Library of Congress has cataloged the printed edition as follows:
Tourism encounters and controversies : ontological politics of tourism development / edited
cby Gunnar Thór Jóhannesson, Carina Ren and René van der Duim.
    pages cm. -- (New directions in tourism analysis)
  Includes bibliographical references and index.
  ISBN 978-1-4724-2436-5 (hardback)
  1. Tourism--Political aspects. 2. Tourism--Politcal aspects--Case studies. 3. Actor-
  -network theory. I. Jóhannesson, Gunnar Thór, editor of compilation. II. Ren,
  Carina, editor of compilation. III. Duim, René van der, editor of compilation.
  G155.A1T59174 2015
  910.68'4--dc23

                                                                    2014044658

ISBN 978-1-4724-2436-5 (hbk)
ISBN 978-0-8153-7804-4 (pbk)

Contents

List of Figures and Tables

Figures

Tables

Notes on Contributors

Martijn Duineveld works at the Cultural Geography chair group at Wageningen University. He is interested in the dynamics of power, people and places. His current research is particularly inspired and influenced by Michel Foucault and more generally by anthropology, and cultural and political geography. His research activities mainly focus on Evolutionary Governance Theory and the contentious nature of place and the various ways citizens, planners and landscape architects use their power to influence the landscape. He is active in both academic and societal debates on citizenship, spatial planning and democratization. Contact: martijn.duineveld@wur.nl

Richard Ek is associate professor at the Department of Service Management and Service Studies (Lund University). In 2003 he concluded his Ph.D. at the Department of Social and Economic Geography, Lund University. He has published on such topics as critical geopolitics, biopolitics, tourism and hospitality studies, and media and communication studies. His current research interests include the politics of social media, the topology of waste and the cultural imagination of nonhuman creatures in contemporary capitalism. Contact: richard.ek@ism.lu.se

Anne-Kirstine Bøcher Ellern is an independent information designer. She holds a Master of Arts (MA) in Design from the Royal Danish Academy of Fine Arts and works with data visualization, participatory design and public engagement in a broad range of projects. Contact: hi.akellern@gmail.com

Anniken Førde is Associate Professor at the Department of Sociology, Political Science and Community Planning at UiT The arctic University of Norway. Her research interests include tourism, innovation and changing landscapes. Among her publications are co-edited books on interdisciplinarity, innovative communities and methodology of place analyses. Contact: anniken.forde@uit.no

Edward H. Huijbens is a geographer and a researcher at the Icelandic Tourism Research Centre which is jointly run by the University of Iceland, University of Akureyri and Hólar University College along with the Travel Industry Association and the Icelandic Tourist Board. Edward also holds a professor position at the Department of Business at the University of Akureyri. Edward has edited four books and published one monograph and one co-authored book on Icelandic tourism. Edward's research interests are geo-philosophy, landscapes, health and wellbeing and innovation. Edward has published his works in journals such as

Annals of Tourism Research, Environment and Planning D, Current Issues in Tourism, Tourism Geographies, Journal of Sustainable Tourism and Scandinavian Journal of Tourism and Hospitality Research. Contact: edward@unak.is

Gunnar Thór Jóhannesson is Associate Professor at the Department of Geography and Tourism, University of Iceland. His research interests are in the areas of entrepreneurship in tourism, tourism policy and destination development as well as research methodologies. He is a co-editor of *Actor-Network Theory and Tourism: Ordering, materiality and multiplicity*, published in 2012 with Routledge and has published his work in journals including *Tourist Studies, Tourism Geographies, Scandinavian Journal of Hospitality and Tourism* and *Current Issues in Tourism*. Contact: gtj@hi.is

Rico Lie is a social anthropologist working at the research group Knowledge, Technology and Innovation, Wageningen University, The Netherlands. He previously worked at the University of Brussels in Belgium and the Universities of Nijmegen and Leiden in The Netherlands. At Wageningen University he is an assistant professor in international communication with an interest in the areas of development communication and intercultural communication. Contact: Rico.Lie@wur.nl

Senna Middelveld is a PhD student at the University of Aberdeen and The James Hutton Institute. Her current interests are in human-animal relations and in particular farm-animal disease. Inspired by actor-network theory, intra-action, and posthumanism she studies multiple realities of sheep scab in Scotland. Contact: senna.middelveld@gmail.com

Claudio Minca is Head and Professor of the Cultural Geography Department at Wageningen University. He is also Visiting Professor at the University of London, at the University of Colorado in Boulder, and at Rikkyo University, Tokyo. His current research centres on three major themes: tourism and travel theories of modernity; the spatialisation of (bio)politics; and the relationship between modern knowledge, space and landscape in postcolonial geography. His most recent books are *On Schmitt and Space* (with R. Rowan, 2014), *Moroccan Dreams* (with L. Wagner, 2014), *Real Tourism* (with T. Oakes, 2011), *Social Capital and Urban Networks of Trust* (with J. Hakli, 2009) and *Travels in Paradox* (with T. Oakes, 2006). Contact: claudio.minca@wur.nl

Anders Kristian Munk is Associate Professor in the Techno-Anthropology group, Aalborg University Copenhagen, and a visiting research fellow at the SciencesPo médialab in Paris. His research focuses on public knowledge controversies and the role of experts in contemporary democracy. He is actively engaged in developing new digital methods for the social sciences and humanities. Anders holds a Ph.D. in Human Geography from the University of Oxford. Contact: akm@learning.aau.dk

Chin-Ee Ong is Assistant Professor at the Cultural Geography Group in Wageningen University. His research focuses on power-knowledge and governmentality in travel, tourism and urban spaces and is largely based on fieldwork in China, Macao, Singapore and the Netherlands. Contact: chinee.ong@wur.nl

Arjaan Pellis is a research assistant with the Cultural Geography group, Wageningen University. He studies whether and how community conservation can be made possible through wilderness based tourism. His case studies have leaded him from Namibia towards similar initiatives taking shape within Kenya, Spain and Portugal. His current research follows the mobility of ideas, production of success, and impacts of tourism upon rural livelihoods. Contact: arjaan.pellis@wur.nl

Felicity Picken is a lecturer in tourism and heritage at the University of Western Sydney, Australia. Her research develops and explores the phenomenon she calls blue tourism and leisure including diving, undersea hotels, museums and art galleries as well as the domesticating of oceanic life to land in aquaria and through mythology. Finding in the ocean a perfect relational materiality, her work seeks to develop these kind of methodologies and to understand the role of pleasurable encounters in performing closer relations with the blue planet. Contact: F.Picken@uws.edu.au

Carina Ren is Associate Professor at the Tourism Research Unit at Aalborg University. Her main research interests are encounters and cultural innovation in tourism, which she ethnographically explores at branding initiatives, in destination development and through mega-events taking a material, relational and multiplicity-oriented approach. She is a co-editor of *Actor-Network Theory and Tourism. Ordering, Materiality and Multiplicity* (2012). She has published her work in journals such as *Annals of Tourism Research, Tourist Studies, Scandinavian Journal of Hospitality* and *Tourism and Ethnologia Europaea*. Contact: ren@cgs.aau.dk

Valerio Simoni received his PhD from Leeds Metropolitan University (UK). After four years as Postdoctoral Researcher at the Centre for Research in Anthropology in Lisbon (Portugal), he is now Research Fellow at the Graduate Institute in Geneva (Switzerland). His current researches, grounded in ethnographic fieldwork in Cuba and Spain, focus on enactments of friendship, love, sex, and commerce in international tourism, the tourism-migration nexus, and the controversial entanglements between intimate and economic relationships. His work has been published in edited books and journals in the fields of anthropology and tourism studies, and his first monograph is due to come out with Berghahn in 2015. Contact: valerio.simoni@graduateinstitute.ch

Lauren Wagner is a Researcher/Lecturer in the Cultural Geography group at Wageningen University. She is part of the Mobilities cluster there, focusing on issues of migration, tourism and leisure. Her research activities focus on emergent categorizations, group belonging, and assemblage in social life. Contact: lauren. wagner@wur.nl

René van der Duim currently works as a Professor of Tourism and Sustainable Development at the Cultural Geography Group at Wageningen University, the Netherlands. His research interests are tourism, conservation and development with a particular interest in Eastern Africa. He is a co-editor of *Actor-Network Theory and Tourism: Ordering, materiality and multiplicity*, published in 2012 with Routledge and has published his work in journals such as *Annals of Tourism Research*, *Journal of Sustainable Tourism*, *Tourist Studies*, *Tourism Geographies*, *Society & Natural Resources* and *Conservation and Society*. He is also chair of the European Association for Leisure and Tourism Education and Research, ATLAS. Contact: rene.vanderduim@wur.nl

Chapter 1

Tourism Encounters, Controversies and Ontologies

Gunnar Thór Jóhannesson, Carina Ren and René van der Duim

1.1 Introduction

In order to address long lasting human–wildlife conflicts and persistent poverty around Bwindi, a small national park in the south-west of Uganda, gorilla tourism was introduced in 1993 (Ahebwa, 2012). The purchase of a US$ 500 permit now enables especially wealthy tourists from the North to visit the gorillas in their natural habitat. Through complex processes of habituation, in which they are getting used to the presence of human beings, gorillas are turned into 'objects of the tourist gaze' and acquire economic value. However, even before this new relationship to tourism and tourists, gorillas have also enacted other networks. For centuries, gorillas of Bwindi have co-existed with and competed for forest resources with hunter-food gathering and farming communities. From the late nineteenth century onwards, they were captured, studied and designated as "man's closest neighbor" in a scientific network of biologists. Also, they eventually became "trophies" in an international hunting network or were poached and – as a reaction to that – protected as "endangered species" in a conservation network, initiated by the work of Dianne Fossey (see Van der Duim, Ampumuza and Ahebwa, 2014)

At this point in time, gorilla tourism has registered considerable success and has gained durability; predominantly by enrolling heterogeneous actors into a complex network. These are tourists with their dollars, travel documents, permits, cameras and other equipment, but also neighboring communities that connect to it through a variety of tourism revenue schemes and direct and indirect employment (see Ahebwa, Van der Duim and Sandbrook, 2012a; 2012b; Ahebwa and Van der Duim, 2013a; 2013b). However, the gorilla tourism network has also remained fluid, as various episodes of instability and controversy burst out. Some are minor incidents or occurrences, others are manifested in continuous negotiations or discourses over a period of time, while there are even examples of hardcore and violent conflicts. Scientists have for instance contested gorilla tourism, pointing at the possible health risks for gorillas due to their encounters with tourists (Sandbrook and Semple, 2006). Laudati (2010, p.726) describes how Bwindi has become 'a product of wilderness, a wild and unspoiled destination marketed to foreign visitors', arguing 'that the "new" relations between people and parks created under ecotourism in Bwindi have in actuality created new forms of control and vulnerabilities'. In 1999, the Interahamwe (a Hutu paramilitary organization) attacked and kidnapped a group of 14 tourists in Bwindi. Eight of the tourists were eventually killed. The story was featured in *National Geographic* with the result that gorilla tourism was clogged for quite a period of time. Last but not least, stability is also threatened by the gorillas themselves as they continue to move outside the park boundaries where they are sometimes killed (Laudati, 2010).

Obviously, this example shows that gorilla tourism is about tourism. But at the same time, it highlights its relations to other things. Following gorilla tourism leads to a number of discourses (on the relation between humans and nature, and between conservation and tourism), to a variety of places and localities (scientific laboratories, zoos, lodges, villages, the forest, the international tourism market), to documents (legislative documents, permits, agreements with communities), objects (guns, dollars, snares, fires), organizations (like the International Gorilla Conservation Programme or the Uganda Wildlife Authority) and people (park staff, iconic conservationists like Leakey or Fossey, international tourists, tour operators, the Batwa and other locals) and to traditional livelihood, hunting, conservation, scientific, and tourism practices (see Van der Duim, Ampumuza and Ahebwa, 2014).

The same applies to this book, which is a book on tourism and tourism research. But it is also about other things. Mostly, it is about the different ways in which tourism interferes with, is shaped by and is entangled to "other things" such as money, future scenarios, food networks, coral reefs, cod fish and casinos and about the implications of such encounters and thus also how tourism is by itself an ordering force (Franklin, 2004; 2012). Our starting point and unifying argument of all the chapters of this volume is that tourism is a relational phenomenon. Tourism comes about and contributes to shaping our world through relational encounters and entanglements of diverse orders. Tourism not only affects and enacts particular "tourism actors" at destinations, such as the gorillas and local communities described above, but even the Earth itself (Huijbens and Gren, 2012). In this book, we wish to explore some of the entanglements of tourism to other things. More precisely, we wish to engage with the diverse ways by which tourism, for instance as a social practice or a business activity, impacts upon and is impacted by other ordering attempts and thus how tourism and "other things" co-constitute each other and work to co-produce the social and the Earth.

Our objective is to move from nouns to verbs (Law, 2009), when we think through the implications of tourism. This means that we must shift our attention from researching and understanding what tourism *is*, to focus on how tourism *works*, how it is accomplished in different relations and how it leads to different impacts. This argument grows out of concerns with how the boundaries between usual organizing concepts of tourism research, tourism experiences and businesses such as the tourist and the host, supply side and demand side, home and away are becoming more and more blurred. As also exemplified in mobility and performativity-inspired studies of tourism (Sheller and Urry, 2004; Larsen, 2008), it is questionable to what degree such distinctions and binaries remain useful to describe tourism in all of its complex richness.

We follow Latour and contend that classical critique of tourism has "run out of steam" (Latour, 2010). If the usual building blocks of the tourist system no longer appear stable and the distinction between production and consumption, home and away, host and guest is becoming increasingly blurred, it is impossible to draw 'precise boundaries' (Latour, 2010, p.473). We therefore cannot build our critique on the possible 'discovery of a true world of realities lying behind a veil of appearances' (Latour, 2010, p.475); we need to find alternative ways to address tourism development in critical ways. One way to do that, we suggest, is to approach it through a relational approach and in terms of ordering.

As a mode of ordering, tourism indeed (re)arranges people, things, technologies, discourses and values in certain, rather than other ways (Franklin, 2004; 2012). However, tourism is not a single mode of ordering. As conveyed by the example of gorilla tourism and many of the chapters of this book, tourism is materially and socially working on the world order in multiple ways, blurring hitherto clear definitions while also creating new and sometimes unexpected boundaries. As a consequence, the implications of tourism are palpable, also in areas which are seemingly external to tourism proper.

While we acknowledge the felt scholarly need and urge until now to carve out an academic space and tools for investigating tourism *in its own right*, we believe that time has come to tear down some of the often restraining disciplinary, methodological, as well as mental, barriers which have characterized much of the research on tourism. There is no such object as tourism lying and waiting for us to experience as consumers or describe as detached academics. As we hope to show in this book, tourism comes about through relational encounters. As such, it is a thing which comes about along multiple lines or threads of life (Ingold, 2008). Ingold draws on Heidegger in his description of the difference between things and objects. In his words: 'The object stands before us as a *fait accompli,* presenting its congealed, outer surfaces to our inspection. [...] The thing, by contrast, is a "going on", or better, a place where several goings on become entwined' (Ingold, 2008, p.6). The thing denotes a gathering, in its ancient meaning (Heidegger, 1951 cited in Latour and Weibel, 2005; and see Pálsson, 2005). While an object can thus be conceived of as a billiard ball that only moves or has agency due to an external force (Emirbayer, 1997; Ingold, 2008) the 'thing has the character [...] of a knot whose constituent threads, far from being contained within it, trail beyond, only to become caught with other threads in other knots' (Ingold, 2008, p.6). Thereby a thing grows or emerges through relational movement that may or may not be ordered into a more or less stabilized form. As we argue in this book, tourism works in such emerging ways, which as we argue, may be studied for instance by taking a closer look at the encounters and controversies were extra concern and attention is devoted to its ordering. We will get back to this shortly.

The study of tourism should therefore not be a rehearsal in pinpointing, delimiting or confining it to one specific area or one kind of research, development approach or management model. Rather, a study of tourism should strive to show ways by which it affects and is affected by various other entities, hence not being a study *of* tourism as an object but rather *through* and *with* tourism understood as a creative and formative process (Ingold, 2008; 2011).

By redirecting the scope from what tourism is (or is not) to how it is made to work, "external" entities are brought to the fore (Callon, 1999). The act of ordering, be it developing alternative methodological approaches to describe tourism or management models to run tourism businesses, always creates externalities that potentially lead to or are manifested in controversies. Rather than reaffirming boundaries between tourism "itself" and "external" conditions, field or actors, we wish to underscore the old anthropological insight that boundaries are the product of relations, but not vice versa (Barth, 1969). Hence, we would like to display how 'everything is entangled with everything else' (Law and Singleton, 2013, p.490) and approach the interferences between different orderings and agendas as generative events (Whatmore, 2009; Mol and Law, 2002; Vertesi, 2014). Such an approach draws attention to how relational ordering has ontological implications, as we will discuss further below.

This chapter proceeds by situating further the general approach of the book and points out some of the derived directions and implications. We first clarify how the notions of encounters and controversies can be described in relational terms. We do so from the approach of (post-)Actor–Network Theory, which has previously been our inspiration to deal with the relationality of tourism (Van der Duim, Ren and Jóhannesson, 2012; 2013). This discussion feeds into a section that addresses the epistemological challenges raised by a relational approach to tourism. The third and last part of this section presents the chapters of the book.

1.2   Tourism Encounters and Controversies: a Relational Approach

By affording and providing the grounds for the unfolding of a plethora of activities and interests by a vast array of actors, tourism continuously conjures controversies. This has been a particular object of study within tourism for decades. Already in 1975, Turner and Ash (1975) discussed the impacts of tourism in their famous book *The Golden Hordes*, arguing that 'international tourism is like King Midas in reverse: a device for the systematic destruction of everything that is beautiful in the world' (p.15). More recently, in their book *Tourism Controversies*, Mouffakir and Burns (2012) discuss controversies related to the impacts of tourism on people and places and show the way particular forms of tourism (hunting tourism, gaming, volunteer tourism, aboriginal tourism or mass tourism) have been subject to debate and polemics centering on processes of commodification, authenticity, participation or limits to growth. Also, the seminal *Hosts and Guests* edited by Smith (1989), as well as Boissevain's (1996) edited volume *Coping with mass tourism. European reactions to mass tourism*, are examples of how the business, development and social activity of tourism are most often framed and perceived as battlefields of differences where the struggles are set between inherently different or oppositional hosts and guests with the tourism developers, entrepreneurs or local authorities as occasional controversy side-kicks (see also Shepherd, 2002).

In order to by-pass a common notion of encounters as clashes between two or more clearly separated orders (Emirbayer, 1997), we move away in this book from impact related controversies and take a next step by providing specific examples of how to study and situate contested events related to tourism in terms which do not replicate and reconfirm it as a clash between (fixed) identities, between insiders and outsiders, between a static or objectified local culture and mobile global flow of tourism, between "internal" and "external" stakeholders of various sorts, between "hosts and guests" or "nature" and "culture". Rather, encounters and controversies are investigated from a poststructuralist and relational approach as complex and emerging, and the roles and characteristics of related actors as co-constituted.

This approach is in line with recent discussion of controversy within science and technology studies (Venturini, 2010; 2012) and geography (Whatmore, 2009). According to Venturini controversy begins 'when actors discover that they cannot ignore each other and controversies end when actors manage to work out a solid compromise to live together. Anything between these two extremes can be called a controversy' (2010, p.261). As creative or generative events, controversies emerge through ordering attempts and arguably offer us 'the best available occasion to observe the social world in its *making*' (Venturini, 2010, p.263, original emphasis; and see Jóhannesson, Ren, Van der Duim and Munk, 2014).

According to this approach, it is by studying relational encounters and controversies that we can partially describe the making of realities or what Ingold (2000) describes as weaving of the world. Relational encounters and controversies in tourism manifest, in other words, the *doing* of tourism and its entanglement to other things. They result from alternative efforts of competing orderings, which frame and enact realities that have multiple implications. They can reach a temporary stabilization and even become an institutionalized social phenomenon between different groups (see Pellis, Duineveld and Wagner in this volume). But still, they should be taken as growing out of heterogeneous relational encounters and as such continuously taking shape as well as shaping future encounters.

This view assigns primacy to processes of formation as opposed to their final products, and to flows and transformations as against states of matter. Importantly, this move does not mean that less attention is given to power relations and politics. On the contrary, we seek to shed light on the complex and political nature of tourism development (see also Jolivet and Heiskanen, 2010), slowing down the process of knowing through tracing the ontological movements of the world. Instead of starting off with predefined entities that more or less clash with each other, a relational approach follows the connections and encounters that may potentially lead to controversy and formation of entities that can be defined as oppositional.

In this book, power appears as a thoroughly relational accomplishment (Latour, 1986) and the spaces of political activities as multiple (Amin, 2004). Every constituent – humans, materials, technologies, buildings – of what we denote as tourism or as another ordering attempt – conservation, development, policy – is a relational accomplishment. The trajectories of diverse constituents are bundled together in diverse topological combinations (see Ingold, 2008). Power and politics relate to how such "bundling" can be affected, ordered and even managed. Lury, Parisi and Terranova (2012) argue that at present we live in a topological society where 'movement – as the ordering of continuity – composes the forms of social and cultural life themselves' (p.6). This is the description of a globalized society where 'it is the mutable quality of relations that determines distance and proximity, rather than a singular and absolute measure' (Harvey, 2012, p.78). It follows that who, or what, is included or excluded in every ordering attempt depending on heterogeneous relations and thus it is imperative to follow, engage with and describe how different modes of relational ordering matter.

This type of research focuses on how ontologies are or may be constructed and enacted in different ways, and how their "overflows" and encounters resulting from multiple tourism and non-tourism enactments, evoke controversies. Hence, it diverts from a predominantly management-oriented view which highly influences, some may argue, current research into tourism, to a multiplicity-oriented approach (Law and Hassard, 1999; Vikkelsø, 2007). Such an engagement enables us to examine and describe the fluxes and flows of many different networks and the enactment of multiple versions of for instance destinations or things, which may seem singular at first (Ren, 2009; 2011). It also opens up for critically addressing how certain (e.g. managerial, political, conservationist or cultural) practices are part of the enactment of certain realities rather than others, but also how different tourism realities and orderings may co-exist and how ultimately, tourism is not and can never become a singular, unambiguous or hegemonic practice.

In relation to the tourist destination, the heterogeneous and fluid processes of enacting not one, but several, realities, challenge common management strategies, which tend to mainstream images and performances, often seeking to create and promote one "unique" selling point by dismissing and muting "destination mess" (Ren and Blichfeldt, 2011). The appreciation of diverse and interwoven modes of ordering also point at the possibility that flexible and fluid development projects that are kept open to diverse connections may be more robust than those dependent on single modes of ordering (Jóhannesson and Bærenholdt, 2008). In a broader perspective, sensitivity towards the material and enacted character of our field of study potentially provides us with a more nuanced understanding of the relations and entities which construct and enable tourism, its actors, objects, cultures and identities, not only in research, but also in the daily practices of managing and promoting the destination.

As stated by Mol (1999) 'the reality we live with is one performed in a variety of practices' (p.74). The implication of such an understanding is that we are not only confronted with different realities created through practices and objects, but also with the option and possibility to choose between them. As Law and Urry note, ontological politics ultimately refer to the question of 'which realities might we try to enact?' (2004, p.396). This is a question we as researchers have to deal with as we go along describing realities in the making. We suggest that it is necessary to slow down our reasoning and research practices (Stengers, 2005; Law and Singleton, 2013) and find ways to account for our work *on* the world as well as our work *in* the world (Law and Singleton, 2013).

1.3   Studying and Enacting Relational Encounters and Controversies

Studying tourism related ordering attempts and the complex socio-material ontology of tourism not only provides close descriptions of how tourism works, but also how the social is constantly emergent and ripe with creative capacities. As Franklin (2004, p.277) argues, tourism has come 'to be a heterogeneous assemblage "at large" in the world, remaking the world anew as a touristic world; a world to be seen, felt, interpellated and travelled'. It is particularly the understanding that researching the social through a concept of tourism is a way to enact the social in a certain way, which we seek to underline and further explore in the present work.

The chapters of this book both illustrate "the making of" tourism realities and yield insights into continuous ordering of the social. The contributing authors not only analyze these encounters and controversies and their effects and implications, but also point to how they may be studied and dealt with in the future. From a relational approach, the ontological and epistemological cannot be clearly separated. As researchers, we are in the business of making particular kinds of realities or worlds more real, other versions are made less so and thus being "othered" (Law, 2004). So, through our processes of knowing we are also engaged in making. There is no innocent method, every method is a framing device, an intervention (Jespersen, et al., 2012) internalizing particular connections at the expense of others. By paying attention to how our research impacts and intervenes into our fields of study, this book raises awareness of how research and knowledge creation is *also* always a matter of doing ontological politics. In the following, we therefore shortly discuss how controversies are brought to the fore in and through research practices and the implications of such a foregrounding.

Tourism controversies not only center on different framings and discourses of people and organizations, but often target at or materialize in contested objects, technologies, spaces and artefacts. We find a post-ANT approach with focus on materiality a useful feature for studying controversies. The (extended) principal of symmetry put forward in ANT insists on treating humans and non-humans equally *in analysis*. The principal of symmetry does not reject the existence of particular categories. Rather, it highlights that their existence is not *a priori*, but effects of an ongoing and cumbersome ordering work carried out by heterogeneous actors. In relation to tourism, handling 'humans and artefacts on a symmetrical footing' (Gad and Jensen, 2010, p.67) broadens the spectrum of what tourism is, who its actors are and what controversies are about.

Seeing tourism not as a material world but a world of materials – an earthly world, of matter in flux – we can follow these materials and how they become actors-enacted (Law and Mol, 2008). As Ingold (2008, p.14) argues:

[T]o follow these materials is to enter into a world that is, so to speak, continually on the boil. Indeed, rather than comparing it to a giant museum or department store, in which objects are arrayed according to their attributes or provenance, it might be more helpful to imagine the world as a huge kitchen, well stocked with ingredients of all sorts. In the kitchen, stuff is mixed together in various combinations, generating new materials in the process which will in turn become mixed with other ingredients in an endless process of transformation.

Seeing tourism as an effect of as well as an addition to a blistering world 'in an endless process of transformation' (Ingold, 2008, p.14) raises concerns of how to go about studying it, let alone how to create valuable knowledge about it. Our suggestion is that we need to be pragmatic. We need to consider what works and what we wish to achieve and bear in mind that most likely no method will work everywhere. That implies that the knowledge produced will not be universal or epistemic but rather phronetic (Flyvbjerg, 2001).

According to Flyvbjerg, phronesis 'is that intellectual activity most relevant to praxis. It focuses on what is variable, on that which cannot be encapsulated by universal rules, on specific cases' (2001, p.57). Phronesis may be translated as prudence or practical wisdom manifested in the capacity for correct judgement of action in particular circumstances. It is based on practical value-rationality and thus revolves around ethics and ethical behaviour. The idea of phronesis may be traced back to Aristotle who formulated it as one of three intellectual virtues important for society, the other two being episteme and techne (Flyvbjerg, 2001). The former refers to scientific knowledge that is context independent and universally applicable. The scientific project of modernity, as for instance described by Latour (1993), is based on episteme. The latter refers to crafts and differs from phronesis as it is oriented towards production and is based on practical instrumental rationality.

To advocate the production of phronetic knowledge is to aim at producing practical knowledge that may balance the power of instrumental and scientific rationality in society. In terms of both research and applied work, phronesis aims at action and developing of skills to connect different kinds of knowledge (Dredge, et al., 2012; Viken, 2014). The objective is to provide partial answers to questions of potential routes for social development or basically 'input to the ongoing social dialogue about the problems and risks we face and how things may be done differently' (Flyvbjerg, 2001, p.61). Phronesis thus revolves around values and how decisions and actions are based on such values (Flyvbjerg, 2004). This approach resonates with Gupta and Ferguson's point about knowledge being a 'form of situated intervention' (1997, p.38). As they state:

We see the political task not as "sharing" knowledges with those who lack it, but as forging links between different knowledges that are possible from different locations and tracing lines of possible alliance and common purpose between them (Gupta and Ferguson, 1997, p.39).

Coming back to our source of inspiration, namely ANT, it is a short step from its modest epistemological claims to phronetic research. Bruno Latour proposes a similar move in his *Compositionist Manifesto* (2010). There he calls for research that can handle "matters of concern" and which is able to compose alternative ways towards the future. Research that takes '… seriously the political task of establishing the continuity of all entities that make up the common world' (Latour, 2010, p.485). This can only be done by following the weaving of the world, the ways in which orders are composed and stabilized and attend to 'the crucial difference between what is *well* or *badly* constructed, *well* or *badly* composed' (p.474, original italics).

Hence, our approach is '… intent on seeking *relational* rather than representational understandings;' (Thrift, 1999, p.304, original italics). It is striving to make partial connections, i.e.: '… to see together without claiming to be another' (Haraway, 1991, p.193). Instead of creating monologues of the experiences of actors or of the researcher, the aim is to produce a version of the field of practice under study, through which '… webs of connections called solidarity in politics and shared conversation in epistemology' (Haraway, 1991, p.191), are established.

Any research is thus a relational effect, produced through the "skilled practice" (Ingold, 2011) of the researcher situated in a particular field of practice. The knowledge produced is about making connections and give examples of possible avenues to take for assembling particular (world)orders to live by. The chapters that follow are primarily based on particular cases that yield insight into various fields of practice and such assembling work. To acknowledge the potentialities of case studies and phronetic knowledge production it is important to clarify how we may approach the idea of "the case" as well as the spatiotemporal connotations of the field.

In most general terms, a case study denotes a close investigation of a particular example. The defining feature of case study is thereby an examination of particular circumstances or the practices that constitute a given field of interest. According to Flyvbjerg (2001), these characteristics make the case study method integral to the practice of phronetic social sciences. The merit of the case study method has been scrutinized especially in regard to if case studies are generalizable or not (Flyvbjerg, 2001). There is no script for choosing the right case to secure generalizability and actually that is far from the objective of much research based on relationalism, at least in the sense of inferring from *one* to *many* (Winthereik and Verran, 2012). Once again referring to ANT, many studies have taken the form of ethnographic accounts based on 'exemplary case studies' (Law, 2009, p.143). The "case" should here not be taken as a small and bounded example of a larger whole but rather understood in its own right, as a sensitizing device that may invoke questions about differences and similarities between sites and circumstances under study. However:

> … a case may still be instructive beyond its specific site and situation, […] but the lessons it holds always come with the condition that, elsewhere, in other

cases, what is similar and different is not to be taken for granted. It remains to be seen, to be experienced, to be investigated (Mol and Law, 2002, p.15).

The idea of the case being a miniature of a larger world demands that it can be clearly demarcated and that its larger counterpart can be described as a stable totality, which is far from the tourism realities discussed in this book. This may seem contradictory to the discussion above about phronetic science and compositionist research practice that more or less explicitly searches for universality. However, the latter's version of universality is different from the episteme knowledge-claims produced by modern science. While the latter believes in a predefined universal state of affairs, be it laws of nature or the working of particular method independent of context, the former view understands universality as something that has to be composed and enacted (Latour, 2010).[1] This applies as well to the field in question. From a relational approach, any given field of research is an effect of research practice and far from the traditionally defined or bounded anthropological field of study as a geographical space that contains holistic cultural objects ripe for researchers to gaze upon (Appadurai, 1991; de Laet, 2000; Gupta and Ferguson, 1997). The present focus on movement and relations implies that the field as a location is not clearly demarcated in Euclidian space but 'should rather be considered as the object's *range*: a space that is performed by the travel of objects and an observer on-the-move' (de Laet, 2000, p.167–8, original italics). Hence, the field can be framed as a topological construct, which is continually emerging due to an array of relational practices that evoke multiple temporalities (Mol and Law, 1994; Law and Mol, 2001; Jóhannesson, 2005; Lury, Parisi and Terranova, 2012).

Through the close empirical examination which ethnographic methods afford, actors and the connections between them, their strengths and importance and their ability to speak, act and represent are established. Detailed descriptions and a (slow) process oriented methodology expose contingencies (Michael, 1996) and deconstruct taken-for-granted categories of analysis. Characteristics or identities such as "local", "foreign", "authentic" or "commercial" emerge as *effects*, rather than pre-given bases of social relations and controversy. This provides a new vision of the research object as assembled in concrete practices and performances involving human and non-human actors, discourses and technologies which are ordered and translated in the network or case under study, revealing a messy entanglement of places, events, phenomena, actors and things. At the same time a slow account runs the risk of being described as too partial, non-coherent or vague. While we acknowledge that vagueness should not be turned automatically into a methodological strength, we argue that it is necessary to run this risk in order to provide politically engaged accounts of tourism realities in the making.

---

1   For a discussion on how ethnographic accounts necessarily are generalisations and different modes of generalisations see e.g. Winthereik and Verran, 2012.

1.4 Themes and Chapters of this Book

Above we have discussed relational tourism research on the basis of our main source of inspiration, namely ANT. Some of the 11 chapters that follow share that entry point, while others approach tourism encounters and controversies from other directions. What they share however, is a focus on 1) how tourism controversies do not spring from some "controversial nature" of tourism, but are rather produced through the relational encounters of people, things, practices, discourses or concerns, and 2) how these encounters are not confined to tourism. All the chapters illustrate and critically address the benefits and challenges of seeing enactments and encounters in tourism as complex, multiple and relational effects. The chapters are divided into four (partly overlapping) sections, each tending to particular aspects of tourism encounters and the way in which they can be described, such as controversies related to how various things shape relations (Chapters 2, 3 and 4), controversial innovations (Chapters 5 and 6), power and politics (Chapters 7, 8 and 9) and controversial ideas of future tourism geographies (Chapters 10, 11 and 12).

Inherently, the study of tourism is a multi-disciplinary field of research which is reflected in the diverse academic backgrounds of the contributing authors. Although all are engaged with tourism research, they have training in geography, anthropology, ethnology and sociology. The cases cover five continents, from Greenland, Iceland and Scandinavia, the island of Cuba, rural Namibia and vampire-ridden American Northwest to the coral reefs of Indonesia and casinos in Macau. The chapters provide different insight into the making of tourism realities and the ways in which society can be studied critically through tourism. Some of the issues which are brought up as closely connected to encounters in tourism include sexual relationships, nature conservation, the meaning and experience of wilderness, bio-politics and future scenarios.

Valerio Simoni sets out to examine the reciprocal constitution of money and relationships in touristic Cuba. According to Simoni, money is a key element in the shaping of relationships between foreign tourists and members of the visited population in Cuba. Rather than simply adopting the view that different deployments of money constitute different relationships, Simoni argues that money and relationships constitute and inform the qualities of each other. Money could therefore appear not as a given, stabilized, and unified object, but as a potentially controversial and plural thing, whose eventual stabilization is itself one of the possible outcomes of the relationship at stake. His ethnographic material shows how different conceptions, uses and values of money can be enacted and refashioned as they become entangled in various sorts of relationships.

Senna Middelveld, René van der Duim and Rico Lie examine another controversial and plural thing: the enactment of coral reefs in Wakatobi National Park, which afford a variety of practices, such as these of fishermen, coral miners, tourists, conservation organizations. By examining the multiplicity of coral reef, they situate reef actors by their ability to influence the reality of which they are part, and their ability to influence other realities that define and use the coral reef in a different way. By focusing on the relations, practices and materials formed around and afforded by the reefs, they make clear how different reef practices are not only made possible by human actors, but also by (informal) rules, laws and regulations (or the lack of it) and objects such as fishing and mining equipment. Viewing coral reefs as multiple and complex, and at the same time acknowledging how this multiplicity is created through different practices, objects and interpretations, provides space for looking at the management of coral reefs and natural resources in new ways.

Moving from the coral reefs of Wakatobi to Snowman land in Målselv, Norway, Anniken Førde examines the intricate processes of tourism entrepreneurship and the many relations, negotiations and controversies involved in tourism development. Through her case study she analyzes the entrepreneurial process of establishing a tourism resort, which provides still another example of what can count as a tourism thing. This process involves creative networking practices, entailing new alliances and configurations. Further, as the project developed to include other regional attractions in the common brand Snowman land, she investigates the challenges related to destination development. Her analysis of tourism development in Målselv seeks to explore how tourism landscapes are produced in complex relations involving multiple types of networking practices. Applying a relational perspective on entrepreneurship, the focus is on networks and negotiations of cultural and symbolic as well as material conditions.

Following the first three chapters discussing multiple controversies related to how particular things are brought together and shape relations, the next two chapters examine the relations between innovations and controversies more specifically. Anders Kristian Munk argues that treating your object of study as a controversy is to insist on deploying it in its maximum heterogeneity and to open it up to specific kinds of inquiry. As such, the controversy approach may work as a deliberate research intervention that affords specific possibilities to the enquiry, for instance by cutting across different domains, creating moments of ontological disturbance. He illustrates this through a controversy mapping of the New Nordic Food phenomenon and debacle, hereby also introducing digital methods as a way to chart and explore such a complex social phenomenon.

Felicity Picken provides a biography of another innovation, the Museo Subaquático de Arte (MUSA), an artificial reef in the Caribbean Sea off the coast of the holiday mecca of Cancún. What makes MUSA unique within the context of touristic encounters is that the requirements for substitution, of a clear distinction between original and copy, natural and artificial, are unable to be met. What MUSA does not do well is fit easily into existing taxonomies of artificial or real, nature or culture and this has implications for its representational validity. Instead of offering a poor copy of the wilderness 'proper', and therefore a poor copy of 'reality', MUSA blurs the distinction altogether. According to Picken, this in turn opens the possibility to acknowledge the creative potential of tourism. Tourism then, is much more than representation; it is rather an experiential mode of being enacted through the deployment of images, bodies, technologies, discourses, nature and objects that are, with varying degrees of success, assembled in the performance of making, or indeed faking, an alternative reality.

Power and politics are central to the next three chapters. Arjaan Pellis, Martijn Duineveld and Lauren Wagner provide a critical reading of some of the dominant literatures concerning conflicts and conflict management in tourism studies. Illustrated by fieldwork in Namibia, where they studied Anabeb Conservancy, one of Namibia's first rural communities that have been legally enabled to constitute themselves as a conservancy taking care of natural resource management, they argue that conflicts should not be studied as 'in betweens' but in their own right, as self-referential entities having their own trajectory through history. According to Pellis and colleagues, conflicts are enabled by their own legacies, their relations to other conflicts and paradoxically also by the powers that aim to overcome, manage, silence or understand them.

Richard Ek's chapter is based on the idea that the tourist, as an ontological figure (the metaphysical imagination of the nature of different faces and functions of the human in Western thought), is not a postmodern or modern creature, but a figure that has been a companion to the central ontological figure in Western metaphysics – the citizen – since the establishment of polis as an ordering principle of society. Ek argues that tourism theory is no stranger to philosophical accounts of biopolitics and power, but that there is more to do here, a need in a political-philosophical way to address the ontological encounter between the citizen and the tourist. Taking tourism seriously implies that ontological figures like the vampire and the citizen are discussed in different ways, not only as a certain approach towards or engagement in the world or as an encounter between the human and the world, but also as an encounter of humans and thus a biopolitical topic.

Biopolitics is also central to the next chapter. Claudio Minca and Chin Ee Ong's chapter focuses on care, custody and tourism and on how their associated spatial arrangements are often controlled, stewarded and monitored by the state. By making reference to two tourism encounters in Asia, they interrogate the extent and the ways in which this involvement represents a deliberate attempt on the part of the state to biopolitically intervene in the lives of their citizenry through tourism. Accordingly, they also investigate how some state-endorsed tourism practices may indeed be bound up with control, surveillance and restrain, despite their appearance as potential fields of freedom and individual self-realization.

The next chapter moves from politics towards policies and different ways in which future tourism geographies are being built up. Gunnar Thór Jóhannesson deals with some of the ways in which the present tourism realities in Iceland have emerged by following relational encounters between tourism policy, flows of tourists and nature. Icelandic tourism policy is addressed as a space of encounters and potential controversy, materialized by heterogeneous assemblages of a wide array of actors. It recounts how tourism and in some sense tourists, have been translated into fish in an effort to conceive tourism as a real sector and eventually a subject of policy making on par with other key industries of the country. At present, the tourism sector has gained an uncontroversial reckoning as a real business, which depends on and iterates a particular relationship to its main resource, namely nature. The chapter also traces some of those relations as manifested in a recent policy tool in a form of multi-site access charge called the Environment Card. Jóhannesson argues that policy making may usefully be analyzed as a process of improvisation that continually encompasses the entanglement of human and more-than-human encounters and which has ontological repercussions. Hence, what seems at present to be an uncontroversial framing of tourism in Iceland as an industry, may create serious challenges for sustainable development of tourism in the near future.

Closely related to the chapter of Jóhannesson is Edward Huijbens' attempt to deal with land-use controversies surrounding tourism development by looking at how landscapes are presented to and encountered by tourists visiting Iceland. Huijbens' aim is to show how wilderness and natural landscapes in Iceland are given voice and agency, thus enabling encounters with the visiting tourist. However, the work that goes into giving wilderness landscapes a voice in marketing and promotion entails the exertion of force upon the earth, molding its surface into marketable form. In order to make sense of this force this chapter draws conceptually on topological imaginaries as presented in literature on cultural topologies and vitalist geo-philosophy.

The chapters by Huijbens and Jóhannesson illustrate how tourism policies implicate controversies and have important ontological repercussions, now and in the near future. By studying the exhibition of Possible Greenland, Carina Ren shows how envisioning the future is also a controversial field. Ren displays how the exhibition themes make use of very different strategies for envisioning the future. She argues that the exhibition may be used as a prism to illustrate how architectural fantasies, political visions and practical concerns get entangled and enrolled in scenarios building. The case of Possible Greenland displays that not only the present or physically existing objects can become controversial or be turned into matters of concern. So can things and issues which are (still) only envisioned or "to be". Ren therefore argues that the acknowledgement of how futuring is intrinsically connected to the present – and how it should be tended to accordingly – holds implication for tourism studies.

Finally, in our postscript (Chapter 13) we first argue to expand the field of investigation when researching tourism in order not to limit our attention to an all too enclosed area of what might be termed 'tourism proper'. Tourism orderings (or ordering attempts) connect or disengage with other ordering attempts and enact different versions of these orders and their relations. Hence, there is no one tourism order as the common description of tourism as a homogeneous sector with relatively clear boundaries, such as oil exports or automobiles, implies. Rather there are many tourism orderings that play part in the continuous becoming of society and space. Second, we argue to focus on controversies when researching how tourism is empirically related to other fields – be it conservation, fisheries, architecture, or wilderness. We abstain from seeing the controversy as a merely counterproductive social phenomenon, as the controversy is also an opportunity, which might show itself as productive. Third, and tightly related, we argue for a relational approach to tracing the connections between tourism and its necessary (but never predefined or presupposed) 'others'. As we have discussed in this introduction, this entails not seeing tourism encounters as a potential clash between already created entities, but rather to look at how the entities and the boundaries between them emerge and are shaped in and through the encounter.

References

Ahebwa, W.M., 2012. *Tourism, livelihoods and biodiversity conservation. An assessment of tourism related policy interventions at Bwindi Impenetrable National Park (BINP), Uganda.* Ph.D. Wageningen University.

Ahebwa, W.M., Van der Duim, V.R. and Sandbrook, C., 2012a. Tourism revenue sharing at Bwindi Impenetrable National Park (BINP), Uganda: A policy arrangement approach. *Journal of Sustainable Tourism,* 20(3), pp.377–94.

Ahebwa, W.M, Van der Duim, V.R. and Sandbrook, C., 2012b. Private-community partnerships: Investigating a new approach to conservation and development in Uganda. *Conservation and Society,* 10(4), pp.305–17.

Ahebwa, W.M. and Van der Duim, V.R., 2012a. The governance capacity of community-based tourism policy initiatives: The case of Buhoma-Mukono model, Uganda. *MAWAZO, the Journal of the College of Humanities and Social Sciences,* Makerere University, 11(1), pp.192–210.

Ahebwa, W.M. and Van der Duim, V.R., 2012b. Conservation, livelihoods and tourism: A case study of the Buhoma-Mukono community-based tourism project in Uganda. *Journal of Park and Recreation Administration,* 31(3), pp.96–114.

Amin, A., 2004. Regions unbound: Towards a new politics of place. *Geografiska Annaler B,* 86(1), pp.33–44.

Appadurai, A., 1991. Global ethnoscapes: Notes and queries for a transnational anthropology. In: R.G. Fox (ed.) *Recapturing anthropology: Working in the present.* Santa Fe: School of American Research Press.

Barth, F., 1969. Introduction. In: F. Barth (ed.) *Ethnic groups and boundaries: The social organization of cultural difference.* Boston: Little Brown and Company, pp.9–38.

Boissevain, J., 1996. Introduction. In: J. Boissevain (ed.) *Coping with tourists. European Reactions to Mass Tourism.* Providence, RI: Berghahn Books.

Callon, M. 1998. An essay on framing and overflowing: economic externalities revisited by sociology. *The Sociological Review,* 46 (S1), pp 244–69

de Laet, M., 2000. Patents, travel, space: Ethnographic encounters with objects in transit. *Environment and Planning D: Society and Space,* 18(2), pp.149–68.

Dredge, D., Benckendorff, P., Day, M., Gross, M.J., Walo, M., Weeks, P. and Whitelaw, P., 2012. The philosophic practitioner and the curriculum space. *Annals of Tourism Research,* 39(4), pp.2154–76. doi: http://dx.doi.org/10.1016/j.annals.2012.07.017

Emirbayer, M., 1997. Manifesto for a relational sociology. *American Journal of Sociology*, 103(2), pp.281–317.

Flyvbjerg, B., 2001. *Making social science matter: Why social inquiry fails and how it can succeed again.* Cambridge: Cambridge University Press.

Flyvbjerg, B., 2004. Phronetic planning research: Theoretical and methodological reflections. *Planning Theory & Practice*, 5(3), pp.283–306. doi: 10.1080/1464935042000250195.

Franklin, A., 2004. Tourism as an ordering: Towards a new ontology of tourism. *Tourist Studies*, 4(3), pp.277–301.

Franklin, A., 2012. The choreography of a mobile world: Tourism orderings. In: R. Van der Duim, C. Ren and G.T. Jóhannesson (eds) *Actor-Network Theory and tourism: Ordering, materiality and multiplicity*. London and New York: Routledge. pp.43–58.

Gad, C. and Jensen, C.B., 2010. On the Consequences of Post-ANT, *Science, Technology and Human Values*, 35(1), pp. 55–80.

Gupta, A. and Ferguson, J., 1997. Discipline and practice: "The field" as site, method and location in anthropology. In: A. Gupta and J. Ferguson (eds) *Anthropological locations: Boundaries and grounds of a field science*. Berkeley, Los Angeles and London: University of California Press.

Haraway, 1991. *Simians, Cyborgs and Women: the Reinvention of Nature*. London, Free Association Books.

Harvey, P., 2012. The topological quality of infrastructural relation: An ethnographic approach. *Theory, Culture & Society*, 29(4/5), pp.76–92. doi: 10.1177/0263276412448827.

Huijbens, E. and Gren, M., 2012. Tourism, ANT and the Earth. In: R. Van der Duim, C. Ren and G.T. Jóhannesson (eds) *Actor-Network Theory and tourism: Ordering, materiality and multiplicity*. London and New York: Routledge.

Ingold, T., 2000. Making culture and weaving the world. In: P.M. Graves-Brown (ed.) *Matter, materiality and modern culture*. London and New York: Routledge. pp.50–71.

Ingold, T., 2008. *Bringing things to life: Creative entanglements in a world of materials.* [online] Available at: <http://www.reallifemethods.ac.uk/events/vitalsigns/programme/documents/vital-signs-ingold-bringing-things-to-life.pdf> [Accessed 19 February 2014].

Ingold, T., 2011. *Being Alive: Essays on movment, knowledge and description.* London and New York: Routledge.

Jespersen, A.P., Krogh Petersen, M., Ren, C. and Sandberg, M., 2012. Cultural analysis as intervention. *Science Studies*, 25(1), pp.3–12.

Jóhannesson, G.T., 2005. Tourism Translations: Actor-Network Theory and tourism research. *Tourist Studies*, 5(2), pp.133–50.

Jóhannesson, G.T. and Bærenholdt, J.O., 2008. Enacting places through connections of tourism. In: B. Granås and J.O. Bærenholdt (eds) *Mobility and place: Enacting European peripheries*. Aldershot: Ashgate, pp.155–66.

Jóhannesson, G., Ren, C. Duim. V.R., and Munk, A. 2014. Actor-Network Theory and Tourism Research: approaches, implications and future. In: J. Widtfeldt Meged, L.A. Hansen, K.A. Hvass and B. Stilling Blichfeldt (eds) *Tourism Methodologies – New Perspectives, Practices and Procedures*. Copenhagen: Copenhagen Business School Press, pp. 119–36

Jolivet, E. and Heiskanen, A. 2010. Blowing against the wind – An exploratory application of actor network theory to the analysis of local controversies and participation process in wind energy. *Energy Policies* 38, pp. 6746 -6754

Larsen, J., 2008. De-exoticizing tourist travel: Everyday life and sociality on the move. *Leisure Studies*, 27(1), pp. 21–34.

Latour, B., 1986. The powers of association. In: J. Law (ed.) *Power, action and belief: A new sociology of knowledge*. London, Boston and Henley: Routledge & Kegan Paul.

Latour, B., 1993. *We have never been modern* (Translated by C. Porter). Cambridge: Harvard University Press.

Latour, B., 2010. An attempt at a "compositionist manifesto". *New Literary History*, 41, pp.471–90.

Latour, B. and Weibel, P. (eds), 2005. *Making things public: Atmospheres of democracy*. Karlsruhe and Cambridge, MA: Center for Art and Media and Massachusetts Institute of Technology.

Laudati, A., 2010. Ecotourism: The modern predator? Implications of gorilla tourism on local livelihoods in Bwindi Impenetrable National Park, Uganda. *Environment and Planning D: Society and Space*, 28(4), pp.726–43.

Law, J., 2004. *After method: Mess in social science research*. London and New York: Routledge.

Law, J. 2009. Actor Network Theory and Material Semiotics. In B.S. Turner (ed.) *The New Blackwell Companion to Social Theory*. Oxford: Blackwell Publishing, pp. 141–58.

Law, J. and Hassard, J. (ed.), 1999. *Actor Network Theory and After*. Oxford: Blackwell.

Law, J., and Mol, A., 2001. Situating Technoscience: An Inquiry into Spatialities. *Environment and Planning D: Society and Space*, 19(5), pp. 609–21.

Law, J., and Mol, A., 2008. The actor-enacted: Cumbrian sheep in 2001. In L. Malafouris and C. Knappett (eds) *Material Agency. Towards a Non-Anthropocentric Approach*. Springer US, pp. 57–77. doi: 10.1007/978-0-387-74711-8

Law, J. and Singleton, V., 2013. ANT and politics: Working in and on the world. *Qualitative Sociology*, 36, pp.485–502. doi: 10.1007/s11133-013-9263-7.

Lury, C., Parisi, L., and Terranova, T., 2012. Introduction: The Becoming Topological of Culture. *Theory, Culture & Society*, 29(4/5), pp.3–35. doi: 10.1177/0263276412454552.

Michael, M.,1996. *Constructing identities: The social, the nonhuman and change*. London: Sage.

Mol, A. (1999). Ontological politics. A word and some questions. In J. Law and J. Hassard (eds) *Actor network theory and after*. Oxford: Blackwell, pp. 74–89.

Mol, A. and Law, J. (1994). Regions, Networks and Fluids: Anaemia and Social Topology. *Social Studies of Science*, 24, pp. 641–71.

Mol, A. and Law, J., 2002. Complexities: An introduction. In: J. Law and A. Mol, (eds) *Complexities: Social studies of knowledge practices*. Durham and London: Duke University Press.

Moufakkir A. and Burns, P.M. 2012. *Controversies in Tourism*. Wallingford: CABI Publishing

Pálsson, G., 2005. Of Althings! In: B. Latour and P. Weibel, (eds) *Making things public: Atmospheres of democracy*. Karlsruhe and Cambridge, MA: Center for Art and Media and Massachusetts Institute of Technology. pp.250–59.

Ren, C. 2009. *Constructing the tourist destination. A socio-material description*, unpublished PhD thesis, University of Southern Denmark.

Ren, C., 2011. Non-human agency, radical ontology and tourism realities. *Annals of Tourism Research*, 38(3), pp.858–81. doi: 10.1916/j.annals.2010.12.007.

Ren, C. and Blichfeldt, B.S., 2011. One clear image? Challenging simplicity in place branding. *Scandinavian Journal of Hospitality and Tourism*, 11(4), pp.416–34. doi: http://dx.doi.org/10.1080/150222250.2011.598753

Sandbrook, C.G. and Semple, S., 2006. The rules and the reality of mountain gorilla *Gorilla beringei beringei* tracking: How close do tourists get? *Oryx*, 40(4), pp.428–33.

Sheller, M. and Urry, J., 2004. *Tourism mobilities: Places to play, places in play*. London and New York: Routledge.

Shepherd, R., 2002. Commodification, culture and tourism. *Tourist Studies*, 2(2), pp.183–201.

Smith, V., ed., 1989. *Hosts and guests. The anthropology of tourism*. Philadelphia: University of Pennsylvania Press.

Stengers, I., 2005. The cosmopolitical proposal. In Latour, B. and P. Weibel (eds) *Making things public: Atmospheres of democracy*, pp. 994–1003.

Thrift, N., 1999. Steps to an ecology of place. In: D. Massey, J. Allen and P. Sarre, (eds) *Human geography today*. Cambridge: Polity Press.

Turner, L. and Ash, J., 1975. *The golden hordes: International tourism and the pleasure periphery*. London: Constable.

Van der Duim, V. R., Ren, C. and Jóhannesson, G.T. (eds), 2012. *Actor-Network Theory and tourism: Ordering, materiality and multiplicity*. London and New York: Routledge.

Van der Duim, V.R., Ren, C. and Jóhannesson, G.T. 2013. Ordering, materiality and multiplicity: Enacting ANT in Tourism, *Tourist Studies*, 13 (1), pp. 3–20

Van der Duim, V.R., Ampumuza, Chr. and Ahebwa, W.M., 2014. Gorilla tourism in Bwindi Impenetrable National Park, Uganda: An Actor-Network perspective. *Society & Natural Resources*. DOI: 10.1080/08941920.2014.901459, 27 (6), pp. 588–601

Venturini, T., 2010. Diving in magma: How to explore controversies with Actor-Network Theory. *Public Understanding of Science*, 19(3), pp.258–73.

Venturini, T., 2012. Building on faults: How to represent controversies with digital methods. *Public Understanding of Science*, 21(7), pp.796–812.

Vertesi, J., 2014. Seamful spaces: Heterogeneous infrastructures in interaction. *Science, Technology & Human Values*, 39(2), pp.264–84. doi: 10.1177/0162243913516012.

Viken, A., 2014. Ski resort development: Scripts and phronesis. In: A. Viken and B. Granås, (eds) *Tourism destination development: Turns and tactics*. Farnham: Ashgate. pp.113–30.

Vikkelsø, S. 2007. Description as Intervention: Engagement and Resistance in Actor-Network Analyses, *Science as Culture*, 16(3), pp. 297–309.

Whatmore, S., 2009. Mapping knowledge controversies: Science, democracy and the redistribution of expertise. *Progress in Human Geography*, 33(5), pp.587–98. doi: 10.1177/0309132509339841.

Winthereik, B.R. and Verran, H., 2012. Ethnographic stories as generalizations that intervene. *Science Studies*, 25(1), pp.37–51.

Chapter 2

Shaping Money and Relationships in Touristic Cuba

Valerio Simoni

2.1 Introduction

Concerns about money, and about the ways in which money affects relationships, are ubiquitous in the realm of tourism in Cuba, and generate a wide range of views and practices. This chapter considers some of these views and practices, showing how they could diverge, converge and be worked over, and highlighting the key role played by money and its deployments in the qualification of relationships.

As argued by Zelizer (2000; 2005), the use of money to distinguish different types of relationships, together with the relational work that people undertake to frame and clarify the meaning of money in relationships, are extremely widespread phenomena, which can be found across a range of socio-cultural and historical contexts. In touristic Cuba, through money – its presence/absence and variegated uses – nuances and differences in relationships were brought about by foreign tourists and members of the visited population. In turn, these relationships contributed to (re)define money itself as well as its purposes. In this sense, money and relationships were in constant dialogue; they relationally qualified and helped people make sense of each other. The issue of whether we are dealing in this context with 'relationships that money can buy' or not,[1] is repeatedly addressed by the protagonists of the encounters considered in this chapter, and different deployments of money and the purposes attributed to it, prompted different answers to this question.

To shed light into the changing entanglements and the reciprocal constitution of money and relationships in touristic Cuba, in the following sections I first start by outlining the connection between tourism, hard currency, and informal tourist/Cuban encounters in this Caribbean island.[2] This leads me to consider some ambiguities

---

1 Such was the title of the conference session for which an early version of this text was originally prepared (*Relations that money can buy: negotiating mutualities and asymmetries in local and translocal social fields*, Workshop 042 of the 2008 European Association of Social Anthropologists Conference).

2 While through this chapter I often employ the general and indefinite plurals 'tourists' and 'Cubans' (meaning 'some tourists' and 'some Cubans'), it should be clear to readers that these 'discursive tropes' do not 'represent an undifferentiated sociological or

concerning the currencies that circulated in Cuba, their value, and their possible uses, and how these ambiguities could be alternatively exploited to 'rip off' tourists, reiterating asymmetries, or to generate narratives of friendship and mutuality. I then look more closely at the frequent tensions emerging between money and friendship, showing how these tensions were sometimes resolved via deployments of the 'right kind' of money, and by reformulating the notion of friendship itself.

By considering in some detail an example that highlights the role of ambiguity and misunderstandings in the working of sexual relationships in which monetary transfers were also involved, I show how discourses and uses of money got entangled in specific moralities and conceptions of mutuality and asymmetry, bringing certain realities to the fore while silencing others. This also leads me to consider how economic asymmetries and the controversial issue of 'buying sex' could be bypassed altogether by making universalizing references to 'ordinary' gendered norms and scripts. Finally, the chapter considers how radical asymmetries were enacted, and different monies and transactional regimes negotiated, in bringing about contentious charitable relationships. The exploration of these different and co-constitutive connections between monies and relationships in touristic Cuba provides a compelling case of the multiplicity of tourism encounters, and of how a diversified range of practices, discourses, materialities, and embodied attachments are being enrolled to bring about different, often competing, tourism-related realities.

2.2 Tourism, *Convertibles*, and Informal Encounters in Cuba

To alleviate the crises that followed the collapse of the Soviet Union, the Cuban government promoted in the 1990s the development of tourism, considered as a sector capable of generating hard currency in relatively short time (*Resolución económica del V congreso del PCC*, 1997, quoted in Argyriadis, 2005, p.31). But in spite of a certain degree of economic recovery after the first years of the 1990s, characterized by dramatic shortages, the economic situation kept being difficult for many Cubans, especially for those who did not have direct access to hard currency through a job in the tourism industry or remittances from relatives abroad (Argyriadis, 2005, p.32). Indeed, most Cubans received their salaries in *pesos cubanos* (CUP, 'cuban pesos', also known as *moneda nacional*, 'national currency'), while many essential household items for instance were only available – formally at least – in *tiendas the recaudación de divisas* ('stores for

---

political reality' (Comaroff and Comaroff, 1997, p.24). Somehow similar to the 'colonial encounters' referred to by Comaroff and Comaroff, in the touristic encounters considered here there was also a tendency 'to force even deeper conceptual wedges into ever more articulated, indivisible orders of relations' (1997, p.26). As we shall see, the deployments of money in the course of these interactions could help strengthen or bridge the divide between tourists and Cubans, (de)stabilizing these relational forms of identification.

the recollection of foreign currency') that operated in *pesos convertibles* (CUC, 'convertible pesos'), the hard currency still in use in present day Cuba.[3]

The circulation and use of both *pesos convertibles* and *pesos cubanos* in Cuba was a source of much confusion for several tourists. Tourist guidebooks gave tips and suggestions on how to deal with this double currency system, generally pointing out that what tourist would essentially need during their trip were *pesos convertibles*, since in hotels and most tourism-related installations this was the only accepted currency. While tourists carried *convertibles*, many Cubans had to *inventar* ('invent', find ways) to get hold of them, as they engaged in their *lucha* ('struggle') – one of the key terms of revolutionary symbolism, which came to indicate Cubans' day-to-day struggle to get by (Palmié, 2004, p.241).

As the numbers of tourists visiting Cuba rose dramatically throughout the 1990s (from 340,000 in 1990 to more than 2 million in 2004), a wide range of tourism-related activities that escaped state regulation flourished on the island, where any interaction with foreigners had the potential of being much more lucrative than any other professional activity. In this respect, policies had been put in place in Cuba which attempted to regulate and frame interactions between tourists and members of the local population, criminalizing some of them and thereby constituting a divide between formal and informal social relations.[4] The exploratory concept of 'informal encounter' draws attention to the implications of such divide, and encourages researchers to address notions of 'tourism harassment', 'instrumentality', or 'friendship' from the perspectives of the various protagonists involved, paying attention to the processes that lead to their emergence, negotiation and eventual stabilization. To give a few examples of such informal engagements, I can mention that in Cuba many people were bypassing the control of the authorities while actively trying to befriend tourists, offering their services as guides or as companions, selling cigars, providing sex, private 'illegal' taxis, accommodation and food. Tourists in Cuba also gave shape to these informal relations as they tried to get in touch with and help the 'locals', buy things more cheaply, 'get off the beaten (tourism) track', listen to narratives of Cubans' everyday lives or get access to products and services formally unavailable (sex and drugs mainly).

---

3   Between 2005 and 2013, one *convertible* could be exchanged for approximately 25 *pesos cubanos*. The use of U.S. dollars was officially banned in November 2004, when convertible pesos became their substitute in a measure designed to counteract what Fidel Castro argued were U.S. attempts to obstruct the sending of dollars to Cuba (Brotherton, 2008, p.268). To curb the circulation of dollars, any exchange was originally charged a 10 per cent commission. In April 2005, the exchange of dollars to convertibles stabilized at a 1:1.18, following an additional 8 per cent revaluation of the CUC (Brotherton, 2008).

4   My Cuban research participants tended to use the expression *asedio del turista* ('siege'/hustling of tourist) when referring to the police accusations of unlawfully engaging with tourists. Officers employed a system of warnings, combined with fines, to penalize Cubans accused of asedio. In the worst case scenario, people could ultimately face time in prison (three years according to most Cubans I heard talking about it).

In Cuba, the terms *jinetero/a* (from the Spanish *jinete*, literally horseman, rider) and *jineterismo* (the activities of the *jinetero/a*) have become essential framing devices when talking about touristic encounters. They evoke notions of tourism hustling and prostitution, of Cubans riding the tourists (see also Palmié, 2004), and are among the key concepts drawing attention to touristic informal encounters on the island and what may be at stake in them. Nevertheless, disputes were frequent among Cubans and tourists alike regarding who was a *jinetero/a* and who was not, making it important to consider how these elusive terms and often stigmatizing categories could be deployed and contested in different situations.[5] In this respect, conceptions and uses of money, and the way they were negotiated in the course of encounters between foreign tourists and Cubans, were among the key elements to take into account, as they informed people's categorizations and their possible self-identifications.

The ethnographic material on which I rely in the following sections is drawn from 12 months of fieldwork carried out in Cuba between 2005 and 2013. During the time spent on the island, data were gathered through participant observation and conversations both with tourists and the Cuban men and women who engaged with them in the tourist poles of Havana (the capital), Viñales (a rural village), and Playas del Este (a beach resort east of the capital). While informal touristic encounters abounded in Cuba, the visitors that engaged in them were more likely to be young independent tourists than people staying in all-inclusive resorts or going on package tours. The former constituted the bulk of my informants, together with those Cubans (generally also in their twenties and thirties) that actively tried to deal with tourists in Havana, Viñales and Playas del Este.

2.3 Qualifying Currencies

2.3.1 'What's this Money?'

Many of the tourists travelling for the first time to Cuba were concerned and intrigued by Cuban currencies and their exchange rates. Among the most striking elements of controversy, was the circulation of more than one currency. Cuban money could not be purchased abroad, and tourists needed to acquire it once in Cuba. Tips circulated about which foreign currencies it was better to bring into the country (e.g. Euros vs. U.S. Dollars), where to change them, which type of Cuban

---

5   Several authors have outlined the porosity (Argyriadis, 2005, p.47), the ambiguities (Berg, 2004; Cabezas, 2004; Fernandez, 1999; Palmié, 2004), and the kaleidoscopic character (Kummels, 2005, p.24) of *jineterismo* and other related phenomena and categories in Cuba – sex work, prostitution, and partnership for instance. Scholars have thus emphasized how *jineterismo* is a complex phenomenon, one which brings issues of morality, nation, race, class and gender into play (Berg, 2004; Cabezas, 2004; Fernandez, 1999; Simoni, 2008a).

currency should be bought – *pesos convertibles* (CUC) vs. *moneda nacional* (CUP) – and in which proportion.

The realm of currency exchange was one in which several Cubans eager to profit from tourists could find much room to manoeuvre, 'riding' ambiguities and the tourists' confusion. According to a self-professed ex-*jinetero* for instance, the true *jineteros*, the ones that made loads of money, were the ones dealing with *el cambio*. This notion – literally meaning 'exchange', and implicitly referring to 'currency exchange' – hinted at something more than the precise moment when currencies where exchanged, and seemed to evoke a whole realm of activity, a sort of informal profession with its own specific skills and competences, which encompassed a wide range of techniques and tricks. According to my informant, these *jineteros* used to hang around the big hotels, befriending tourists who had just arrived on the island. Once they had gained some of the tourists' trust, they would then suggest them a 'profitable' exchange of 'Cuban money'.

I heard several stories from tourists about such exchanges of currency, which generally started as a 'fortuitous' encounter with a friendly Cuban on the streets of Havana. These were occasions where values and equivalences between currencies would be talked about and enacted, and which often ended up with the tourists exchanging their euros or dollars with 'Cuban money', 'the money one would need here', at a 'favourable rate'. The recurrent problem, as it were, was that while the rate may have been very favourable for *pesos convertibles*, what was sold to tourists were *pesos cubanos*, whose value was 25 times lower. As a result, some tourists I met confessed having lost up to a thousand euros. I also heard of situations in which the Cubans at stake managed to convince tourists of the existence of three types of currencies in Cuba: the deal here was cast as a unique occasion to buy the most convenient of them – which again, turned out to be the *pesos cubanos*.

These were situations in which monies and their values were enacted and constituted ad hoc, bypassing the stabilizing endeavours of the formal institutions that fixed currency exchanges. Rather than a well settled and clearly objectified material entity, as one would expect money to be, Cuban currencies emerged here as a gathering of discourses, skilful techniques and materialities that were able to work over value 'on the spot', exploiting confusion and the lack of knowledge of tourists (see also Simoni, 2012). What these *cambios* brought forward was a view of tourist/local relationships as highly asymmetrical, as potentially contrived and exploitative, and as predetermined and influenced by inequalities of knowledge and money (Simoni, 2008a; 2008b).

2.3.2 Deploying Pesos Cubanos: Becoming an Insider?

Another deployment of the two Cuban currencies and their connotations that contributed to shape relationships and notions of (in)equality between and among tourists and Cubans, related to the visitors' decision to acquire and use *pesos cubanos*. Such decision could become an element of distinction between tourists, with some of them emphasizing for instance how they were relying on the 'local currency' to get by during their journey – buying food in local markets, eating pizzas and sandwiches from little stalls and shops, using public transport in CUP, frequenting 'local', 'Cubans only' bars. Their familiarity and use of *pesos cubanos* would be portrayed and valued as a proof of integration into 'local Cuban life', an expression of their effort to reach out and experience the life of ordinary Cubans, avoiding the tourists' circuit. Following this line of reasoning, the 'tourist bubble' would be equated and exemplified by the places and selling points where only *convertibles* were accepted.

In this sense, the difference between *convertibles* and *moneda nacional* could become a crucial device to delineate and draw boundaries between the touristy and the 'really Cuban', and to give shape to different relationships between tourists and Cuban people. The willingness to avoid as far as possible the 'touristy' expressed by several tourists, and the importance of money to signify and materialize such desire, did not go unnoticed to the Cubans who wished to engage with them. Indeed, such preferences were frequently acknowledged and brought forward to conjure a 'special relationship', one imbued with a sense of mutuality, like was the case for friendship.

2.4 Money and Friendship

2.4.1 A Friend Wants no Money

<blockquote>
I am not interested in your money
Money, you can gain it or lose it. A friendship is for life!
</blockquote>

These sort of expressions were recurrently addressed to tourists by their Cuban companions, as a way to convince them that what they valued most was genuine, sincere friendship (*una amistad sincera*), rather than ephemeral money. To exemplify such statements, the Cubans at stake could deny getting any cash-commissions in the places they frequented with tourists. Another common endeavour emphasized how tourists guided by such Cuban friends were gaining access to 'the places of the Cubans', where one could pay in *moneda nacional*, save money and not being ripped off as those 'other tourists' going in touristy locations where only convertible pesos were accepted. These expressions of help and solidarity with the tourists, which relied on specific deployments of money, could be portrayed as proofs of sincere, disinterested friendship, and contrasted with the undertakings of *jineteros* who brought tourists to expensive tourist bars and restaurants just to get their commissions in *convertibles*.

In a similar vein, Cubans who were used to the company of young travellers and backpackers could emphasize the value of a simple Cuban lifestyle, while criticizing the commercialism of tourist installations and pointing out their aversion for touristy places in Old Havana and the countless venues of prostitution or the selling of expensive *mojitos*. As an alternative, they could suggest to gather some money from people who wanted to share – Cubans and tourists alike – and go get some cheap clandestine rum in a place nearby – something to 'share, the Cuban way' (*compartir, a lo cubano*), which could be paid in *moneda nacional*. Generosity and reciprocity were emphasized and seemed to play a very important part on these occasions, as people shared their drinks without any hint of calculation.

What can be drawn from such examples, and which applied to a wide range of interactions between tourists and Cubans, are the widely shared assumptions on the 'socially corrupting' status of money – and particularly *pesos convertibles* – and its problematic entanglement with notions of friendship. References to monetary gain would generally be avoided by Cubans who were trying to establish friendship with tourists, except perhaps while condemning the exploitative practices of 'other', commission-driven Cubans. The emphasis was instead on having a good time together, between friends, occasionally sharing drinks and food. Delineating a moral hierarchy that closely linked types of goods and forms of exchange, a fundamental distinction was thus made between monetary transactions on the one hand, and the offering of other products (such as food and beverages) on the other – the latter being far easier to entangle with constructions of friendship.

2.4.2   Economic Asymmetries and Emerging Notions of Friendship

Several tourists told me that they had no problem at all in offering drinks and food to their Cuban friends or acquaintances. What was important for them was to have the feeling that they were giving things out of their own will, as opposed to any sort of pressure for 'having to' give. Tourists also disliked the notion that the main motive of the Cubans they were inviting and sharing with was to gain commission in cash. While this seems to confirm Tucker's remarks on the dichotomy tourists construe between friendship and money (1997, p.121) – an actualization of Zelizer's (2000; 2005) 'hostile worlds' perspective – in the course of some fascinating discussions I had with tourists on these matters I also realized that the terms of this dichotomy could also be reconciled to make room for other views of friendship, or at least companionship, which were not necessarily incompatible with interest or instrumental economic transactions. Puzzled by the motivations of Cubans they had met during their journey, some tourists ended up admitting the possible coexistence of a desire to improve material and economic conditions through relationship with tourists on one side, and to be friends with them on the other.[6] Friendship would thereby be portrayed as compatible with economic asymmetries and interests, normalizing relationships where interests and instrumentality could go hand in hand with positive emotional involvement.

---

6   This may be also seen as a way, for these tourists, of preserving the impression of having built meaningful relations of intimacy and friendship with Cubans who nonetheless showed interest for their economic possessions. Adopting a less cynical stance, I think it is more fruitful to take seriously these tourists' insights on their relationships with Cubans.

Outlining a kind of general theory of sociality, other tourists I met reached the conclusion that relationships themselves, in general, were hardly conceivable without some kind of interest moving the parties involved.

The Cubans I talked to, on their side, would seldom get as far in entangling friendship and interests. As shown by Argyriadis (2005) and Palmié (2004), the opposition between interests and affection (*interes y cariño*) is a salient one in contemporary Cuba, where critiques of the increasing predominance of '*relaciones de interés*' – as opposed to 'real' relationships (Fosado, 2005) and 'true love' (Lundgren, 2011) – have gained much ground (see also Simoni, 2014c). Bringing into the picture notions of gift-giving and reciprocity, some of my Cuban informants admitted that friendships' potential for mutual gratification and satisfaction could eventually also entail the free-willing exchange of gifts and presents. These material exchanges, however, ought never to be the main motive of a 'true' friendship (Simoni, 2014a; 2014b). Again, this attitude could be contrasted with that of other Cubans/*jineteros* who just wanted the tourists' money, who were only looking for interested friendships (*amistad por interés*) and who did not care about more noble feelings or long-lasting relationships.

The distinctions between types of goods (e.g. money, food) and forms of exchange (e.g. commodity, gift) also played a particularly important role when sexual relationships were at stake. In this case too, the ways in which money made its appearance, the modalities and temporalities of its circulation, could greatly influence the sort of relationship that could take shape.

2.5 Money and Sexual Relations

2.5.1 *A Wide Range of Possibilities?*

Regarding more generally sex and romance between tourists and members of the visited population, a tendency to avoid discussions about money and economic gain – at least in the first stages of these relationships – has been observed in several parts of the world (see for instance Cohen, 1993; Philip and Dann, 1998; Günther, 1998; Dahles and Bras, 1999; Frohlick, 2007; Herold, Garcia and DeMoya, 2001). This same tendency is also pointed out in relation to Cuba (Cabezas, 2004; Kummels, 2005; Fosado, 2005). According to Cabezas: 'Studies confirm that most *pingueros*, *jineteros/-as*, and *shanky pankys* prefer to accept gifts or clothing, jewelry, and meals from tourists rather than to negotiate money for sex, because direct commercial transactions foreclose other possibilities and because direct commercial transactions confirm an identity as prostitute that they do not desire' (2004, p.999). As clearly shown by Cabezas (2004) and Kummels (2005), Cuban *jineteras* could be well aware that many tourists did not like to construct their relationship in terms of 'sex for money'. In Cabezas' terms: 'It is a preferable strategy to distance oneself from commercial sexual exchanges in order to procure more stable and lucrative social roles, such as that of a girlfriend or wife' (2004, p.1000).

On their side, tourists also had their own clues and recipes to make sense of these potentially ambiguous intimacies and the contentious role of money in them. In internet forums, people who have travelled to Cuba could for instance compare their experiences and debate vehemently on the character of their engagements with Cubans. During fieldwork, several tourists shared with me their knowledge and intuitions, some expressing doubts, others speaking with more confidence about 'how things were' on the island as far as the entanglements between sex and money were concerned. For instance, an experienced tourist who had been visiting Cuba regularly in the past three years, and had just come out of two intense relationships with Cuban women from whom he now felt betrayed, explained to me that there were three kind of 'girls' in Cuba.

> The ones that you meet and ask you straightforward for money, say 40 dollars [U.S.] ... The ones with whom you make love and only afterwards ask you for some money for a taxi to get home ... And the ones who don't ask you anything ... generally the most beautiful ones ... and that when you come back to your country you can't stop thinking about them, about their needs and poverty, and you keep writing to them, sending them money, 100, 200 dollars ... while in the meantime they are here in Cuba enjoying their [Cuban] boyfriends ... and fucking other tourists.

Other tourists with whom I discussed these issues kept it simpler, warning me that all that Cubans wanted from tourists was money. Foreigners who had visited the island on numerous occasions tended to regret the changes that were taking place in terms of the commoditization of sexual relationships. One of them was sorry to say that people in Cuba were not naive anymore: they were becoming more and more 'like us', 'money oriented', and in the process of 'capitalize' [sic] (*capitalizzare*) themselves. Echoing a narrative I was starting to become familiar with, the same man talked with more enthusiasm about the less touristic areas of the island where he spent most of his holidays, places where one could easily reunite with a local girlfriend year after year, and where relationships with Cubans were generally less tarnished by money and economic considerations than in the touristic centres of the island.

Following the accounts of several male tourists I met, what happened in many situations ridden with ambiguity was that references to money would be avoided in the first instances of an encounter, leaving the question suspended at least until the end of the intercourse. This issue could reappear later on, more likely as a request by the Cuban woman at stake for some money to get home by taxi, or as a help in her struggle to overcome the economic hardship she was suffering. Alternatively, after a first successful encounter, the couple could continue going out together all through the tourist's stay in Cuba. Again, invitations and the offering of presents like clothes and shoes, or food and drinks during the time spent together would acquire a different connotation than the payment of cash for sex. We can agree with Cabezas here, when she argues that '[w]ith gifts seen as expressions of love and not as payment for services rendered, men and women hope to obscure the dichotomy between love and money' (2004, p.1000). But even as ambiguities were dissipated and controversies settled between the parties, and when romance seemed the proper term to define their relation, the protagonists involved would still have to confront the sceptical gazes and remarks of fellow friends and peers, who could easily mock their ingenuity, question the sincerity of their partner, and hint at the inevitability of cheating and deception (see Simoni, 2013; 2014a). Facing these insinuations, doubts could be kept at bay only via constant reassertions of the parameters of the relationship, requiring for instance reiterated proofs of a sincere engagement in it.

2.5.2   Indexing Money, Playing with Ambiguity

The practices and discourses of Gianluca, Daniele and Marzio,[7] three young men from Italy that I repeatedly met on the beach of Santa Maria, can help shed more light on the nuanced, controversial, and changing entanglements and connotations of sexual relationships and monetary exchange. While discussing their predispositions to engage with Cuban women, these tourists repeatedly drew and re-drew moral boundaries between commoditized sex/prostitution and what they referred to as more 'genuine', 'spontaneous' sexual relationships. By discussing with them both before and after their concrete experience of sex with Cuban women, I could follow how such experiences informed changes in their discourses and justifications, and the way they could manipulate ambiguity and deploy misunderstandings in their favour (see also Simoni, 2014c).

When I talked to Gianluca, Daniele and Marzio for the first time, our conversation progressively moved to the topic of Cuban women and of sexual relationships, with Gianluca arguing that Cuban women were indeed what he had come to Cuba for. He then went on summarizing his holiday's drives in three words: 'the beach, the sun, and the babes' ('*la spiaggia, il sole, e la gnocca*'). Immediately, this admission was tempered by other remarks which specified the nature of his predisposition, and drew some boundaries between various types of sexual engagements – most notably in relation to the role of money:

> But I mean, if we have to pay [for sex], like to pay 20 Euros, then no way! I can do that in Italy if I want, I just pay 25 Euros. There was no need to come all the way here.

After his comment, I provocatively mentioned the potential difficulty of having sex without getting money involved, as I was wondering how they had planned

---

7   All the personal names of research participants are fictional.

to solve such dilemma. Gianluca replied, emphasizing the skilfulness of it all – of engaging in sex without paying for it.

> Yes but you know, the taxi driver who brought us here, told us that first you have to get to know them [Cuban women] a bit, talk with them, slowly, and you will find a solution. I mean, ok, you pay them the food, the drinks, you go out together at night … He [taxi driver] told us that you can do that. You just need to know how to do it … Yeah, I wouldn't mind having a Cuban girlfriend, like, for 5 days.

The establishment of a temporary girlfriend–boyfriend relationship was therefore cast as a challenge requiring certain skills and abilities, among which patience and a know-how on how to properly deploy money, generosity, and enact a suitable masculine self.

Marzio had already been in Cuba in 1999, and told me how things had changed since then:

> Yes you know, the last time, you just went out with a girl, you bought some drinks to her, you went dancing together. A bit like in Italy I mean. And then you would fuck her.

It was via a parallel with Italy that boundaries were drawn here, and that the road to an ideal, normal sexual relationship was outlined. This kind of narrative, which came up repeatedly in conversations in Santa Maria (Simoni, 2014c), posited as the norm for men to sponsor drinks, food, entrance fees to potential partners as a way to access sex. In this line of reasoning, sex became a way for women to reciprocate men's invitations.

Referring to the money given to a Cuban woman after a night together – 15 CUC for a taxi to get back home – a young Italian man assessed the cheapness of the deal when compared with Italy: 'I mean, by us [in Italy], you bring her out for lunch a couple of times, and already [you have spent much more than that] …'. These grids of legibility made of sex a matter of calculation, something that could be accounted for in terms of economic equivalences. Even the payment of a taxi or invitations for lunch could thus become objects of calculation, translated into monetary value. Countering the need to justify payment for sex, these discourses strived to emphasize the normality of it: yes, an economic transaction was at stake, but this was just like in Italy, with Italy representing here 'everyday', 'normal' situations. But while monetary equivalences were drawn, cash was not overtly given for sex. Instead, money becomes entangled in a broader paternalistic approach to gender relations, which saw men sponsoring meals, drinks, and taxis as part of a normal and normative 'order of things', and women reciprocating with sexual availability. The asymmetries that such deployments of money brought about here were indexed to gender norms rather than to a 'rich tourist – poor local' divide. The unequal economic position of tourists and Cubans was downplayed and this could eventually also enable the protagonists involved to escape the stigmatizing identifications of 'client' and 'prostitute'. Instead, the partners were portrayed as gendered beings enacting 'ordinary', 'normal' gender roles.

But economic inequalities could also be brought into the picture by the visitors who engaged in sex with Cuban women. In the case of Gianluca, Daniele and Marzio, this, however, did not question their resolution not to pay for sex. As Gianluca put it:

> No, if all [Cuban women] ask me for money, [there is] no way I will go with them. Sure, I will not go with any of them. I will rather just do a holiday here, on the beach, it doesn't matter. It's not that I do not want to give them money. That's not the point. It is not that I don't want to help them. I know they need. But not money to make love. What's that, I pay and then ... [mimicking the act of having sex]. No, that's squalid/sordid (*squallido*)!

At stake here were issues of self-perception and self-esteem, and of one's moral way of engaging in sex. Gianluca did not like the idea of seeing himself paying for it, and would not be able to do it that way. Nevertheless, he was aware of the needs of Cuban people, of their difficult economic situation. His problem lay not so much in the fact of giving something, of being charitable and generous, but specifically in engaging in commoditized sex.

Two days after our first exchange, I met Gianluca, Daniele and Marzio again in Santa Maria. They started telling me about the adventure they had had with three Cuban women. Everything went fine, Gianluca told me. Marzio confirmed it had been all right, 'apart from the end'. To Daniele then to clarify:

> Yes, there was a misunderstanding (*quiproquò*). Because, yes, she [the Cuban woman he met] asked for money. I mean, she did not tell me before, the evening before ... I told her, 'you did not tell me the night before, and I am not paying you!' ... And then, we gave the money for the taxi and they left.

In the course of the conversation that followed, Gianluca elaborated further:

> I mean, last night you [referring to the Cuban partner in question] did not tell us anything. If you had told me yesterday, maybe I would not have even gone out with you. I mean, it's not that I do not want to give her the money, but, if she had told me before ... Then, I can also choose the girl I want. If I have to pay, it's me who decides, I also decide the girl with whom I want to go.

We can perceive here the double edge in which Cuban women could be caught as they tried to establish a relationship with tourists and draw some economic resources from it. The Italian men had told me two days earlier that they would not have engaged with someone asking money for sex. If not openly contradicting such views, here they seemed at least to add an additional clause to their reasoning:

their preference for an open and explicit behaviour. However, I would argue that it was precisely the non-explicit and ambiguous character of relationships that had ultimately enabled them to have sex with these Cuban women. Most likely, the women too had speculated on the affordance of such ambiguity, in the hope that the foreigners would turn out to be generous, but also exposed themselves to the risk of not being given anything in return for sex. Any explicit hint to payments beforehand could have led the tourists to move on to other potential partners. With the request of payment coming only after sex, Gianluca and his friends had been able to play, retrospectively, the 'misunderstanding'. In this sense, we may argue that while ambiguity and the productive potential of misunderstanding (Tsing, 2005) had allowed the relationship to happen, the tourists seemed to have benefitted the most from it.

The tourists' account also revealed a change in attitude towards the general principle of paying for sex: if they had to pay – the reasoning now went – they expected at least to be able to choose with whom to have sex. Payment seemed to have entered the range of possibilities, perhaps once they realized the challenges of having sex otherwise. This moral shift was confirmed a few moments after. 'Shit! Look at this one! What a beauty! This one ... I would even give her fifteen ... For this one, I would even pay fifteen euros', had been Marzio's comment when a young Cuban woman passed beside us. Ironic or not, his remarks indicated a renewed openness and moral disposition to pay for sex. I could perceive these shifts in perspective in the discourses of other male tourists, notably people who had some experiences of sexual relationships with Cuban women. In this respect, many were those who seemed to reach the conclusion one could not get around paying for sex in Cuba. Once they subscribed to this state of affairs, the tourists' skilfulness would then reside in how best to deal with it, and playing with ambiguity and misunderstandings was certainly a valued way to do so.

2.6 Money and Charitable Relations

The idioms of friendship and sexual relationships examined above saw money deployed in ways that tended to downplay the importance of economic asymmetries in the establishment of relationships. Another relational idiom in touristic Cuba would, instead of silencing such asymmetries and inequalities, call for appropriate moral behaviours to make up for them. In charitable relationships, the protagonists of interactions were encouraged to inhabit the positions of destitute beneficiaries on one side, and of powerful benefactors on the other. In a relational way, the former called for the latter, evoking the 'coercive subordination' described by Appadurai in the case of Hindu India (1990), whereby 'beggars seek to trap (...) [their (potential) benefactors] in the cultural implication of their roles as superiors, that is, the obligation to be generous' (p.101). In touristic Cuba, the taken for granted implication on which these practices relied was that tourists were extremely privileged, in economic terms, when compared to the Cuban population, and that their journey also ought to have resulted in a redistribution of their wealth to the poorest and most vulnerable within such population.

Children, elderly people, and women with infants predominated among the Cubans that addressed foreign tourists on the streets of Havana with explicit requests for help, be it material goods or money. Marks of poverty and vulnerability would in this case be emphasized, as people lamented their condition and drew the tourists' attention, for instance, to disabilities, lack of nourishment, or their worn out and shattered clothes. Rumours circulated among my Cuban interlocutors about mothers 'renting' someone else's baby in order to follow the tourists' trail and ask for money, following the rationale that a mother and baby where more likely to induce feelings of pity and compassion among the foreigners. The attitudes of tourists towards these requests could vary greatly. Some assumed the role of benefactor ascribed to them, while others categorically refused to engage in it, arguing for instance that charity produced begging, and condemning the other tourists' responsibility in reproducing and fostering such practice.

Being repeatedly confronted with these endeavours, I noticed that various deployments of money could also be at stake in them. For instance, I repeatedly came across a woman that refused the tourists' money when she deemed that the amount was too small and/or in the 'wrong kind' of currency – i.e. *pesos cubanos*. Complaining about the meanness of such donations, coming as they were from *convertibles*-carrying tourists, she lamented that she would not be able to 'do anything' with a few Cuban pesos, leaving the visitors perplexed, if not offended, by her refusal.[8]

A common request saw women asking for powdered milk for their new-born babies. Tourists were then encouraged to follow the women into a nearby *tienda*, the state run shops running in *convertibles*, and buy the milk powder together, so as to make sure that the money was spent appropriately. Nevertheless, arrangements between shop attendants and those who brought tourists there seemed to be the rule, so that the milk could be reimbursed as soon as the parties split. Occasionally, Cuban men too could ask for money to buy baby milk. In such cases, I found it significant that some men emphasized how they would not employ the cash to buy rum or cigarettes, but just this essential item for their infants at home. Such were the norms governing these requests for help, which delineated a hierarchy between different entanglements of money, its purpose, and the morality of it.

Enticing gifts from tourists could become a very reflexive and carefully calculated endeavour, and several other tactics could be deployed to that effect. An ex-*jinetero* once explained me that in order to bring about feelings of pity and generosity among his tourist companions, he would wear the same worn out clothes during all the days they spent together. His calculation was that once the tourists' noticed it, this would have given him a good pretext to complain about

---

8   See Palmié's (2004,) reflection on a similar instance of refusal by a Cuban man engaged in an Afro-Cuban possession ritual: 'The deity took a good look at the bill, and returned it to me with the comment that this was not the right kind of *owo* [money]' (p.237).

his lack of economic resources and his inability to buy what he needed. Back in the 1990s, he explained, when tourists were less circumspect and cynical in their interactions with Cubans, he and his friends had managed to receive several suitcases full of clothes, which they then went on to sell for much needed cash.

As this last example shows, there could be different shades and variations of the benefactor–beneficiary dyad: from more upfront and explicit begging, to generosity enticing tactics that could easily blur into evocations of reciprocal exchanges of gifts and favours. The Cubans' efforts to bring about gift-giving and reciprocity could become particularly evident when tourists were about to leave. In these moments, the Cuban companion could draw attention to the amazing things that the tourist had been able to do thanks to their guidance and their insider knowledge, which had granted them access to the secrets of a Cuba beyond the 'tourist bubble' – a more real, safer and cheaper Cuba. Pushing relationships beyond the realms of friendship or charity, these discourses could move towards the objectification and commoditization of prestations like guiding, with the pricing of a service and the establishment of monetary equivalences being the ultimate step in this direction. This could lead from friendship, charity, and the moralities attached to them, to a relation more akin to a market transaction, one in which money was explicitly given as payment for a well demarcated service rendered.

2.7 Concluding Remarks

As the various examples discussed in this chapter have shown, money was a key element in the shaping of relationships between foreign tourists and members of the visited population in Cuba. Rather than simply adopting the view that different deployments of money constituted different relationships, we may argue that money and relationships tend to constitute and inform the qualities of each other. Money could therefore appear not as a given, stabilized, and unified object, but as a potentially controversial and plural 'thing' (Latour, 2005; Henare, Holbraad and Wastell, 2007), whose eventual stabilization was itself one of the possible outcomes of the relationship at stake. My ethnographic material shows how different conceptions, uses and values of money could be enacted and refashioned as they become entangled in various sorts of relationships. I have followed Maurer's call here for an anthropology of money that reorients itself 'from meanings to repertoires, pragmatics, and indexicality' (2006, p.30). Helping shape specific relationships, and being in turn (re)qualified by them, money and its deployments became key devices to produce different and demarcated realities. They brought to life a variety of competing instantiations of tourism encounters, making a good case for their multiplicity.

To understand the reciprocal constitution of money and relationships and their variegated outcomes, it is certainly important to consider the transactional orders (Maurer, 2006, p.22; Bloch and Parry, 1989) – 'gift' or 'commodity' exchange for instance – in which money became entangled. But also differences and boundaries between transactional orders were not always clear and stable. Accordingly, these boundaries could themselves become the object of reflexive manipulations, prompting shifts between forms of transaction, which in their wake produced yet other shifts and re-qualifications of the relationships at stake, and vice versa. Money could be indexed and performed as a gift rather than a payment, producing qualitatively different relationships, but the partners involved did not always see things the same way, and this could bring unexpected turns in relationships, changing money as a result. And when tourists and Cubans were led to keep ambiguities alive, this opened up further space for different realities to take shape.

Different deployments of money also served to negotiate mutualities and asymmetries. A tricky currency exchange could (re)assert the tourist's status of 'naïve outsider', placing the 'local insider' in a temporary position of superiority. A relation of mutual friendship could find expression in the use of *pesos cubanos* as opposed to *pesos convertibles*. Sexual partners could deploy and index money's deployments as payment, help, form of reciprocity, or ordinary manifestation of gender relations –these different indexations being potentially at play, in different moments, even in the same relationship – thereby drawing mutualities and asymmetries along different lines, and reshaping intimate engagements accordingly. Charitable relationships emphasized asymmetries, albeit they could also easily shift (with money once again protagonist) and be recast as exploitative expressions of scrounging, forms of reciprocity, or commoditized prestations of service. The fact of not settling the meanings of transactions explicitly and once and for all could also enable the people involved to (re)conceive relationships in their own ways and for their own purposes. Thus, from an encounter, different monies and different relationships could take shape, outlining different moral orders and hierarchies of value, and making the encounter no longer count as one, but as plural and multiple.

References

Appadurai, A., 1990. Topographies of the self: Praise and emotion in Hindu India. In: C.A. Lutz and L. Abu-Lughod (eds) *Language and the politics of emotion*. Cambridge: Cambridge University Press, Paris: Editions de la Maison des Sciences de l'Homme, pp.92–112.

Argyriadis, K., 2005. El desarrollo del turismo religioso en La Habana y la acusación de mercantilismo. *Desacatos* 18, pp.29–52.

Berg, M.L., 2004. Tourism and the revolutionary new man: The specter of *Jineterismo* in late 'special period' Cuba. *Focaal – European Journal of Anthropology*, 43, pp.46–56.

Bloch, M. and Parry, J., 1989. *Money and the morality of exchange*. Cambridge: Cambridge University Press.

Brotherton, S., 2008. We have to think like capitalists but continue being socialists: Medicalized subjectivities, emergent capital and socialist entrepreneurs in post-soviet Cuba. *American Ethnologist*, 35(2), pp.259–74.

Cabezas, A.L., 2004. Between love and money: Sex, tourism and citizenship in Cuba and the Dominican Republic. *Signs*, 29(4), pp.984–1015.

Cohen, E., 1993. Open-ended prostitution as a skilful game of luck: Opportunities, risk and security among tourist-oriented prostitutes in a Bangkok soi. In: M. Hitchcock, V.T. King and M. Parnwell (eds) *Tourism in South East Asia*. London: Routledge, pp.155–78.

Comaroff, J.L. and Comaroff, J., 1997. *Of revelation and revolution vol. 2: The dialectics of modernity on a South-African frontier*. Chicago and London: University of Chicago Press.

Dahles, H. and Bras, K., 1999. Entrepreneurs in romance: Tourism in Indonesia. *Annals of Tourism Research*, 26(2), pp.267–93.

Fernandez, N., 1999. Back to the future? Women, race and tourism in Cuba. In: K. Kempadoo (ed.) *Sun, sex and gold: Tourism and sex work in the Caribbean*. Lanham: Rowman & Littlefield Publishers, pp.81–9.

Fosado, G., 2005. Gay sex tourism, ambiguity and transnational love in Havana. In: D.J. Fernández (ed.) *Cuba transnational*. Gainesville: University Press of Florida, pp.61–78.

Frohlick, S., 2007. Fluid exchanges: The negotiation of intimacy between tourist women and local men in a transnational town in Caribbean Costa Rica. *City and Society*, 19(1), pp.139–68.

Günther, A., 1998. Sex tourism without sex tourists. In: M. Oppermann (ed.) *Sex tourism and prostitution: Aspects of seisure, recreation and work*. New York: Cognizant Communication Corporation, pp.71–80.

Henare, A., Holbraad, M. and Wastell, S., 2007. Introduction: Thinking through things. In: A. Henare, M. Holbraad and S. Wastell (eds) *Thinking through things: Theorising artefacts ethnographically*. Oxon and New York: Routledge. pp.1–31.

Herold, E., Garcia, R. and DeMoya, T., 2001. Female tourists and beach boys: Romance or sex tourism? *Annals of Tourism Research*, 29(4), pp.978–97.

Kummels, I., 2005. Love in the time of diaspora. Global markets and local meaning in prostitution, marriage and womanhood in Cuba. *Iberoamericana*, 5(20), pp.7–26.

Latour, B., 2005. *Reassembling the social: An introduction to Actor-Network-Theory*. Oxford: Oxford University Press.

Lundgren, S., 2011. *Heterosexual Havana: Ideals and hierarchies of gender and sexuality in contemporary Cuba*. Ph.D. Uppsala University (unpublished).

Maurer, B., 2006. The anthropology of money. *Annual Review of Anthropology*, 35, pp.15–36.

Palmié, S., 2004. *Fascinans* or *tremendum*? Permutations of the state, the body and the divine in late-twentieth-century Havana. *New West Indian Guide*, 78(3/4), pp.229–68.

Philip, J. and Dann, G., 1998. Bar girls in central Bangkok: Prostitution as entrepreneurship. In: M. Oppermann (ed.) *Sex tourism and prostitution: Aspects of leisure, recreation and work*. New York: Cognizant Communication Corporation, pp.60–70.

Simoni, V., 2008a. Shifting power: The (de)stabilization of asymmetries in the realm of tourism in Cuba. *Tsansta: Journal of the Swiss Ethnological Society*, 13, pp.11–19.

Simoni, V., 2008b. 'Riding' diversity: Cubans'/Jineteros' uses of 'nationality-talks' in the realm of their informal encounters with tourists. In: P. Burns and M. Novelli (eds) *Tourism Development: Growth, Myths and Inequalities*. Wallingford, Cambridge MA: CAB International, pp.68–84.

Simoni, V., 2012. Tourism materialities. Enacting cigars in touristic Cuba. In: R. Van der Duim, C. Ren and G.T. Jóhannesson (eds) *Actor-Network Theory and tourism: Ordering, materiality and multiplicity*. London: Routledge, pp.59–79.

Simoni, V., 2013. Intimate stereotypes: The vicissitudes of being *caliente* in touristic Cuba. *Civilisations: Revue Internationale d'Anthropologie et de Sciences Humaines*, 62(1–2), pp.181–97.

Simoni, V., 2014a. Revisiting hosts and guests: Ethnographic insights on touristic encounters from Cuba. *Journal of Tourism Challenges and Trends*, 6(2), pp.39–62.

Simoni, V., 2014b. The morality of friendship in touristic Cuba. *Suomen Antropologi: Journal of the Finnish Anthropological Society*, 39(1), pp.19–36.

Simoni, V., 2014c. Coping with ambiguous relationships: Sex, tourism, and transformation in Cuba. *Journal of Tourism and Cultural Change*, 12(2), pp.166–183.

Tucker, H., 1997. The ideal village: Interactions through tourism in central Anatolia. In: S. Abram, J. Waldren and D.V.L. Macleod (eds) *Tourists and tourism. Identifying with people and places*. Oxford and New York: Berg, pp.107–128.

Tsing, A., 2005. *Friction: An ethnography of global connection*. Princeton: Princeton University Press.

Zelizer, V.A., 2000. The purchase of intimacy. *Law and Social Inquiry*, 25(3), pp.817–48.

Zelizer, V.A., 2005. *The purchase of intimacy*. Princeton, NJ: Princeton University Press.

Chapter 3
Reef Controversies: The Case of Wakatobi National Park, Indonesia

Senna Middelveld, René van der Duim and Rico Lie

3.1 Introduction

In southeast Asia 80 per cent of the coral reefs, being complex mosaics of marine plants and animals, are ecologically degraded due to practices such as coral mining, bomb-fishing, trap-fishing, and overfishing to name a few (Clifton, 2003, also see Green, et al., 2011; Caras and Pasternak, 2009; Elliott, et al., 2001). Because of these ecological threats, in 1996 the government of Indonesia designated Wakatobi as a Marine National Park and in 2002 as a Marine Protected Area (Caras and Pasternak, 2009). Since 2005 it has also been listed as a tentative World Heritage site. In turn this encouraged tourism, since World Heritage sites are more often visited by tourists than other destinations (Jimura, 2011; Buckley, 2004).

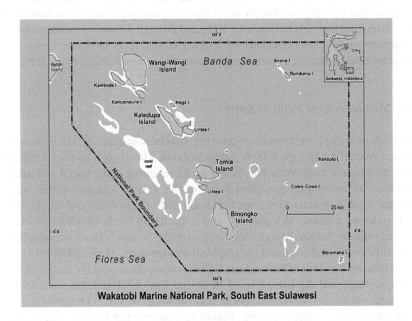

Figure 3.1 Wakatobi Marine National Park, South East Sulawesi
Source: Operation Wallacea

Wakatobi consists of four larger islands (Wangi-Wangi, Kaledupa, Tomia and Binongko), as well as smaller islands located at the southeast of Sulawesi, Indonesia. Wakatobi includes 25 groups of coral reefs, amongst others barrier reefs, atolls and fringing reefs with a total of 600 km^2, and comprising almost 400 species of coral belonging to 68 genera and 15 families. Figure 3.1 shows the park and its boundaries. Approximately 80,000 people live in Wakatobi of which 92 per cent are land people (people mainly engaging in pastoral and arable activities), and a minority Bajo ("sea people") (Clifton, 2003). Bajo are very closely connected to the reefs as 'they rely almost exclusively on marine resources' (Clifton, 2003, p.390).

Inspired by Actor–Network Theory (ANT), this chapter examines how coral reefs in Wakatobi are enacted in multiple ways. We closely trace some of the networks, alignments and orderings of the reefs to provide new ways of understanding how the reefs enable, are actively used by and connected to different actors, interpretations, practices and performances. By tracing these networks we aim to explore multiple and sometimes controversial enacted realities of the reefs, examine how tourism and other reef practices go together, and discuss how to deal with complex and messy objects, such as coral reefs.

Below, we first briefly introduce our theoretical and methodological points of departure. Second, we distinguish different realities of coral reefs. These different realities co-exist but also engage with each other through networks, interpretations and practices in distinct (but partially connected) ways. Third, we present the main controversies resulting from the multiplicity of reef enactments and discuss the consequences of the existence of different realities. Finally in the conclusive part we argue that viewing coral reefs as multiple and complex, and at the same time acknowledging how this multiplicity is created through different practices, objects and interpretations, provides space for looking at coral reefs and natural resources, and at the relation between tourism and conservation, in new and unexpected ways.

3.2   Methodological Point of Entry

Our study of multiple enactments of coral reefs has been inspired by Actor–Network Theory. According to Law (2009) Actor–Network Theory is a distinct family of material-semiotic tools and methods that treat everything in the social and natural worlds as an incessantly generated result of the web of relations within which they are located. It thus 'describes the enactment of materially and discursively heterogeneous relations that produce and reshuffle all kinds of actors including objects, subjects, human beings, machines, animals, "nature", ideas, organizations, inequalities scale and sizes and geographical arrangements' (Law, 2009, p.141).

Following the work of for example Callon (1986), discussing the domestication of the scallops and the fisherman of St Brieuc Bay, ANT scholars have looked at natural resources. As Jepson, Barua and Buckingham (2011) recently argued, while introducing Actor–Network Theory to conservation biology, the concept of an actor should be broadened to include nonhumans, such as animal or plant species, because they are actors-enacted (Law and Mol, 2008) and can influence project goals and outcomes. By challenging the purification of the world in two distinct categories, Nature–Society, a range of 'hybrid' entities have been rethought as relational achievements and this relational ontology is increasingly linked to conservation biology (see Lorimer, 2012)

This is for example illustrated by a study of Thompson (2002; see also Law, 2009) about the way elephants at Amboseli National Park in Kenya should be handled. In this case, the realities of animal behaviourists and conservation biologists are counterpoised, and these realities 'are heterogeneous, combining and enacting the natural, the social, and the political' (Law, 2009, p.154). Related studies focussing on natural resources provided new insights in the organization of Norwegian fisheries (Johnson, et al., 2009), the domestication of Atlantic salmon (Lien and Law, 2011), and the development of whale and dolphin watching in New Zealand (Cloke and Perkins, 2005).

Recent ANT inspired studies also highlight and illustrate the multiplicity and heterogeneity (Law and Singleton, 2005; Law, 2009; Van der Duim, Ren and Jóhannesson, 2012; 2013) of actor-networks, as well as their capacity to enact reality (Mol, 1999; 2002; Law, 2009). In that sense ANT reshapes ontology and our understanding of how 'the reality we live with is one performed in a variety of practices' (Mol, 1999, p.74). Because of ANT's multiplicity assumption, different and valid knowledges appear that can be neither entirely reconciled nor dismissed (Mol, 2002). Examples of such a treatment of multiplicity can be found in the literature related to topics such as liver cirrhosis (Law and Singleton, 2005), the human body (Mol, 2002), elephants (Whatmore and Thorne, 2000) and gorillas (Van der Duim, Ampumuza and Ahebwa, 2014). The main argument is that, instead of thinking about multiple interpretations of the same object, we should think about – in this case – coral reefs as multiple objects themselves (Law and Singleton, 2005). These coral reefs are enacted in different versions (Ren, 2011).

Following Law and Mol (2008), in this chapter we explore how practices of fishing, bombing, tourism and conservation each enact "reefs" in different ways. This tells us that what a "reef" is can only be known if we explore these practices – that it is not given outside them. But this is not to say that exploring a few practices in a few pages gives us an exhaustive answer to the question "what is a reef?" Our inquiries are necessarily partial. We might say a lot more about other – fishing, tourism, or conservation – practices and we might also go on to investigate other practices. The list is endless. The reality of an entity is never exhausted. A reef-enacted does not exist all by itself and neither does it act alone. Indeed, as Law and Mol (2008, p.72–3) argue:

> an actor-enacted acts in collaboration with others to such an extent that it is not always clear who is doing what. Action moves around. It is like a viscous fluid. What each actor does also depends on its co-actors, on whether they allow it to act and on what they allow it to do, on rules and regulations. But this is not to say that an actor-enacted is determined by its surroundings. It has its

own stubbornness and specificities: it is full of surprises. So the difference an actor makes is not predictable. Indeed, on the contrary: what actors-enacted do is essentially indeterminate. So much comes together in the collaborative webs of complex practice.

In order to examine this complexity and multiplicity, we discern a number of 'materials' involved in the enactment of the coral reefs (see Callon and Law, 1995). First there are people, like fishermen, coral miners, tourists, conservationists, scientists or government officials. Second, there are coral reefs, in different shapes, white and colored, growing or shrinking, "alive" and "dead", and the fish or turtles swimming in the reefs. Third, there are devices, technologies, licenses and papers. As we shall see bubus, bombs, lingis, diving equipment and laws, and many more, are playing their respective roles in the enactment of coral reefs. Their properties and identities are the result of being part of "collectifs" of materially heterogeneous bits and pieces. *Collectifs* which in turn are emergent effects by the interactions of the heterogeneous parts that make it up (Callon and Law, 1995).

To study these *collectifs* and trace the multiple enactments of the reefs, the first author "followed the actors" to unfold how reefs are enacted. In a first round of fieldwork (October 2011), (participant) observations, note making, and in-depth (open-ended) interviews were conducted. Besides working with the initially selected respondents, the connections they mentioned with other actors, materials or networks were also investigated. During this field work at least 25 different reef practices were identified, of which fishing-techniques are the majority. Based on these findings and due to time limitations, the decision was made to follow a smaller number of different and potentially interesting and contrasting practices. During a second round of fieldwork (November 2011), the first author again conducted semi-structured interviews, visited the market, talked to sellers and renters of equipment and attended meetings and educational workshops organized by conservation organizations, but also more closely "followed the reefs" and how they enable particular practices, as she for example sailed with fishing boats and made reef walks (for full methodological account see Middelveld, 2012). By following these actors, many other actors and materials showed up, as well as relations between them. Even though many connections outside of Wakatobi were mentioned by respondents, for this research Wakatobi National Park was the boundary surrounding the fieldwork.

3.3 The Multiple Enactments of Coral Reefs

Natural objects like coral reefs "afford" certain possibilities. They do so because of the particular ways in which they are entangled with people, technologies and materials. Given certain past and present relations, particular "objects" like reefs afford a range of possibilities and opportunities; they owe certain affordances (see Harré, 2002; Van der Duim, 2007). Coral reefs as actors-enacted are disposed towards many different usages. Coral reefs enable coral miners and fishermen to "making a living". But the reefs are also enacted by tourists and tourism facilitators, for example by diving, and by conservation organizations and the government, with as common goal the protection of the reefs. We first examine how reefs afford production and consumption. After that we discuss how reefs are protected.

3.3.1   Fishing and Coral Mining

In our research, we first followed different types of fishermen and coral miners. The bubu-fishermen make or buy square bamboo traps (bubus), which they place on top of or near the reefs. The trap and the live coral pieces are thus essential for this fishing-technique and the fish are used domestically or sold at the market. This technique has its roots in land people's history (i.e. bamboo-farming). It is used by "land people" only. To find a suitable spot to catch their target-fish, they walk over the reefs at low tide. They cover the trap with living coral pieces. It is explained in this way: '*The fish are just too smart. First we used dead rocks only, but then the fish found out that shelters made of these rocks are often a trap so they started to avoid the traps. The dead rocks are white, so they stand out too much from the colorful corals. That's when we decided to use living coral, and then the trap is just better camouflaged*'. Because the trap does not contain bait, camouflage is needed to avoid detection by the fish. Yansen, one of the fishermen, described bubu-fishing as follows: '*The idea of the bubu is that you create a nice resting place for the fish, so that it will enter your trap*'. After 24 hours the trap is checked and the caught fish are removed. Besides the trap itself, fishermen evaluate tides and weather before they decide whether or not to set the trap again. They only set traps with low tide because it is very dangerous to walk on the reefs if the tide is high or the weather rough. The high waves can easily cause loss of balance and injuries during the reef walk.

   Menyulu is a spear fishing technique used at night, for which fishermen use a boat, an oil lamp and spears made of bamboo sticks (farmed by land people) and five-pointed spear points made of iron by blacksmiths (land people). This technique is practiced by Bajonese only. A weather assessment is done before fishermen leave for menyulu. Rain, wind, high tide and waves reduce visibility of the water and menyulu is thus mainly performed during the dry season. Depending on the lunar-cycle and spawning season squid, crab or fish are the main target, but everything that swims or walks by on the sea-bottom is speared. A bad catch is eaten together directly, whereas a good catch is sold at the market. During one of the trips, it was full moon and Ridwan, one of the Bajonese, explained why fish was not the main target this evening: '*Fish are more difficult to catch with full moon, because they can see the spear reflect in the water which gives them a bigger chance to escape. Besides that, October and November are spawning months for fish, so many fish have moved to their breeding grounds away from the living reefs*'. Instead, squid and crab were targeted, because both squid and crab are more active when it is full moon (crab walks around more and squid comes to the surface), which makes them both easier targets to catch.

A third fishing practice is carried out by bomb-fishermen, who order bomb-materials (manure, wicks) from Kendari, Singapore or Malaysia. One of the fishermen emphasized the importance of paying the right price to the authorities from Singapore, Malaysia and Indonesia for a successful import of bomb-materials: '*If not enough money is given, then you have a problem. So first you have to get acquainted and create a good relationship before you can import your bomb-materials*'. The fishermen build the bombs themselves from these materials, and they prefer to use them at remote reefs (which are less frequently checked) to avoid problems with other fishermen and the government. When they arrive at the reefs, they select a site where a lot of large and favoured fish species are seen. Three to five bombs are detonated sequentially on site with only a few minutes in between, after which they collect the dead floating fish of preferred species and size. Small species are left behind. After collecting the fish, the fishermen sell the fish at the market or to a middleman. Because bomb-fishing has been illegal since 1996, the market for bomb-materials went 'underground'. Several strategies are present to bypass authorities: first a warning system (if informants see a joint patrol leaving the harbour they call the bomb-fishermen at remote reefs to warn them), and second by throwing all bombs overboard when they see a patrol arriving to avoid detection. After the check the bombs are dived up and used after the authorities have left.

The final practice observed is coral mining. The coral miners use a lingis to remove coral stone from the sea. A lingis is a long iron spear that was originally used as an agricultural tool for planting seeds (often it is longer than the spear used for agriculture). None of the coral miners referred to the stones as coral. So instead of referring to "karang mati", dead coral, they refer to it as "karang batu", or coral stone. In other words, dead coral is not coral; it is stone that can be mined and used as building material. One of the miners explained: '*We never bring corals to the shore, because we know that if we take the corals the fish will also disappear. So we only take the stones, not the corals*'. The separation between stone and coral is made by looking at the presence of mucus: '*Living coral has mucus if you hit it, whereas dead coral has no mucus. And we only take the dead coral because that is suitable as a building material, so only spots where the corals are covered with sand are searched. And only those stones are taken*'. With their boat they leave early in the morning at low tide for mining sites, often near their home. Mining is only done by Bajonese, and especially in the harbour area near Mola. While standing at chest level in the water next to their boat, they hit the lingis on the sand-covered bottom until they hit hard surface. Then they cuff the piece until it is loosened from the bottom, before picking it up and placing it in their boat. This process continues until the boat is filled. The stones are only removed if they are covered with sand, otherwise they are not hard enough to be used as building material. The stones are domestically used, sold to the government or to local or land people. The coral stones are used as building material for houses, roads, government buildings, harbours, bridges and canals.

During the interviews all fishermen emphasize that living reefs are needed to enable their reef practices, because the fish and other targets live near the reefs and they need the living reefs to survive. The living reefs are thus essential for the fishermen to make a living, as are dead reefs for the coral miners. Furthermore, remote and local reefs are described as "disconnected" by the fishermen, as are dead and living reefs by the coral miners. Thus, practices occurring at reefs near the shore do not influence the remote reefs and vice versa, just as (dead) reefs that are used for mining do not influence the (living) reefs used for fishing. None of the fishermen and coral miners consider their practices as damaging to the reefs or as interfering with other reef-users.

3.3.2 Tourism

Next to fishermen and coral miners, tourists also frequent the reefs, as the reefs enable snorkelling and diving. Often tourists are attracted to Wakatobi by websites showing beautiful reef pictures or by advertisements and flyers from the government. They expect to enter a national park well-protected by authorities, with a high biodiversity, for which an entrance fee is paid and where visible signs of protection are present. However, entering the national park they encounter a lot of waste and plastic in the seawater, only little fish, no sharks or turtles and a bad reef condition near and around Hoga island (the main island used to facilitate tourists and researchers). One of the tourists described his disappointment about the reefs: '*If I had known the reefs were in this condition before I arrived, I would not have come here. It really is misleading advertising they do for this area ... I have seen much better reefs than the ones out here*'.

Other tourists staying at Patuno resort were more enthusiastic about the reefs and its condition, but were very disturbed by the bubu-trapping and bomb-fishing. Tourists consider bubu-traps, placed on the reefs covered with live coral, and bombs used for fishing, to be very destructive objects. The traps break coral parts that take a long time to restore, and the living coral pieces are damaged by picking them up. One of the tourists mentioned that he '*untrapped one of the traps, because it was placed on the coral, so we placed it on the sand. When we retrieved the trap we saw a tiny hole in it, but we did not make it bigger when we moved the trap. Some of the fish did get out, but not all of them*'. Other tourists break the traps to release the fish: '*Actually I broke one of the traps myself. There was a beautiful fish inside and "accidentally" my elbow happened to hit the trap and let the fish out. I saw large and small traps, with beautiful colored fish inside, I really felt sorry for them*'. Tourists thus act against bubu-trapping by breaking or relocating the traps, and they report bomb-fishing. Some tourists also had to abort their dive because the concussions caused by bombs underwater were too dangerous.

3.3.3 Conservation

Then there are people and organizations, both governmental and nongovernmental, who try to protect the reefs. They patrol, monitor and research the reef or educate about it. The Nature Conservancy (TNC) and World Wildlife Fund (WWF) are the most influential actors in the region. They were the first organizations involved in conservation after the national park declaration. They decided to cooperate in a joint program, where TNC is responsible for research, monitoring and patrolling and WWF for the translation of these results to the local people, fisheries, other conservation organizations and the government. Quickly after TNC and WWF started their cooperation, TN (Taman Nasional) also joined them in an MOU (memorandum of understanding) in which TNC-WWF's role is to support TN wherever they can. Operation Wallacea, a research network that collects data to assess the effectiveness of conservation management interventions, is also tightly connected to TNC-WWF, because TNC-WWF facilitates students of this operation to do reef-research. The students and researchers have become spokespersons for the reef, informing conservation and governmental organizations on the state of the reefs (Steins, 2001)

   TNC-WWF, TN, navy and the marine police execute three types of patrols: 1) joint patrols (patrolling local and remote reefs every month together); 2) incidental patrols (patrolling the reefs when reports are filed about illegal reef practices) and 3) independent patrols. In practice the joint patrols only take place a few times per year. In 2011 they only checked the remote reefs once. The incidental patrols are officially done immediately after a report is filed, but in practice this does not happen very often due to insufficient funding to protect the marine national park. TN Wakatobi receives the same funding to protect the coral reefs as a terrestrial national park, while protecting a marine national park is more expensive because of speedboat maintenance and fuel to completely cover the park. All conservation organizations agree that because of budget issues the park is insufficiently protected. TNC-WWF has a leading role in educating the other conservation organizations and government about how they should patrol, and what are 'good' or 'bad' reef practices. They also educate local people about the negative consequences of coral mining and bomb-fishing. Their main argument against coral mining is that the dead stones taken from the sea still fulfil important ecological functions for the living reefs as dead reefs are spawning areas for fish. Also, dead reefs can recover if a certain algae returns to the area and finally, mining causes rising sea-levels which has negative consequences for seabirds and seaweed. These effects cause a decrease in fish, in seabirds and impacts seaweed farmers and fishermen. By representing these "silent actors" (fish, seaweed, seabirds, fishermen and seaweed farmers), TNC-WWF tries to convince the miners to stop coral mining. The other conservation organizations and government support this explanation of mining being harmful for the reefs.

   The Indonesian government designated a law in 1996 forbidding coral mining. Miners are only allowed in the harbour area near Mola, a lagoon with a large dead reef in front of it. The dead reef is blocking ships to leave or enter the harbour during low tide; therefore mining was seen as a good solution. However, miners found outside the harbour face consequences. TNC-WWF only give miners a warning when they encounter them elsewhere. TN gives them a warning and after three warnings a jail sentence follows. Sara (a local organization protecting Liya territory) confiscates the miners' boat and equipment to make sure they cannot resume mining. Sometimes only a warning is given by the marine police and the navy, because they are convinced by the miners' arguments that they work for the government in providing them building materials. To reduce the dependency on corals as building material, the government is also using mountain rocks, which, although more expensive than coral, often can be delivered quickly.

Unlike law implementation for coral mining, clear implementation plans are present for bomb-fishing. Often the marine police deals with them because they are armed (bomb-fishermen are known to have thrown bombs at the authorities when detected). Bomb-fishermen's equipment is taken by the police to gather evidence for them in court.

COREMAP also performs monitoring and patrolling, but in a different way. COREMAP trains local people to do monitoring and patrolling for them, and they are mainly focused on Marine Protected Areas near the shore. In patrolling there is no cooperation between COREMAP and TNC-WWF or TN, nor with the navy, marine police and the government. Lack of communication between these organizations leads to different organizations patrolling the same reefs at the same time. TNC-WWF together with TN are pressuring government, COREMAP, marine police and the navy to sign an MOU in which budgets are opened to find out who has which capacities to protect the reefs, and to reach agreements about who should do what to improve reef protection and monitoring.

3.4   Consequences of Multiple Reefs

The coral reef collectifs, as described above, co-exist but also engage with each other in distinct (but partially connected) ways. This leads to controversies as well as ways in which actors and networks concord. Different practices and interpretations are negotiated, enacted and sometimes aligned or contested. The main controversies stem from conflicting enactments of coral reefs by bomb-fishermen and other reef-users; by bubu-fishermen and tourists; and by coral miners and the government; and finally between conservation organizations and government. The main concordance and alignments are between practices of menyulu-fishermen, government and conservation organizations; the government and bomb-fishermen; and also between conservation organizations and the government. We begin with the latter.

3.4.1   Co-enacting the Reefs

Menyulu-fishermen, the conservation and government organizations all accept menyulu as a nonharmful reef-practice, and therefore menyulu as a reef practice is allowed in reef-zones appointed for local use. Second, there is a similar alignment between the bubu-fishermen, the conservation organizations and the government. Bubu-trapping is also assigned as a nondestructive reef-practice and therefore allowed on reefs designated for local use. The fishermen, the government and the conservation organizations, share a definition of 'good' local reef practices, the objects used for these practices and the location where these practices are performed.

Third, there is an alignment between the government and bomb-fishermen. Bomb-fishermen are only able to make and use bombs if they can obtain bomb-materials that are not obtainable in Wakatobi. For a successful import and transport of bomb-materials a good relationship between government officials and bomb-fishermen is thus needed. This relationship is mainly financial in the form of bribing government officials, who then circumvent checking the boat with bomb-materials. Both the fishermen and government officials gain from these arrangements; the officials are financially supported, whereas the bomb-fishermen are supported by not being checked. The bomb-materials play a central role in this transaction, because they are constantly (re)negotiated by government officials and bomb-fishermen and are enacted as objects crossing the border for a particular price. These practices are at the same time othering the interpretation of others, arguing bombs being harmful for the reefs.

Finally, conservation organizations support each other wherever they can, and often share resources (boats, organizing joint patrols, share monitoring, results of research and patrolling, educational information on how to perform patrols and on good or bad reef practices). Local organizations such as FORKANI and Sara are encouraged by TNC-WWF to join their growing network of conservation organizations. TNC-WWF provides resources in the form of money, education and gasoline and they are invited to joined patrols. Because TNC-WWF is the spider in the web for all these practices, they can easily disseminate their readings of the reefs; what kind of reef practices are allowed and where; and what kind of materials are tolerable or not. They have become important representatives of the reefs and are central in many processes of negotiation about bomb-fishing and coral mining. However, information is only shared with the government on request.

3.4.2   Controversies

As the Wakatobi coral reefs are used in multiple ways by different users, the reefs have also become a site of struggle, a relational effect that recursively generates and reproduces itself (Steins, 2001). These struggles at least partially result from differences in framing. On the one hand tourists, menyulu-fishermen, conservation organizations and the government frame bombs as harmful objects. Bomb-fishing is discussed as damaging the reefs, and thus considered an unacceptable practice. The framing rests on an interpretation of the reef itself as fragile, connected and in need of protection for scientific reasons (conservation organizations), enjoyment (tourists) or making a living (menyulu-fishermen). Practices to reduce bomb-fishing include: reporting bomb-encounters to conservation organizations or the government (menyulu-fishermen, tourists), enforcement of the law (conservation organizations and government), and creating awareness amongst locals of the negative consequences of bomb-fishing (conservation organizations).

Bomb-fishermen on the other hand do not frame their practice as damaging for the reefs at all (but mainly as a quick way to make money). They are not aware of how their practices and interpretations of the remote reefs (disconnected from local reefs, and as a resource for fish) and bombs (as fishing equipment) are conflicting with other reef users' interpretations and practices. Even though they claim there are no conflicts with other reef-users, they are aware of the illegality of their practice based on the presence of their warning systems, the fact that they only frequent remote reefs, their ways to avoid detection of bombs, and the underground market for bomb-materials.

There are also encounters between bubu-fishermen and tourists. Both tourists and tourism operators attempt to present bubu-trapping as a damaging reef practice in need of attention from conservation organizations and the government. The bubu is thus interpreted as a harmful object that needs to be banned by law. Practically, tourists sabotage or relocate the bubus to reduce its negative impacts on the reefs. As the tourists' representative, tourism operators pressure conservation organizations to act against bubu-trapping by reporting reef damage as a consequence of bubu-trapping. Even though bubu-fishermen are portrayed as performing destructive reef practices, they are neither aware of this representation, nor of actions aimed at reducing their practices. Even though bubu traps are occasionally sabotaged by tourists, it is not uncommon that bubus are damaged by sea snakes or large fish biting their way out of a bubu, or in stormy weather by strong currents. Similar to bomb-fishermen, bubu-fishermen interpret the bubu as fishing-equipment and the reefs as a resource for fish.

Coral miners and the government also conflict. According to coral miners spawning fish are absent from mined reefs, seabirds are not affected, and the mined reefs are (dead) stone. Contrary, for government and conservation organizations mined reefs are a place for fish to spawn, seabirds are negatively affected, and finally the mined reefs are alive and can be restored if a certain type of algae returns. The governmental practices are nevertheless ambiguous as they are the largest buyer of corals, while at the same time accepting and partially implementing a law (in 1996) that forbids mining. Currently, government and conservation organizations restrict miners by patrolling and punishing mining outside 'designated' areas. Through education miners are encouraged to stop mining. This completely disregards the interpretation of reefs by the miners, and miners show their discontent by continuing mining in the no-take zones, and by emphasizing that they work for the government to (successfully) avoid punishment.

This ambiguous position of the government causes new controversies with conservation organizations who pressure the government to enforce the laws for mining. The lack of a clear implementation plan forced conservation organizations to create their own rules and practices to deal with mining. The conservation organizations insist that the government should set an example by outlawing the purchase of corals, as only a ban on coral purchasing can enable conservation organizations to act firmly against mining. In the current situation they are undermined by a government that acts against its own laws.

3.5 Conclusion

In this chapter we examined the enactment of coral reefs in Wakatobi National Park and found that reefs afford a variety of practices of fishermen, coral miners, tourists, conservation organizations and most probably many others, as it is important to realize that our story is a particular one. By studying other reef practices and objects, other realities could have become visible that are now not taken into account. As Jóhannesson, Ren and Van der Duim (2012, p.12) argue, 'research and knowledge creation is always a matter of doing ontological politics, i.e. bringing certain realities into being', while othering others. That is also the case here.

Nevertheless, our study of the different affordances and related practices of the reefs show that the enactment of a coral reef is constantly constructed, renegotiated, and influenced by actors present in the same or other versions of the reef. By examining the multiplicity of coral reefs, we situated reef actors through their ability to influence the reality of which they are part, and their ability to influence other realities that define and use the coral reef in a different way. By focusing on the relations, practices and materials formed around and afforded by the reefs, it became clear that different reef practices are not only made possible by human actors, but also by (informal) rules, laws and regulations (or the lack thereof) and objects such as fishing (bamboo traps, five-pointed spears, bombs), and mining equipment (lingis). These connections between different human and nonhuman entities illustrate how different reef practices are performed through shifting connections between coral reef, people and objects, new developments such as reef protection and tourism, and reef practices that have been enduring (bubu, menyulu, coral mining and bomb-fishing).

Examining different reef practices and interpretations in combination with different reef users in Wakatobi shows how different enactments of the reefs construct and change relationships, connections and associations between different actors (both human and nonhuman). Even though different versions of the reefs were presented, these versions are not mutually exclusive; they coexist in more or less consistent enactments of the reefs (Ren, 2011).

As can be seen from the pressure of certain actors to align other actors with their version of the reefs, it is clear that the realities themselves do not have strict borders but that they are influenced, rearranged, reconstructed and changed through processes of translation. During these processes of translation some practices, interpretations and actors are present and taken into account, whereas others are othered. A number of interpretations (reefs as dead or alive, reefs as (un)protected, reefs for making a living, reefs as (dis)connected), practices (fishing, coral mining, diving, snorkelling, patrolling, monitoring, researching), nonhuman actors (fishing/mining equipment), places (remote or local reefs), human actors (fishermen, coral miners, tourists, tourism facilitators, government officials, conservationists), agreements between human actors, and laws and law-implementation engage with each other simultaneously, resulting in seeing coral reefs performed as a resource for making a living, as an attraction for tourism and as a fragile ecosystem in need of protection. Viewing coral reefs as multiple and complex, and at the same time acknowledging how this multiplicity is created through different practices, objects and interpretations, provides space for looking at coral reefs and natural resources in a new way. Acknowledging multiplicity and thus viewing the reefs in a broader perspective enables a better understanding of what a natural resource is and confronts a more invariable look at natural resources like coral reefs (Lorimer, 2012). It also could lead to finding new solutions for complex problems surrounding natural resources.

References

Buckley, R.C., 2004. The effects of World Heritage listing on tourism to Australian national parks. *Journal of Sustainable Tourism*, 12(1), pp.70–84.

Callon, M., 1986. Some elements of a sociology of translation: Domestication of the scallops and the fishermen of St Brieuc Bay. First published in: J. Law (ed.) *Power, action and belief: A new sociology of knowledge?* London: Routledge, pp.196–223.

Callon, M. and Law, J., 1995. Agency and the hybrid collectif. *The South Atlantic Quarterly*, 94(2), pp.481–507.

Caras, T. and Pasternak, Z., 2009. Long-term environmental impact of coral mining at the Wakatobi marine park, Indonesia. *Ocean & Coastal Management*, 52, pp.539–44.

Clifton, J., 2003. Prospects for co-management in Indonesia's marine protected areas. *Marine Policy*, 27, pp.389–95.

Cloke, P. and Perkins, H.C., 2005. Cetacean performance and tourism in Kaikoura, New Zealand. *Environment and Planning D: Society and Space*, 23, pp.903–24.

Elliott, G., Mitchell, B., Wiltshire, B., Manan, A. and Wismer, S., 2001. Community participation in marine protected area management: Wakatobi National Park, Sulawesi, Indonesia. *Coastal Management*, 29(4), pp.295–316.

Green, S.J., White, A.T., Christie, P. Kilarsky, S., Meneses, A.B.T., Salmonte-Tan, G., Karrer, L.B., Fox, H., Campbell, S. and Claussen, J.D., 2011. Emerging marine protected area networks in the coral triangle: Lessons and way forward. *Conservation and Society*, 9(3), pp.173–88.

Harré, R., 2002. Material object in the social world. *Theory, Culture & Society*, 19(5/6), pp.22–33.

Jepson, P., Barua, M. and Buckingham, K., 2011. What is a conservation actor? *Conservation and Society*, 9(3), pp.229–35.

Jimura, T., 2011. The impact of world heritage site designation on local communities – A case study of Ogimachi, Shirakawa-mura, Japan. *Tourism Management*, 32(2), pp.288–96.

Jóhannesson, G.T., Ren, C. and Van der Duim, V.R., 2012. Gatherings: Ordering, materiality and multiplicity. In: V.R. Van der Duim, C. Ren and G.T. Jóhannesson, (eds) *Actor-Network Theory and tourism: Ordering, materiality and multiplicity.* London: Routledge, Ch.11.

Johnson, J.P., Holm, P., Sinclair, P. and Bavington, D., 2009. The cyborgization of the fisheries: On attempts to make fisheries management possible. *Maritime Studies,* 7(2), pp.9–34.

Law, J., 2009. *Unknown Actor-Network Theory and material semiotics.* City?: Blackwell Publishing Limited.

Law, J. and Singleton, V., 2005. Object lessons. *Organization,* 12(3), pp.331–55.

Law, J. and Mol, A., 2008, The actor-enacted: Cumbrian sheep in 2001. In: L. Malafouris and C. Knappett (eds) *Material agency: Towards a non-anthropocentric approach.* Berlin: Springer, pp.57–77.

Lien, M.E. and Law, J., 2011. Emergent aliens: On salmon nature and their enactment. *Ethnos,* 76(1), pp.65–87.

Lorimer, J., 2012. Multinatural geographies for the Anthropocene. *Progress in Human Geography,* 36(5), pp.593–612.

Middelveld, S., 2012. *Coral reefs in Wakatobi National Park Indonesia: Insights from Actor-Network Theory.* MSc thesis Wageningen University.

Mol, A., 1999. Ontological politics: A word and some questions. In: J. Law and J. Hassard, (eds) *Actor Network Theory and after.* Oxford: Blackwell, pp.74–89.

Mol, A., 2002. *The body multiple: Ontology in medical practice.* Durham, NC: Duke University Press.

Ren, C., 2011. Non-human agency, radical ontology and tourism realities. *Annals of Tourism Research,* 38(3), pp.858–81.

Steins, N.A., 2001. New directions in natural resource management. The offer of Actor-Network Theory. *ISD Bulletin,* 32(4), pp.18–25.

Thompson, C., 2002. When elephants stand for competing models of nature. In: Law, J. and A. Mol (eds) *Complexity in Science, Technology and Medicine.* Durham, NC: Duke University Press, pp. 166–90

Van der Duim, V.R., 2007. Tourism, materiality and space. In: I. Ateljevic, A. Pritchard and N. Morgan (eds) *The critical turn in tourism studies. Innovative research methodologies.* Amsterdam: Elsevier. pp. 149–63

Van der Duim, V.R, Ren, C. and Jóhannesson, G.T., 2012. *Actor-Network Theory and tourism: Ordering materiality and multiplicity.* Oxon: Routledge.

Van der Duim, V.R., Ren, C. and Jóhannesson, G., 2013. Ordering, materiality and multiplicity: Enacting Actor-Network-Theory in tourism. *Tourism Studies,* 13(1), pp.3–20.

Van der Duim, V.R., Ampumuza, Chr. and Ahebwa, W., 2014. Gorilla tourism in Bwindi Impenetrable National Park, Uganda: An actor-network perspective. *Society & Natural Resources.* doi: 10.1080/08941920.2014.901459.

Whatmore, S. and Thorne, L., 2000. Elephants on the move: Spatial formations of wildlife exchange. *Society and Space,* 18, pp.185–203.

Chapter 4

Entrepreneurship and Controversies of Tourism Development

Anniken Førde

4.1 Introduction

Entrepreneurship and innovation is seen as a central element to the emergence of tourism economies (Hall and Williams, 2008; Van der Duim, Ren and Jóhannesson, 2012). Innovation is pervasive in tourism, and takes many and complex forms. Entrepreneurship creates disturbance through innovation, and can lead to the reshaping of an entire tourism landscape (Hall and Williams, 2008). As it becomes difficult to separate the tourism landscapes from the inhabited landscape of local people (Ingold, 2000; Knudsen, Soper and Metro-Roland, 2008), tourism innovations can also reshape the landscapes of the locals. As argued by Saarinen (1998), the development of tourism destinations can be an on-going process of producing spaces. This activity is neither neutral nor passive, but a spatial struggle. Multiple meanings, interests and values are involved. Knudsen, Soper and Metro-Roland (2008) emphasize that contestations over meaning occur in every landscape, tourism landscapes being no exception.

This chapter addresses entrepreneurship and controversies of tourism development in Målselv, and the struggle over the emerging tourist landscape. Målselv is a rural community in north Norway of about 6,500 inhabitants. Tourism is not a new phenomenon in this community, which has long traditions of salmon angling in the river Målselva and hiking in the national park Dividalen. But the last decade tourism development has gathered headway, much based on the establishment of the ski resort *Målselv Fjellandsby* (Målselv Mountain Village) in 2008. The establishment of Målselv Fjellandsby included regulation and sale of lots for vacation homes, construction of ski slopes, building of cottages and flats, a restaurant and an amusement park. It was by many seen as a rescue for Målselv, experiencing depopulation mainly due to the withdrawal of the military forces. The municipality has been an important site for military activities during the Cold War, but lost its vital position with the new political situation after the fall of the Soviet Union and the Berlin Wall. Tourism was seen as a possible way out of the decline, and establishing a ski resort became an area of priority in local development. The ski resort created a lot of new activity in the community, and people tell stories of seduction, enthusiasm and optimism. But stories are also told of scepticism and resistance. As the project grew bigger, and the need to enlarge the market became critical, a new brand was created to attract foreign tourists: *Snowman area*, locally called Snowman Land. This implied collaboration between the ski resort and several other tourist attractions in the region. The resort was renamed to Snowman resort Målselv Fjellandsby, and a marketing company, Visit Snowman, was established to market the new destination. As a part of this process, the local airport was given the label Snowman International Airport. This caused a heated debate in the community. Whereas some celebrated the development of a joint regional destination, others contested the new brand; not everyone in Målselv wanted to live in Snowman Land. The transformation into a destination entered into broader discourses of regional development and social identities (Førde, 2014). Scrutinizing these complex processes, opposing stories unfold and new configurations emerge.

Before taking the reader to Målselv, I will discuss the theoretical and methodological implications of applying a relational approach to entrepreneurship. Then I will present an analysis of the entrepreneurial process of establishing a ski resort, and of the strategies and contestations of transforming Målselv into Snowman Land. Emphasis is on the complex relations, negotiations and struggles involved.

4.2   A Relational Approach to Entrepreneurship

This chapter applies a relational perspective on entrepreneurship. Entrepreneurship is seen as embedded practice and innovation as a relational activity. Entrepreneurial processes are socially situated, relying on a variety of social relations. Entrepreneurs are only so due to their relations (Van der Duim, Ren and Jóhannesson, 2012), and entrepreneurs' creativity is inseparable from the relations in which they are embedded (Ingold and Hallam, 2007). The many relations are further situated in particular contexts (Hall and Williams, 2008). Establishing tourist enterprises involves the production of tourist places in complex relations involving multiple types of networking practices. Relations are here understood as the interactions of specific, situated actors and contexts. These relations need to be described and analyzed in order to explore innovative processes of tourism development. As argued by Van der Duim, Ren and Jóhannesson (2012), tourism should be understood as emergent through relational practices connecting cultures, natures and technologies in multifarious ways. This implies putting an emphasis on processes rather than products. For, as Ingold and Hallam (2007) argue, if we want to reveal the productive forces of innovation we need to shift the focus from the results to the processes that create them.

Traditional accounts of entrepreneurship have tended to focus on single actors and their efforts and skills. These have produced notions and storylines of the individual, heroic and creative entrepreneur, where the role of the individual is often overplayed (De Laet and Mol, 2000; Ingold and Hallam, 2007; Hall and Williams, 2008; Jóhanneson, 2012; Van der Duim, Ren and Jóhannesson, 2012). Within this hegemonic understanding of entrepreneurship the cultural and institutional as well as material contexts are reduced to given conditions or constraints for the entrepreneur. Shifting the focus from the individual heroes to relations and networks at play allows for alternative stories where the narrative of the individual hero is replaced by new understandings of agency accounting for multiple actors and hence multiple versions of tourism development and tourism landscapes.

As the performative turn has reached entrepreneurship studies, there is an increased emphasis on the cultural context and complexity of entrepreneurial processes (Lindh de Montoya, 2000; Hjort and Steyaert, 2004; Ingold and Hallam, 2007). Studying tourism entrepreneurship as social processes and networks at work implies a broad understanding of entrepreneurial processes. It involves studying innovative processes not only within the economic field but also within the variety of social fields that tourism development initiates from and enters into; cultural work, voluntary work, politics and public management, as well as business activity (Førde, 2009). Bringing in inspiration from socio-material approaches, it also allows cultural and material environments to be seen as active co-players in entrepreneurial processes. Because the social is always material, and the real is relationally enacted practices (Law, 2008).

As Lindh de Montoya (2000) demonstrates, entrepreneurship is not simply a matter of "discovering opportunities", but more a matter of creating opportunities along the way. These are created through complex relations and networks, and in continuous negotiations. Innovation processes set places in motion, and established patterns of interaction and meanings are challenged. Norms and normalities are brought in a state of flux, and therefore become subject to negotiation. As tourism entrepreneurship processes often involve new constructions of place images, new negotiations and negotiators enter the stage. The complex making of tourist places involves different actors drawing different histories, values and lifestyles into the product (Burns and Novelli, 2006). As argued by Bærenholdt, et al. (2004), tourist places are produced in complex relations where the material production of place intersects with imaginative place production; they are hybrids of mind and matter, imagination and presence. Tourism places are landscapes subject to continual transformation and reformation; they emerge, change, disappear and re-emerge in varied forms (Saarinen, 1998). And the reading of tourism landscapes will always be open to multiple interpretations (Knudsen, et al., 2008).

Accepting that tourism and tourism places are always in the making, we need to focus on the spatial, temporal and relational aspects of tourism entrepreneurship. Rather than seeing innovation as a new present, broken off from a past that is already over, creativity always involves motion (Ingold and Hallam, 2007). Entrepreneurial practises imply both novelty and conventions as invention is created in the interaction between conventions and innovations. Entrepreneurs bring together traditional and new practices, they use and combine experiences and skills from different social fields and place their repertoire of knowledge into new projects. By studying how they enter complex relations of situated actors and contexts, we can grasp how tourism development contributes to the maintenance as well as transformation of local practices, representations and nature. Often, tourism entrepreneurship is created through new and unconventional liaisons and working methods of community development. These imply new local alliances as well as extended networks, and new combinations of tradition and invention, nature and culture, the local and the global (Førde, 2009; 2011). In our attempt to grasp such complex entrepreneurship processes, we as researchers face the challenge of tracking the most fluid aspects of reality, at the same time as we seek to convey how the fluidity of social life is insolubly connected to the struggle to "make things stick" and become durable (Barber, 2007).

4.3   Methodological Reflections

Accepting that our theory and methods are intertwined, and that our methods are performative as they work to create knowledge about and in relation to the object of study, it becomes urgent to reflect upon our research practices. If we understand entrepreneurship as complex relational practices, how can we study tourism entrepreneurship, and how do we establish stories of entrepreneurship through our research design? Different research practices not only produce different perspectives of entrepreneurship, but also different realities (Mol, 2002; Law, 2004). Our methods are thus not innocent techniques, but play a creative role in constructing specific knowledges and realities (Law, 2008; Jóhannesson, Van der Duim and Ren, 2012).

Complex realities demand more creative methods (Alvesson, 2011; Law, 2004). Law argues that in order to study complexity and messy realities, we need to focus less on order. A way of facing this challenge is to increase our sensibility towards ambiguities and multiple meanings. In the following analyses of tourism entrepreneurship in Målselv, I aim at challenging the interpretations produced through exploring more than one set of meaning. The analyses are based on a qualitative case study in Målselv, conducted from 2011–2012 by a team of researchers related to the CHAIR Arctic tourism project.[1] We have carried out individual interviews and focus group sessions of persons involved in tourism development and community development in different ways; people from the tourism industry, other local industries, the voluntary sector, the local government administration, leaders of the local council, the Norwegian Armed Forces, teachers, high school pupils and retired people. The structure of the interviews and focus group sessions was open, aiming at inviting different stories of tourism development. By explicitly searching for multiple stories and meanings, and focusing on the imaginative as well as the material production of Målselv as a tourist place, we have tried to meet the request for more complex-sensitive methods.

---

1   The research team consisted of Per Kåre Jacobsen (Finnmark University College), Arvid Viken, Torill Nyseth and Anniken Førde (University of Tromsø). Perhaps needless to say, the tourism development processes in Målselv continues and have taken on new forms after our fieldwork. These are not accounted for in my analyses.

This broad approach to studying tourist entrepreneurship makes it possible to reveal some of the complexity of relations and networks involved. It allows for challenging the implicit conceptions of relevant relations and coherences. Doing fieldwork together with other researchers contribute to increased sensibility towards multiple meanings as our interpretations were constantly negotiated. Using the focus group as a method, interpretations were also constantly challenged as common constructions and dividing perceptions became explicit. The group sessions revealed shared stories as well as conflicting understandings, and sometimes provoked debates where meanings were negotiated explicitly. Entering into such negotiations, the researchers also contribute to start new processes (Viken, 2013). Creating and participating in arenas for discussion, the research team entered into and became part of the complex negotiation of place, community and tourism development. Talking of ontological politics, Mol (1999) underlines the ways "the real" and the "political" are interlinked. Accepting that reality is done and enacted rather than just observed entails questions of the ways we as researchers are involved in the processes of reshaping it. Through our research practices – our theories, methods and descriptions – we take part in the configuring of the field of study. In this case, by intervening in and describing intricate processes of tourism development, the research itself contributes to multiple stories of tourism development in Målselv being brought to life. Co-creating a multiple reality might also imply tensions, in ways we are not aware of. As Mol (1999) argues, various performances of reality have tensions between them, but are interconnected in complex ways.

4.4   The Entrepreneurial Process of Establishing a Ski Resort

At the foot of the mountain Myrefjell, 450 km north of the polar circle and 14 km from the small town Bardufoss, we find the ski and vacation resort Målselv Fjellandsby. Situated 380 m above sea level, the ski resort benefits from a great view over the valley and the surrounding mountains. The hilly landscape and the inland climate with long winter seasons provide good opportunities for skiing.

Målselv Fjellandsby is located half an hour drive from Bardufoss airport/ Snowman International airport, and two hours from the city Tromsø. The resort consists of a number of cottages and apartment buildings – about 350 beds altogether – and holds several downhill slopes and ski lifts, as well as tracks for cross-country skiing. It has a pub, a restaurant, a conference center, a Blue Elf adventure house and small sport and souvenir shops. In addition, the resort has many small scale subcontractors, offering activities like dog sleds, reindeer sleds and "Sami experiences", horse riding and guiding. Målselv Fjellandsby also provides visits to other attractions in the region such as the Polar Zoo. The resort has 15 permanent employees, 45 during the winter season.

While conducting our study, we were told many stories of how the ski resort came into being. The master story – the one presented in public and most often

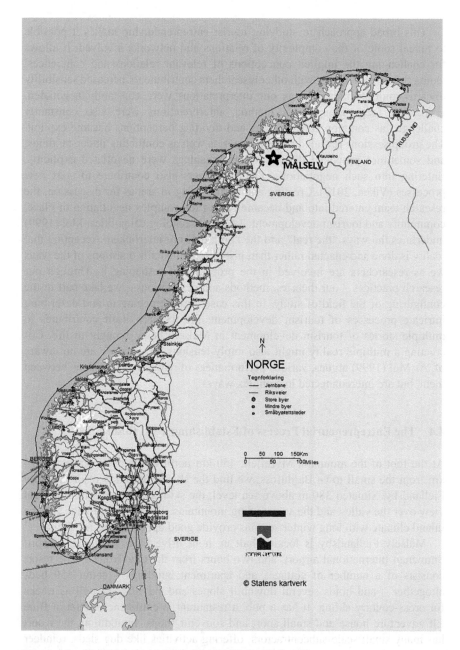

Figure 4.1 Map depicting the location of Målselv Fjellandsby

Figure 4.2 The children's ski tow (Courtesy of O.M. Rapp)

referred to by local actors – is that of the heroic entrepreneur from Voss in western Norway entering the community with great plans, experience from creating ski resorts, the necessary capital and capability to realize big projects. Looking closer into the entrepreneurial process of establishing the ski resort shows that there are numerous actors and relations involved, and that there are multiple versions of this process. In the following, I will outline some of what I see as key aspects in these stories, concerning readapting of the community through innovation, but also of emerging controversies related to negotiation of space, speed, scale and visions of the future.

4.5 Enforced Innovative Municipality and the Heroic Entrepreneur

> We talk about the burdensome peace that occured here. (…) We lost 15–1600 people. So we had to do something to create jobs, to get people back.

This quote from the mayor indicates how "the burdensome peace" and the withdrawal of the military forces from Målselv constitute an important context for the municipality's priority accorded to tourism. As the military forces were reduced, the population decreased and people in Målselv became nervous about the future. The municipality was forced to search for alternatives, and had to 'give all ideas a chance'. Seen as a possible rescue, tourism became a core issue in discourses of local development (Førde, 2014). In 2007 Målselv was awarded as the most innovative municipality in Norway. What was specially emphasized was the establishment of a film camp and the ski resort. According to the mayor this development work was a result of a thorough work of readapting a military community.

Målselv has long traditions for tourism, based on the salmon fishing in the river Målselva that has attracted British nobility since the nineteenth century. This was tourism for people of rank, the leader of a regional destination company explains: '*The role of the locals was to whisk away the mosquitos from the tourists with birch branches*'. The river still attracts many tourists, and the waterfall Målselvfossen, elected the National Waterfall of Norway some years ago, receives about 90,000 visitors a year. Målselv has been famous for hunting, angling and hiking. Until 2008, the tourism businesses in Målselv consisted of a hotel, some guesthouses, a camping site and several small-scale enterprises offering accommodation, dogsledding, horse riding and guided tours. As part of the readjustment process, ideas of developing fish tourism and establish ski slopes were discussed.

During this period, the municipality, and especially the mayor, played an active role in the tourism development process. The idea of creating the ski resort came as a result of an initiative from the municipality. In 2005 they invited an entrepreneur and investor from the ski district of Voss, in the southwest part of Norway, to evaluate the possibilities in Målselv. Hegbom, the entrepreneur, who happened to be a former classmate of the community planner in Målselv, had experience with establishing ski resorts. The municipality provided a helicopter and showed him the river and the mountains. He was impressed by what he saw, and became interested in tourism development here.

This was the start of a fast-going process, resulting in the establishment of Målselv Fjellandsby. Many emphasize the impact of Hegbom's entry into the project. '*He was the one who got things started*', one of the local managers says, explaining how he managed to persuade people of the project: '*When he gets to talk, then it's like – people get hypnotized. He's like Messias, like a preacher!*' The story of the heroic entrepreneur is much drawn upon in Målselv. Many in Målselv talk about "before and after Hegbom", and the mayor claims he deserves a statue. Hegbom is seen as the one who came with the experience of creating ski resorts, and as the one capable of convincing authorities, landowners and investors. We were told many stories of how he seduces people, how he '*manages to create enthusiasm*' by getting in direct contact with everybody involved: '*He sits down with them, drink and talk!*' We were also told stories of how he strategically uses his position to achieve his means; he offered Målselv his investments and competences given the right conditions. But looking closer at the process, other versions emerge, revealing a multiple reality. Behind the story of the "preacher", the realization of the resort establishment has involved many actors. Many new relations and networks were created. Unconventional alliances and creative working methods were applied, and many aspects of local development were negotiated.

Many communities now look to what they have done in Målselv, and the initiators have been traveling around to tell their story. As also demonstrated by Bærenholdt, et al. (2004), local authorities play many and significant roles in tourism development overseeing physical planning, establishing destination organizations and coordinating business, infrastructure and landscape management. In Målselv the municipality worked hard and in unconventional ways – both politically and administratively – to support the realization of the ski resort. This account from Målselv is in most versions a story of successful readjustment work from the municipality; a story of an innovative and flexible municipality able to create new opportunities in a period of recession. But there are also other stories involved; accounts of an ailing municipality willing to invest a lot in a new grand project, and once into it left with no choice but to accept the premises set up by external investors. Common to the diverging versions is an emphasis on the ski resort becoming of principal concern in local development in Målselv, and thus entering into a complex of other development processes.

4.6   Negotiating Space; Struggles and New Alliances

Establishing a ski resort implies intervention in nature and landscape, and influences on the many actors involved in this landscape. In Målselv, the area selected for the ski resort was wooded hills and graze lands, owned by nine farmers and the State Forest Company. In addition, reindeer herders had pasture rights in the area. The process of developing the resort entered into struggles of land use and implied many new alliances – taking on different forms.

The first alliance that was made was between the landowners and the initiators of the ski resort. Hegbom introduced a model for how to cooperate with the landowners, adopted from the establishment of ski resorts in Trysil and Voss. '*We were told that in Trysil he locked in the land owners together with the mayor in a cabin, and said they were not leaving until they had an agreement on co-operation. I think the same tactic was used here*', explains the mayor. The landowners were also invited to Voss, to look at the model there. '*He made us believe that it was possible here too*', says one of the landowners. Hegbom insisted on the landowners handling over the ground to a company taking care of the development and management. This model, described by Viken (2014) as the common estate model, introduced new ways of organizing land ownership in the region. In the new company, Målselv Development, all the landowners got an equal share. In addition, the Sami reindeer herders were given a part in the landowner company. The landowners still own their land, but the common company decides on the use of it. For each lot sold, the partners get paid according to an agreed formula. In this new configuration grazing land is transformed to shares in a tourism enterprise.

An alliance with the Sami reindeer herders was crucial to the ski resort entrepreneurs, as they were in a position to stop the project. In order to gain construction license for the ski resort, the reindeer herders had to accept it. An interesting aspect of this alliance is the way the resort development entered into an old conflict between the reindeer herders and the National Defence over a shooting field. For decades the reindeer herders had been fighting against the military's plan of expanding their training areas directly through their grazing land. In negotiations over land-use, the reindeer herders' claimed that if they were to accept the establishment of a ski resort, the military had to reduce their expansion plans. The initiators of Målselv Fjellandsby, who claimed they 'got the power in relation to the municipality', made the municipality engage in this conflict. By drawing on his contacts and involving the Ministry of Defence, the mayor in particular managed to find a solution for the long-lasting shooting field conflict. This story illustrates how new alliances can move issues such as reindeer pastures. With the introduction of new plans in the area, the seemingly stuck conflict between the Sami reindeer herders and the National Defence attained new bargainers. And the bargaining counter was no longer just pasture rights, but the future tourism industry in the community. As this conflict was solved, the reindeer herders accepted the establishment of a ski resort. They entered the alliance, where they were made partners with the landowners. They were also invited to develop a tourist operation based on reindeer sledding and the exposure of Sami culture. But the reindeer herders entered this alliance reluctantly. They felt in a squeeze; in order to get the conflict with the National Defence solved, they had no choice but to accept the resort development. They saw expropriation as a probable alternative. Again new configurations emerge, where pastures become part of political negotiation of other issues, and reindeer herding becomes part of commercial experiences. Some of the reindeer herders express discomfort by having been "bought and paid for" by the tourism industry, and are worried about the future consequences.

Another important alliance was with the local and regional government. Hegbom explains how he initially talked to all the politicians, from all parties: '*We held incendiary speeches about possibilities, and made a lot of publicity*'. Belief in new growth and activity in the municipality was created. At the same time, the municipality was put under pressure; Hegbom made it clear from the very beginning that without good conditions he would rather invest elsewhere. Even though Målselv is an indebted municipality, a united local council supported the establishment. '*The politicians have been courageous, to be able to think big*', the mayor states. The municipality, and especially the mayor, is seen as playing an important role in this process. The local managers of Målselv Fjellandsby talk of the mayor as 'a co-player for the local businesses', and emphasize his engagement for new ideas. '*He believes in people, when somebody has an idea, the mayor says; let's try it!*' The mayor himself explains how they have been working in 'untraditional ways' to establish new activities; '*I use all the networks I have, I write many letters, and then I keep running along the letters and make sure the right persons read them*'. He admits that they have 'been tempted to make some short-cuts' to make things happen, and claims that 'the aim of increasing the population is more important than the bureaucracy'. While the municipality's unconventional working methods regarding this project are celebrated by the mangers, it has been met with much criticism from other local actors. Many claim the emphasis on the ski resort has been at the cost of other issues crucial to local development; that local development has become equated with ski resort development.

Raising the necessary investment capital also demanded yet other alliances, and brought about some interesting configurations of private and public, external and local capital. It started with the establishment of a company called Målselv Development, led by Hegbom. The company had a rather small starting capital of 100,000 NOK. Then local and regional investors entered the team, investing 12 million NOK. After a share capital augmentation, where yet other local investors were invited in, the financial platform of Målselv Development valued 24 million NOK. For Hegbom, involving local investors was also a strategy to gain legitimacy in Målselv, '*It was an important signal to the community*'. For the local investors, who were all in the construction sector, these investments were seen as a strategic means to provide further activity for their companies. Public capital was also involved, as the municipality undertook a loan of 60 million NOK for the development of infrastructure, including roads, sewage and cabling. One thousand, five hundred new vacation-home lots were regulated, and the agreement was that the loan should be repaid as the lots were sold. The sale of real property should also finance the ski lifts and give income to the landowners. In 2012 about 300 lots were sold, 148 cabins were built, and 48 flats have been constructed. About 600 million NOK have been invested during the first five years. The basic idea of Målselv Fjellandsby is to combine a ski resort with real estate development and tourism, and to create a modern high standard second home area – with 1,500 mountain chalets for the regional market. Through new alliances of local constructors, regional investors and the municipality, as well as pre-sale of lots, the required capital to realize the project was raised. This amalgamation of capital interests makes this land a complex area where many concerns are at stake at the same time. Which again entail many forms of contestation.

4.7 High Speed Development; Success and Expenses

There was supposed to be an opening ceremony. We sat in the local council to approve the plans. At the same time there was a meeting within the reindeer herding district (that also had to approve the plans). (…) And there were grab-dredgers and the county mayor, ready to unveil a stone over there. A lot of people, champagne and everything. They were waiting for the local council to come. And then, half an hour late, a journalist called and said 'you have a resolution (from the reindeer herding district)' – and then bang – the gavel fell, we all drove over (…) The grab-dredgers started digging immediately!

This is how the mayor describes the start of what is now Målselv Fjellandsby. This event took place on the 6 October 2006. The local council could not confirm the regulation plan before the reindeer herding district had accepted. As soon as they had got the necessary decisions, the construction work started. A representative for a destination company in the region states: '*They must have beaten the national record – or world record – in rapid administration of land management – to get those lots and everything*'. Time – speed – has been a crucial issue for negotiation in the development process.

The high speed that has characterized the establishment of the ski resort was given as a criterion from the start. Based on earlier experience, Hegbom feared that regulations could be too slow and expensive: '*The mayor promised me that if I needed a political decision, within 15 minutes, even on a Sunday, I would get it. Then the bureaucratic barriers were cleared away. Then it became possible*'. The municipality accepted quite an unaccustomed rhythm of bureaucratic and political work. One of the local managers states: '*It would not have been possible without the municipality showing this understanding for the process*'. In addition to the strong alliance with the mayor and local council, alliances were made with the regional authorities. Hegbom personally contacted the county governor before the drawings were made. In this way they paved the way for the decisions that had to be made, and made it possible to rush the process.

The managers of Målselv Fjellandsby have put much effort in gaining publicity and brand the resort, in a high speed. '*All publicity is good publicity*', they argue – and they have organized their public communication by this rule. There have been numerous features in local, regional, national and international media from the very beginning. Ideas have been launched with a lot of bravura before anything was even realized. This has been a strategy to "make it big", and to make people – investors as well as customers – believe in the project. From the beginning they have been selling products not yet developed. Hegbom tells how he sold the rights to lots before they had any regulations: '*I was just selling numbers!*' When he had sold many 'numbers' of 50,000 NOK each, he could prove the interest of the project to potential investors. Their next step is foreign tourists. The manager responsible for abroad marketing explains that this is still how it works: '*First I sell something, and then we have to think, what does it require? Because we've sold it!*' As the project grew, Målselv Fjellandsby decided to put a stake on charter tourism and made plans for constructing a hotel. But as a hotel is still not built they have challenges of housing people. The same manager explains: '*When I book a charter, I have to find all available beds around. We build at the same time as we sell*'.

But the speed also has expenses – and has led to controversy. Some of the price is directly related to mistakes in the constructive work. Målselv Fjellandsby has been criticized for many defects, especially in the ski slopes. Many also claim that the restaurant is constructed '*the wrong way*', with the kitchen and not the dining hall facing the spectacular view of the valley. The managers recognize many of the mistakes, and blame it on the high tempo: '*It is the price for the speed. Never mind the restaurant facing the wrong way*'. They claim that the quality of the services will improve as they move along. Another consequence of presenting ideas before they are settled is that it creates a lot of expectations, and not all of them are met. New labels have also been presented throughout the developing process, resulting in a confusing myriad of names on the resort; Myrefjell, Blåfjell, Målselv Fjellandsby and Snowman resort.

While the high speed has been celebrated by the resort managers, it has been questioned by others. It has led to the local planning section being overburdened, and many claim that it has been at the sacrifice of other building applications. Many claim that the local government's strong emphasis on the ski resort has overshadowed other development tasks in the community: '*Målselv is more than Målselv Fjellandsby!*' The establishment of the ski resort seems to have transformed the local discourses of development and place. There are many issues at stake, entailing controversies over land use, scale and speed. And, as will be discussed in the next section, it also involves negotiating visions of the future in and of Målselv.

4.8 'Welcome to Snowman Land'. The Controversies of Producing Tourist Places

The process of developing the ski resort has gained much support in the community. '*It has created new activity in the village. It is a meeting place for many people. There they can meet friends and neighbors*'. Others emphasize that '*people have become more interested in skiing*', and that the ski resort has made Målselv '*a more attractive place to live for young people*', because there is more activity. At the resort the local youth meet young people from the city during the weekends, and some claim it has made Målselv '*more urban*'. But with the introduction of Snowman Land more critical voices were raised.

'*Finland took Santa Claus. What else is known out there? The snowman!*' This quote from one of the local managers is one version of how the idea of the Snowman came about. We were also told different stories. The managers of Målselv Fjellandsby give much credit to a British tour operator, who visited the resort together with his family. As he realized how fun it was for the kids to play in the snow, he stated that this was what they should go for; playing in the snow! Their vision is to become best in the world in snow experiences. The snowman is chosen as a symbol, since 'everybody knows the snowman'.

The creation of Snowman Land is often explained by the competition with Finland, and their successful ski resort Levi. '*Everything we do, we copy from Levi*', says one of the marketers. They have been studying Levi's concept, both regarding the ski resort and the branding through Santa Claus. In Rovaniemi they have named the airport Santa Claus International Airport. This gave the idea to name the local airport at Bardufoss Snowman International Airport.

'*What we need now is volume!*' the manager states. The creation of Snowman Land is a response to the need for more visitors. The managers of the ski resort stress that the local and regional market has become too small. The aim now is to attract foreign tourists, and charter is their main priority. Visit Snowman is a sale company for several attractions in the region; Snowman Resort, Hamn in Senja, Polar Zoo and Målselvfossen. The idea is to take in charters, create packages and spread the tourists across the region. They mostly pursue the British market, but also Russia, Ukraine, Kazakhstan and the Netherlands.

Those marketing the Snowman tell of a tremendous response. They have participated at several fairs dressed as the snowman: '*When the snowmen walked the streets of Berlin, it attracted a lot of attention. People go like "wow!"*'. The manager responsible for abroad marketing says it has made sales increase: '*To travel the world with the Snowman opens new doors*'. In 2011 Bardufoss airport got the label Snowman International Airport. A proud mayor tells that they won an international competition of profiled and exiting airports in Kuala Lumpur.

When the idea of Snowman Land was first launched in 2007, people in Målselv were mobilized to create snowmen all over the community. The local newspaper arranged a competition where people were asked to send in pictures of their snowmen. Local artists working with snow and ice were also mobilized. But the enthusiasm seems to have faded, and the local artists are no longer included in the development process. The managers explain that the product Snowman Land is produced as they go along: '*At the same time as we are selling, we expand the destination*'. Until now the focus has been on creating the brand and selling charters. The content of the brand seems to be weakly developed. '*We will make our own history around the Snowman*', one of the resort managers tells. They also have plans of constructing a Snowman park. But the resort managers' story

Figure 4.3   The opening of Snowman Airport (Courtesy of O.M. Rapp)

of Snowman Land is not drawn on blank paper. It is a story of a land which also comprises other stories and other story tellers. And the new story of Snowman Land also acts upon these.

4.9 Living in Snowman Land?

Snowman Land?! It just sounds silly. Who wants to live in Snowman Land?

The quote from a high school student illustrates the skepticism many of the young express. They think the brand is kitschy, and do not want to relate to it. We also find this resistance among elder people. This has especially been expressed in the debate about renaming the airport. In establishing the Snowman International Airport, the airport has been given a make-up, and stands out more touristic, with a big snowman painted on the front of the terminal building. A woman working for a destination company tells of the reaction from her neighbor: '*Snowman International Airport?! What kind of nonsense is that?!*' Like several other locals, her neighbor found the idea not only stupid, but also offending to the existing local name. Many have claimed that Bardufoss Airport has an important history, which they feel is being put aside by the new label.

The involved tourist actors have tried to meet these protests by explaining that the labels Snowman Land and Snowman International Airport are only meant for foreigners. Hegbom says he understands that it sounds silly to Norwegians, and that he does not expect that local people will buy lots in Snowman Resort or travel to Snowman International Airport. The names Målselv Fjellandsby and Bardufoss Airport are therefore kept, and the resort tries to use the two different labels in abroad and domestic marketing. But the new destination label nevertheless enters into local discourses of place identity.

Among those representing the creative industries we find critical voices expressing skepticism to the content of this new brand. In a focus group with people in Målselv working with film, music, ice sculpturing and teaching art, it was claimed that by just copying Finland, we lose sight of the unique things that we have here: '*There are just a lot of copycats. And for every copy, the quality aggravates*'. Snowman Land, to these local actors 'does not at all signalize where we are in the world'. Some of them were involved in the early phase of developing the destination, contributing to discussions of the content. Here snow art and literature about the snowman was highlighted. But they feel the content fell off along the road. They point to Jukkasjärvi, where they have made an ice hotel based on the work of ice sculptors: '*But here they started with grab-dredgers and a lot of capital!*' This, they claim, has leaded to the Snowman being 'an empty label'. As one of them states: '*What is visualized is a snowman of rubber sponge, which they travel the world with. Apart from that it's nothing!*'

Those promoting Snowman Land connect the opposition to cultural resistance to 'anything new'. We are explained that 'here are some strong "museum guards"', and that these opponents '*are from the valley, really conservatives, they only think*

about woods, the river and the mountain. Moose, salmon and cloudberries ...'
In the dominating discourse of development in the community, the conditions
for critical voices are difficult. They are stamped as traditional, reactionary and
opposed to innovation and development, even if they also come from young
people and the creative industries. And their perceptions of development are not
made relevant in the destination development process.

4.10   The Melting Snowman

> They go for the snowman, but for every tourist they bring in to look at it, the
> snowman will melt this much (showing some centimetres with the fingers), right?

A small scale tourism actor expresses worries of the development. The development
of Snowman Land represents a shift from small scale to mass tourism in Målselv.
The vision is to become "the coming destination for alpine skiing". A local manager
states: '*The idea from the beginning was to create mass tourism. They (Hegbom and
his companions) saw the potential here to build something big. We had the airport, the
infrastructure, the mountains, the Samis, everything you needed to succeed*'. Nature
and people are seen as part of the tourism product. But when places and people are
being transformed into what Picard (2011) calls "magical gardens" in which human
life is cultivated for tourist consumption, new configurations emerge – entailing new
encounters and controversies. Examples are reindeer herders expressing worries
about the consequences of pastures being turned into economic and political assets in
tourism, and young people questioning the future of living in Snowman Land.

Among those expressing worries about this development are small-scale
tourism actors. In a focus group of several local actors involved in small tourism
enterprises, emphasis was put on how mass tourism threatens existing local
practices and the distinctive characteristics of the community (Førde, 2014).
It was claimed that the municipality, the public support system and regional
destination companies '*have lost small scale actors out of sight*'. These actors
also question the environmental aspects of this development. Mass tourism, they
claim, will contribute to climate changes and global warming, and threatens to
'melt the snowman' on which it is based. They emphasize that until now tourism in
Målselv has been nature-based and based on short travels and express anxiety over
the development of mass tourism. The encounters and controversies of tourism
development constitute competing discourses of development and place identity,
where time, space, scale and visions for the future are at issue.

4.11   Conclusion

In this chapter I have been concerned with the multiple relations and negotiations
involved in tourism entrepreneurship, and with the struggles enacted in emerging

tourist landscapes. Tourism entrepreneurship processes contribute to reshaping places – materially, socially and discursively. The reshaping requires renegotiation of social identities and struggles over representations and practices.

Through a case study of the establishment of a ski resort in Målselv, I have aimed at accounting for the multiple reality of tourism development. I argue for a relational approach to entrepreneurship, where entrepreneurship is studied as the relational activity of specific situated actors and contexts. Acknowledging the relationality of entrepreneurship allows for the complexity of entrepreneurial processes in our studies, which again allows for multiple versions and controversies. By emphasizing the multiple relational practices involved in entrepreneurial processes, hegemonic narratives – like the one of the heroic entrepreneur – can be challenged.

Further, I have strived to show that destination development must be understood in relation to broader development processes. The attempt to create a destination brand through the Snowman to attract foreign tourists to Målselv, illustrates the controversies of mirroring tourist desires in tourism development. The process of communicating places and destinations influences both tourists' and locals' perceptions of place. As a tourist destination Snowman Land was designed to project an appealing image, as a representation of what tourists seek. But locally the snowman led to controversies of social identities; not everybody in Målselv wanted to live in Snowman Land. The development of tourist destinations leads to new representations, meanings and practises, and can be seen as an on-going process of producing spaces. This activity is neither neutral nor passive, but a spatial struggle. The presence of some things and activities depends on the absence of others. Like any other place, Målselv is inhabited by different actors with different interests, histories and values. The process of destination development does not comprise the multitude of practices and identities present here. Through stories of encounters and controversies of various forms, I have tried to show some of this multiplicity. "The melting snowman" may serve as a metaphor for the need of a more inclusive and integrated tourism development, where the multiple realities are taken into account.

Tourist places are dynamic, always in play. They are fragile constructions, produced through multiple networking practices (Bærenholdt, et al., 2004). This complexity is difficult to grasp. As Law (2008) argues, our only access to complex and messy realities is through dealing with specific practices and acknowledging difference and non-coherence. The case study from Målselv demonstrates a complex relationality of places and people. It also demonstrates how multiple realities may play off against each other. Tourism constantly (re)produces place through processes where spatial boundaries are marked out and meanings of place and who belong in it are confirmed. Defining and performing a destination thus becomes an on-going struggle and process of contestation. Tourism research should continue the search for productive ways of exploring these processes. I have suggested to apply a relational perspective on entrepreneurship and tourism development, and provide descriptions of multiple realities. If we manage to produce more multiplicity in our accounts, it will add to the realities of the tourism development we search to understand.

References

Alvesson, M., 2011. *Interpreting interviews*. London: SAGE Publications.
Barber, K., 2007. Improvisation and the art of making things stick. In: E. Hallam and T. Ingold (eds) *Creativity and cultural improvisation*. Oxford and New York: Berg Publishers.
Burns, P. and Novelli, M., 2006. Tourism and social identities: Introduction. In: P. Burns and M. Novelli (eds) *Tourism and social identities. Global frameworks and local realities*. Oxford: Elsevier.
Bærenholdt, J.O., Haldrup, M., Larsen, J. and Urry, J., 2004. *Performing tourist places*. Aldershot: Ashgate.
De Laet, M. and Mol, A., 2000. The Zimbabwe bush pump: Mechanics of a fluid technology. *Social Studies of Science*, 20(2), pp.225–63.
Førde, A., 2009. Creating the land of the big fish. A study of rural tourism innovation. In: T. Nyseth and A. Viken (eds) *Place reinvention. Northern perspectives*. Aldershot: Ashgate.
Førde, A., 2011. From fishing industry to 'fish porn'. Tourism transforming place. In: D. Macleod and S. Gillesppie (eds) *Sustainable tourism in rural europe*. Oxon: Routledge.
Førde, A., 2014. Integrated tourism development? When places of the ordinary are transformed to destinations. In: A. Viken and B. Granås (eds) *Destination development in tourism: Turns and tactics*. City?: Ashgate.
Hall, M. and Williams, A., 2008. *Tourism and innovation*. Oxon: Routledge.
Hjort, D. and Steyaert, C., 2004. *Narrative and discursive approaches in entrepreneurship: A second movement in entrepreneurship*. Cheltenham: Edward Elgar.
Ingold, T., 2000. *The perception of the environment – Essays on livelihood, dwelling and skills*. London: Routledge.
Ingold, T. and Hallam, E., 2007. Creativity and cultural improvisation: An introduction. In: E. Hallam and T. Ingold (eds) *Creativity and cultural improvisation*. Oxford: Berg Publishers.
Jóhannesson, G.T., 2012. To get things done: A relational approach to entrepreneurship. *Scandinavian Journal of Hospitality and Tourism*, 12(2), pp.181–96.
Jóhannesson, G.T., Van der Duim, V.R. and Ren, C., 2012. Introduction. In: V.R. Van der Duim, C. Ren and G.T. Jóhannesson (eds) *Actor-Network Theory and tourism. Ordering, materiality and multiplicity*. Oxon: Routledge.
Knudsen, D., Soper, A. and Metro-Roland, M., 2008. Landscape, tourism and meaning. An introduction. In: D. Knudsen, M. Metro-Roland, A. Soper and C. Greer (eds) *Landscape, tourism and meaning*. Hampshire: Ashgate.

Law, J., 2004. *After method. Mess in social science research*. Oxon: Routledge.

Law, J., 2008. On sociology and STS. *The Sociological Review*, 56(4), pp.623–49.

Lindh de Montoya, M., 2000. Entrepreneurship and culture. The case of Freddy, the strawberry man. In: R. Swedberg (ed.) *Entrepreneurship. The social science view*. Oxford: Oxford University Press.

Mol, A., 1999. Ontological politics. A word and some questions. In: J. Law and J. Hassard (eds) *Actor Network Theory and after*. Oxford: Blackwell.

Mol, A., 2002. *The body multiple: Ontology in medical practice*. Durham: Duke University Press.

Picard, D., 2011. *Tourism, magic and modernity. Cultivating the human garden*. Oxford: Berghahn Books.

Saarinen, J., 1998. The social construction of tourist destinations: The process of transformation of the Saariselkä tourism region in Finish Lapland. In: G. Ringer (ed.) *Destinations. Cultural landscapes of tourism*. London: Routledge.

Van der Duim, V.R., Ren, C. and Jóhannesson, G.T., 2012. Tourismscapes, entrepreneurs and sustainability. Enacting ANT in tourism studies. In: V.R. Van der Duim, C. Ren and G.T. Jóhannesson (eds) *Actor-Network Theory and tourism. Ordering, materiality and multiplicity*. Oxon: Routledge.

Viken, A., 2013. Fokus på sted – Fokusgruppesamtale som metode i steds- og destinasjonsanalyser. In: A. Førde, B. Kramvig, N.G. Berg and B. Dale (eds) Å finne sted. Metodologiske perspektiver *i stedsanalyse*. Trondheim: Academica.

Viken, A., 2014. Ski resort development: Scripts and phronesis. In: A. Viken and B. Granås (eds) *Destination development in tourism: Turns and tactics*. City?: Ashgate.

Chapter 5

Mapping the New Nordic Issue-scape: How to Navigate a Diffuse Controversy with Digital Methods

Anders Kristian Munk and Anne-Kristine Bøcher Ellern

5.1 Introduction

By most standards, the New Nordic Food phenomenon is not a controversy. At least not in the sense that its stakeholders are mobilized by their desire to dispute new knowledge claims, question political decisions, or voice their concerns about some emerging or untested technology. Unlike climate change, fracking, GMOs, or immunization schemes, the involvement of actors in the New Nordic Food movement is not primarily defined by their distrust or their alarm, their skepticism or their disagreement, but by rather more laudatory impulses like culinary experimentation or social innovation. And yet it would be a mistake to think that these actors are not engaged in some form of political undertaking. The New Nordic Food movement has an explicit agenda of changing not only the state of affairs in, but also the premises on which we perceive and engage with, a range of contemporary issues, many of which are traditionally controversial, such as sustainability, rural development or public health. It is a form of politics that does not take place in the established political arenas, but in the everyday laboratories of growers, consumers, chefs, tourism professionals, food scientists, and nutritionists. In the vocabulary deployed by the editors of this book, it is an ontological form of politics.

We want to argue that such distributed and emergent phenomena can be fruitfully treated as controversies in order to acquire an analytical handle on them, even though they do not appear contentious or divisive in and of themselves. We want to show that this opens them up to inquiry in ways that are useful but also challenging to the researcher, because it allows them to be deployed in their fullest possible heterogeneity. This can be useful if the research question that motivates the inquiry relates to the ways in which a phenomenon like New Nordic Food make otherwise disparate entities and situations matter to one another. In the context of this book the interesting question could for example be how the experimental invention of a new cuisine and a new diet is of any consequence to destination development and the tourism sector in rural Scandinavia? To answer such a question it is first necessary to map the territory in which it makes sense to ask it; the territory of the New Nordic Food movement and its heterogeneous issue-scape, that is. This is a challenging task, for a variety of reasons that we will elaborate below, and we will try to show how the use of digital methods and online datasets can provide some of the navigational aids necessary to manage it. Mapping the New Nordic Food phenomenon as a controversy, we contend, provides important clues about the complexity that makes it simultaneously both interesting and difficult to study.

5.2   What Difference does it Make to Call Something a Controversy?

A dictionary will tell you that the word controversy is akin to dispute, discussion, disagreement or debate; that it denotes a situation where different views are advanced on the same topic. Contemporary social theory, and the sociology of science and technology in particular, goes a bit further than that and typically takes controversies to mean something more complicated and harder to resolve. Tommaso Venturini suggests that we can pragmatically define controversies as situations in which the actors not only agree to disagree (although this is of course a prerequisite), but also frequently disagree on the substance of their disagreement; controversies are, as he puts it, resistant to reduction (Venturini, 2010, p.262). In such situations it is by no means trivial to establish what the relevant questions are to ask, or who the trustworthy experts are to answer them. Discussions ensue about the rights to speak on different aspects of an issue, and about the kinds of evidence and testimony that can be admitted in support of differing opinions and positions. It is understood that controversies are particularly difficult (and perhaps also particularly interesting to the social theorist) when they become, in this way, the scene of "ontological politics" (Mol, 1999); when they become a battleground, that is, for a struggle to define what belongs to an issue and what does not. Taken from this point of view, which is what the present book proposes to do, the act of labeling something as a controversy signals at least an interest in a particular object of study. Arguably, however, there is more at stake than that.

The sociology of science and technology has a long and rich tradition for studying controversies spanning from an interest in the trajectory of scientific discovery (e.g. Collins, 1975; 2010; Pickering, 1984; Latour and Woolgar, 1986; Pinch and Bijker, 1987, Latour, 1988) to much broader questions about the role of experts and the status of expertise in contemporary society (e.g. Martin, 1988; Epstein, 1996; 2009; Nowotny, Scott, et al., 2001; Mitchell 2002; Callon, Lascoumes, et al., 2009; Horst and Irwin, 2010). In much of this work, despite its changing focal points, the act of labeling something as a controversy implies specific, constructivist ideas about the ways in which that something should be studied; it implies a specific methodological stance (Pinch, 2014). Techno-scientific work is, crudely put, assumed to be best described and understood by following the intricacies of a controversy, because it is in the absence of consensus and stability that construction work becomes traceable, black boxes temporarily reopened, and the implicit made explicit through contestation. Cast in this way, the active use of controversies as a research instrument traces a direct ancestry back to Harold Garfinkel's breaching experiments in the 1960's (Garfinkel, 1964) and has been repeatedly employed in constructivist strands of the STS literature over the past four decades (see also Callon, 1986; Wynne, 1992; Latour, 1996; Law, 2006).

It is a stance that features with particular force if we begin to consider ontology as something fluid and political. Here controversies become invested with a specific creative potential when they are seen as the "generative events" (Whatmore, 2009, p.588) that energize participation, ferment situations in which knowledge claims can be scrutinized and new identities acquired, or, as Noortje Marres puts it, "spark a public into being" (Marres 2005). So much so that controversies are taken, in a fairly general sense, to display the social in its making. In the more recent work of Bruno Latour this assertion is at the heart of what he envisions his sociology of associations to be about, namely to inquire into the assemblage of the social (as an empirical question) by following controversies, rather than using the social (as a theoretical abstraction) to explain away phenomena (Latour, 2005). Seen through this lens, to treat your object of study as a controversy is to insist on deploying it in its maximum heterogeneity and to open it up to specific (often actor–network theoretical) modes of inquiry.

It follows that a distinction must be made between controversy as an *ethno* term – i.e. as a label that actors put on their own disputes – and controversy as a *technical* or *methodological* term – i.e. as an analytical instrument employed by the social scientist. Whereas actors themselves rarely perceive what they are engaged in as controversial (even when disagreements are apparent they can be construed as resulting from simple misunderstandings or lack of information), the situations in which the analytical treatment of a phenomenon as a controversy can serve to open it up to inquiry are potentially endless. What is important to understand, however, is that in this latter sense the term controversy no longer refers to any substantial feature of the object of study and that this imports a series of practical challenges into the research design. It not only complicates the question of where and how to end the description and "cut the network" (Strathern, 1996, see also Latour, 2004), or how to acquire the time, access and resources necessary to trace all interesting associations, but it fundamentally raises the question of how to bring out the controversy in something that is not necessarily and always overtly controversial, at least not in the sense of being a hotly contested topic.

We came face to face with these challenges when we were preparing the first draft of this text. We were away on fieldwork in the Swedish Baltic and we had been treating New Nordic Food as a controversy for some time. Not because it had been a spectacularly contentious issue generating fierce debates or arousing conflicting political passions, but because it had been a convenient way for us to conceptualize our research design. There had been occasional discussions about the ethics of eating live shrimps at Noma, for example, or the identity project that would ally the invention of a new regional cuisine with a dogmatic commitment to local ingredients, but the reason we had begun thinking in terms of controversies had little to do with these debates. More than anything it was a basic attempt to understand what we were doing. We had promised in our research proposal that we would be "mapping the New Nordic Food phenomenon, its diffusion, development and socio-technical variation"[1] and so the immediate problem that presented itself to us was how to define New Nordic Food? What should count as belonging to this rather diffuse denomination? The actor–network theoretical impulse is always to solicit such a question to the actors themselves. We reasoned that if New Nordic Food was an emergent socio-technical phenomenon then the actors would already be asking themselves – and be trying to answer – what it was. To treat it as a controversy was not only to acknowledge that such a definition was a matter of concern to them (or rather, as we shall see, to insist that it might be), but also to give it pride of place in the research design. It became, from the outset of the project, one of the central questions for us to explore.

We had come to Gotland and Öland to do just that, and so we had arranged to talk to growers, chefs and tourism professionals involved in their regional food networks. From the perspective of someone living in Copenhagen this made sense, we thought, since both islands were frequently staged as prime examples of Nordic terroirs delivering high quality products like the Gotland truffle or the rediscovered Öland wheat to the Scandinavian food scene. In Copenhagen, at least, these places came through as quintessentially New Nordic, but it was an entirely different story to visit the islands themselves. Few of our informants on Öland had ever heard about Öland wheat, and although both Öland and Gotland were teeming with quality conscious local growers and producers, virtually none of those we talked to mentioned New Nordic Food as something they cared particularly about, had a specific interest in, or felt especially influenced or inspired by. It was, with very few exceptions, not the easiest place in the world to solicit a question about New Nordic Food to the actors themselves. Arguably because the people we were talking to were in fact *not* the actors, at least not in the pragmatic sense that they themselves were trying to make a difference to whatever New Nordic Food was, should or could be. On the other hand, their vegetables, and their lamb, their wild herbs, truffles, and berries, all ended up in restaurants, farmers markets, and cook books where they were praised for their unique Nordicness and their sense of terroir. The context in which they were produced, albeit without explicit reference to something New Nordic, was also focused on combining sustainable rural development with business innovation in the agri-food and tourism sectors, a hallmark shared with the New Nordic Food movement. And yet it was plain to see that New Nordic Food was not an issue here. The controversy that we had been claiming as a fundamental part of our research design appeared blatantly absent.

This was put especially to the point when a public debacle on New Nordic Food did in fact break out back home in Copenhagen only a few days into our fieldwork. It

---

1   The project is supported by the Carlsberg Foundation and runs between January 1st 2012 and July 1st 2014: http://vbn.aau.dk/files/91666688/Project_Description_Mapping_New_Nordic_Food.pdf, accessed October 17, 2013.

was sparked when a former doctoral student on a 13€m dietary intervention project called OPUS[2] came out with allegations that he had been forced by his steering committee to tweak conclusions in his dissertation.[3] The project was investigating the potential health benefits of the so-called New Nordic Diet and it was co-chaired by the food entrepreneur, celebrity chef and major stakeholder in the New Nordic Food movement, Claus Meyer. The doctoral student had been responsible for evaluating the new diet in everyday use practice and assessing the possible barriers for its adoption. In the media he described how the steering committee had tried to convince him to soften up his conclusions before sending them off to peer-review, and kept criticizing what they perceived as his own negative and politicizing attitude towards the diet, also after the paper came back accepted for publication (published in *Appetite* as Michelsen, Holm, et al., 2013). It was a situation that offered numerous opportunities to the actor–network analysis because it immediately forced some of the leading researchers, not just on OPUS, but in a wider research community, to publically articulate their differing ideas about sound and robust knowledge production.[4] It was, if you will, a rare case of controversy figuring as an ethno term in the field, but of course not a situation that we could rely on materializing in every phase and site of our field work.

The contrast to our work on Öland and Gotland was stark. In the OPUS case we had been served a situation where it did not feel like a stretch to treat New Nordic Food as a controversy (on the contrary, that was exactly what it had become with or without us calling it so) and it was undeniably easier to follow actors that already had obvious stakes in the phenomenon we were interested in. The problem was, of course, that there were real and tangible reasons why we had come to Gotland and Öland to map the New Nordic Food phenomenon and, as we will try to substantiate below, why we were treating this task as an exercise in controversy mapping (following Rogers, Marres, 2000; Marres, 2004; 2012; Venturini, 2010; 2012). The situation we found ourselves in was essentially illustrative of a practical problem that follows directly from the idea that controversy mapping is a methodological stance that can be actively taken *even when there are no immediate debacles in sight*. To deliberately treat something as controversial can be fruitfully understood as a research intervention that affords specific possibilities

---

2 OPUS: Optimal well–being, development and health for Danish children through a healthy New Nordic Diet, http://foodoflife.dk/opus/english/about/, accessed October 6, 2013.

3 http://videnskab.dk/kultur-samfund/nedtur-millionprojekt-vi-gider-ikke-lave-ny-nordisk-mad, accessed on October 6, 2013, http://videnskab.dk/kultur-samfund/forsker-i-millionprojekt-ledelsen-forsogte-pavirke-mine-resultater, accessed October 16, 2013.

4 http://politiken.dk/videnskab/ECE2057524/claus-meyer-madforskning-er-studentikost-og-uden-kontakt-til-virkeligheden/, accessed October 15, 2013, http://videnskab.dk/kultur-samfund/arne-astrup-vi-gjorde-forskningen-bedre, accessed October 15, 2013, http://www.ifro.ku.dk/debatindlaeg/debat_svartilclausmeyer/, accessed October 16, 2013.

to the enquiry, but it also presents the researcher with an equally specific problem, namely how to deploy that controversy without the willing help of antagonized, concerned groups. Below we will show how a set of digital techniques for charting online activity in the New Nordic issue space became instrumental to the way in which we were eventually able to deal with that problem, but first it is necessary to substantiate our interest in this phenomenon.

5.3 The Manifesto for the New Nordic Cuisine and the Complex Origins of a Fractionally Coherent Phenomenon

The emergence of the New Nordic Food movement can be conveniently dated to the publication of the *Manifesto for the New Nordic Cuisine* in November 2004. Signed by a group of chefs from Denmark, Sweden, Norway, Finland, Iceland, the Faroe Islands, and Åland, it marked the first attempt to unite a range of existing agendas under the same aegis. The manifesto thus declared that the aims of New Nordic Cuisine would be:

1. To express the purity, freshness, simplicity and ethics we wish to associate with our region.
2. To reflect the changing of the seasons in the meals we make.
3. To base our cooking on ingredients and produce whose characteristics are particularly excellent in our climates, landscapes and waters.
4. To combine the demand for good taste with modern knowledge of health and well-being.
5. To promote Nordic products and the variety of Nordic producers – and to spread the word about their underlying cultures.
6. To promote animal welfare and a sound production process in our seas, on our farmland and in the wild.
7. To develop potentially new applications of traditional Nordic food products.
8. To combine the best in Nordic cookery and culinary traditions with impulses from abroad.
9. To combine local self-sufficiency with regional sharing of high-quality products.
10. To join forces with consumer representatives, other cooking craftsmen, agriculture, the fishing, food, retail and wholesale industries, researchers, teachers, politicians and authorities on this project for the benefit and advantage of everyone in the Nordic countries.[5]

You will notice that the manifesto reads like an open invitation to those already concerned by issues like rural development, sustainability, regional identity,

---

5   http://nynordiskmad.org/om-nnm-ii/koeksmanifestet/om00/, accessed on October 17, 2013.

public health, biodiversity, nature conservation, or animal welfare, not to mention fine dining and culinary heritage. It is a call for them to join forces. And in many ways that was exactly what happened in the following years. Crucially, though, it was never simply about giving a range of pre-existing concerned groups a new banner to rally under, but about finding the means for them to take each other into account in ways that would allow a new common ground to emerge (for a discussion of the ways in which such projects might energize controversy, see also Petersen, Munk 2013). Think about it: the world in which Michelin starred haute cuisine can become a natural ally of animal welfare and public health is not a straightforward construction. One needs only utter the words "foie gras" to put the whole construction in jeopardy. What was needed was a comprehensive rearrangement of the political *things* (in the sense of Latour, 2005) that mobilized the issue publics in question and defined the terms of their commitment; what was needed was an effective ontological politics.

These material rearrangements are to be taken quite literally. They involved the investment of a host of Scandinavian ingredients with new potentials for health, tastiness, sustainability, or even edibility, and they required practical work in the laboratories of research institutions, on the plates and palates of chefs and food professionals, in the fields of growers, and on the hunting grounds of foragers and fishermen. Sea buckthorn, for instance, a berry found in Denmark and along the Baltic coasts of Sweden and Finland, was successfully recast as a super fruit rich in vitamin C, beta-carotenes and polyunsaturated fatty acids, and is currently being tested for its beneficial effects on weight loss.[6] It is available fresh, frozen, dried, juiced and pickled in retail stores and frequently stars on the gastro-pages of newspapers and lifestyle magazines. This was certainly not the case ten years ago. At Noma it has been served up with sea urchin and scallops, vegetables and gooseberries, as a mousse, or in a beetroot cream puff. Sea buckthorn has even become a favorite foraging item for many ordinary Danes who venture out to pick them in autumn and share their advice on social media on where to find them, or how to best avoid the thorns (the last bit of wisdom circulated in our network was to freeze an entire branch of the bush and then beat the berries loose inside a plastic bag).

Far from being banal everyday undertakings, or perhaps precisely because they are banal everyday undertakings, for the analysis that claims to be actor–network theoretical in its origin, these rearrangements are exactly what we are interested in tracing. And that means going to places like Gotland and Öland, even if the humans who are harvesting the vast swaths of sea buckthorn on those islands would never dream of using the terminology of New Nordic Food to describe their work. They are still materially engaged in the ontological politics from which New Nordic Food has emerged as a phenomenon. With the sprawling issue-scape suggested in the manifesto in mind, it quickly becomes clear that the potential range of everyday practices that could be said to be interesting from this point

---

6 http://foodoflife.dk/nyheder/2012/972_havtorn/, accessed October 17, 2013.

of view is immense, which makes it virtually impossible to manually trace every association. This is by no means a new problem in actor–network analysis, rather something that has been with it since its inception, and thus already in the 1980's Michel Callon and others suggested that quantitative scientometrics could play a role in the qualtitative study of dynamics in science and technology (Callon, Courtial, et al., 1983; Leydesdorff, 1989), an effort which was followed up in the 1990's with attempts at computerizing the analysis (Latour, Mauguin, et al., 1992; Teil, Latour, 1995). Most recently, profiting from the wealth of new digital traces, and the techniques for harvesting and analyzing them that have become available online, it has been suggested that this kind of associational sociology might be able speed up and work at scale without defaulting on its promises to follow the actors and let them deploy their worlds on their own terms (Venturini, Latour, 2010; Venturini, 2012; Yaneva, 2012). It was with these new potentials in mind that we had dared take on the task of mapping the New Nordic Food phenomenon, and it is with some of the resulting navigational aids in hand that we will now try to wriggle our way out of the impasse from which we began this chapter: how to deploy New Nordic Food as a controversy?

In a general sense the problem was how to study a swarm of disparate practices and locations as part of the same, but only very fractionally coherent, phenomenon. Or in more concrete terms: how to make New Nordic Food matter to the practices we were observing on Gotland and Öland? The American anthropologist George Marcus has famously suggested in his plea for multi-sited ethnography that it is the job of the field worker to posit the logics of association that bring disparate cultural locales together and enable an analysis of the translations that take place between them (Marcus, 1995, for a specific application to the notion of terroir, see Hoyrup, Munk, 2007). We were looking to digital methods, online datasets, and a cartography of food related websites to help us construct that multi-sited field. What emerged was a map of an overlapping New Nordic issue space that allowed us to locate what was happening on Öland and Gotland vis-à-vis our experiences from Copenhagen and to attain a line of inquiry with our informants.

5.3 Mapping the New Nordic Food Phenomenon Online

One of the first things we noticed when we became involved in this project in early 2012 was the proliferation of different terms with the prefix 'New Nordic' to them. These differences appeared to be significant, if for no other reason than because words like 'cuisine' or 'diet' are etymologically quite far apart, but perhaps more importantly because different actors seemed to favor the use of some of these 'New Nordic' terms over others. Since these terms were frequently used by actors on the web, usually in connection with other issue terms like 'sustainable development' or 'healthy school meals', and since tracing them was relatively easy, their mention in different online documents became the basis for our first cartographic experiments on the web.

One of the most obvious traces that actors leave online is text. Be it in the form of tweets, blog posts or 500 page reports, texts proliferate across the web and New Nordic Food is of course no exception. For the most part these documents are also full-text searchable through engines like Google, which allows you to find them and segment them based not only on who wrote them or when they were written, but on the stuff they talk about, i.e. the terms used in the text. Our first step was therefore to compile a corpus of online text for each of the terms we wanted to explore; a collection of documents, that is, in which each of the terms were mentioned. We did this using the following five Google queries that returned a total of 207 pdf's in English ranging from reports, papers and conference presentations to tourist guides and promotional material produced at various points in time:

These queries produced five discrete sets of documents that were *exclusively* mentioning *either* New Nordic Food, New Nordic Cuisine, New Nordic Diet, New Nordic Kitchen, or New Nordic Cooking somewhere in the text, but *never* making use of two or more of the terms at the same time. As a result of our query design we left out all documents which were generically making use of several issue terms at the same time. Since the terms never co-occurred it made

Table 5.1 Query design used with Google to retrieve English language.pdf documents citing either "New Nordic Food", "New Nordic Cuisine", "New Nordic Diet", "New Nordic Kitchen", or "New Nordic Cooking", but never citing two or more of the terms at the same time. The top three queries (marked in black) were the ones eventually used for the analysis.

Google query (Google.com was queried for English language pdf's in May 2012. A manual query was subsequently carried out within the documents to verify the quality of the search result and cleanse for errors)	Number of documents returned	Tag (All documents were tagged according to their query)
"New Nordic Food" -"New -Nordic -Cooking" - "New -Nordic -Cuisine" -"New -Nordic -Diet" - "New -Nordic -Kitchen" filetype:pdf	82	New Nordic Food
"New Nordic Cuisine" -"New -Nordic -Food" - "New -Nordic -Cooking" -"New -Nordic -Diet" - "New -Nordic -Kitchen" filetype:pdf	74	New Nordic Cuisine
"New Nordic Diet" -"New -Nordic -Food" - "New -Nordic -Cuisine" -"New -Nordic -Cooking"- "New -Nordic -Kitchen" filetype:pdf	32	New Nordic Diet
"New Nordic Kitchen" -"New -Nordic -Food" - "New -Nordic -Cuisine" -"New -Nordic -Diet" - "New -Nordic -Cooking" filetype:pdf	26	New Nordic Kitchen
"New Nordic Cooking" -"New -Nordic -Food" - "New -Nordic -Cuisine" -"New -Nordic -Diet" - "New -Nordic -Kitchen" filetype:pdf	3	New Nordic Cooking

sense to consider the text gathered in each set of documents as a sample of what actors talk about when they talk about, for example, New Nordic Cuisine *or* New Nordic Diet, and subsequently compare these discourses to one another and explore their differences. What became possible, you could say, was to compare the discursive spaces forming around different issue terms and explore their differences and overlaps, even though this was of course an artificially static mapping that could not take into account the possible developments over time across these spaces.

Once we had gathered and categorized the documents we used a piece of software for semantic analysis called ANTA (the Actor–Network Text Analyzer) to find out what kind of language was associated with the use of each issue term. ANTA was developed at the Sciences Po médialab for use in actor–network inspired research (Venturini, Guido, 2012) and allows for automatically extracting recurrent expressions (word entities that are being 'named' in the text) from a set of documents, and subsequently merge what the researcher considers to be equivalent expressions. ANTA thus works by suggesting to us possible relations between two main types of entities: those doing the naming, which is in our case the documents talking about cuisine, cooking, food, diet or kitchen respectively, and those being named or enunciated, which is in our case institutions like the Nordic Council, actors like Claus Meyer, concepts like sustainability, or materials like sea buckthorn.

The first insight that this analysis yielded was that the discourses on New Nordic Cooking and New Nordic Kitchen had very little unique language associated with them. The terms extracted in these documents were also extracted from other sets of documents and did not make it possible to exclusively associate kitchen or cooking with specific issues or specific actors. The terms extracted from the documents talking about cuisine, food, and diet were on the other hand distinctly unique in ways that suggested substantial differences between them. Figure 5.1 shows an initial selection of the most frequent unique terms extracted from each of the corpora. Already here it is noteworthy that names of famous chefs like René Redzepi or Rasmus Kofoed only appear in documents talking about New Nordic Cuisine alongside typical tourist destinations and culinary events like Copenhagen Cooking. New Nordic Food is rife with the Nordic dimension, innovation and business development, rural areas and genetic resources, while New Nordic Diet is distinctly technical with terms like human nutrition and sensory perception. It was with the two first discourses that our experiences at Gotland and Öland had resonance, while the controversy around the OPUS project appeared to be mostly related to the latter.

This relatively crude mapping affords limited opportunities for placing issues vis-à-vis one another, but a spatialized visualization not only enhances that potential, it also allows us to explore shared language and to assess the relative importance of terms. In figure 5.2 we have visualized the relationship between documents and extracted terms as a citation network (sets of documents citing terms). It has been spatialized using a spring-based algorithm which allows you

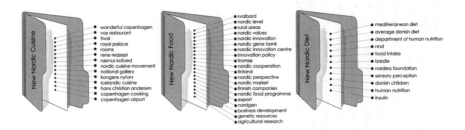

Figure 5.1 Unique language in documents mentioning 'New Nordic Cuisine', 'New Nordic Food', and 'New Nordic Diet' respectively. Terms have been extracted using the Actor–Network Text Analyzer (https://github.com/medialab/ANTA).

to see which terms are shared and which terms are unique, which terms are cited by more documents (have stronger edge weights and will appear closer to the set of documents citing it), and which terms appear with higher frequency (bigger nodes). We have left out terms shared by all three sets of documents, and we have very significantly reduced the amount of terms to make the visualization readable in this format. Although this means that terms like Claus Meyer have been left out because they are cited by all three sets of documents, the OPUS project and its characteristic language is still clearly identifiable around New Nordic Diet. This is where controversy conveniently emerged as an ethno term. Gotland, on the other hand, is located alongside concepts like entrepreneurship, Nordic cooperation, organic production, tourism and green growth in the language shared between New Nordic Food and New Nordic Cuisine.

What is the use of a mapping like this? Can it serve as a way of staging New Nordic Food as a matter of concern on Gotland and Öland? First of all it shows how these Islands are being enunciated alongside issues like tourism development and organic production in documents about New Nordic Food and New Nordic Cuisine, which provides a line of inquiry when you are talking to local organic producers or tourism professionals. It also shows the almost complete absence of health and dietary concerns in documents talking about Gotland and Öland, which again suggests that the controversy around the Opus project happened in an altogether different issue space although all part of the loosely assembled agendas that make up the New Nordic movement. This thus provides clues, if you will, about the fractional coherence that simultaneously makes Nordic Food an interesting topic to study and a difficult phenomenon to account for.

Just take a look at the few ingredients that are still to be found (many more appear in the full mapping). Musk ox, foie gras and fresh mountain lamb are mentioned alongside tourist attractions, destinations and famous chefs and restaurants, while cream, milk protein and Nordic fruits go together with medical journals, lifestyle diseases and randomized control trials. It makes it possible to engage in a kind of

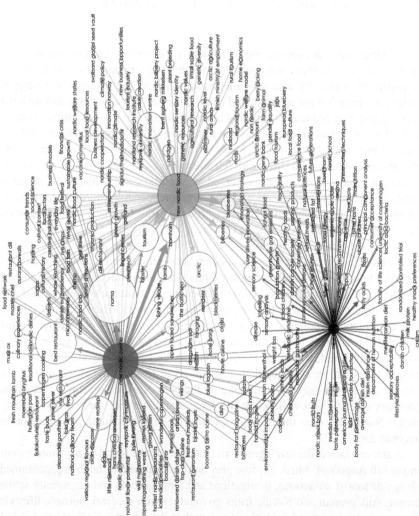

Figure 5.2 Terms cited by documents mentioning 'New Nordic Cuisine', 'New Nordic Food', and 'New Nordic Diet' respectively. Terms have been extracted using the Actor–Network Text Analyzer (https://github.com/medialab/ANTA). Node size represents the frequency with which terms appear in each document, edge weight represents the number documents in each set citing each term. Spatialized in Gephi using ForceAtlas2.

associational profiling of each of these terms. While bilberries and blueberries, for example, puts us in the borderland between dietary intervention trials, children's health and consumer research, and Nordic cooperation, rural development and biodiversity, the use of the technical term for bilberries, *vaccinum myrtillus*, is exclusively associated with the latter. The term organic production appears to be associated with green growth, entrepreneurship and Nordic food culture, while organic products appear alongside school food, traceability and greenhouse gas emissions. Cuisine documents talk about taste buds while diet documents talk about sensory experiences, and Heston Blumenthal and molecular gastronomy appears to provide a link between fine dining and dietary intervention. This is an exploratory exercise that is potentially endless and can be revisited over and over again with new questions in mind. Just like any other map. These visualizations are basically useful to generate hypothesis, rather than proving or confirming them, through what John Tukey called "exploratory data analysis" (1977).

5.4   Navigating the New Nordic Issue-scape

So far we have been mapping discursive formations around three issue terms in three collections of documents. To be able to root these formations in a map that tells us something about specific actors and to find out who is making use of these issue terms and how, a different approach is necessary. To try and accomplish this we turned our attention to another trace that is left in force by actors online, and possibly one that holds more currency to an analysis that claims to be associational in character: the hyperlink. Contrary to a term found in a text, a hyperlink is always an act of association. In Figure 5.3 we have used a web-crawler to harvest the hyperlinks from the website of the Nordic Council of Ministers' New Nordic Food program (nynordiskmad.org), and subsequently harvest the hyperlinks from all its neighboring sites. All the websites you see are thus pointed to by nynordskmad.org, which makes an interesting list in itself, considering that it has in practice been suggested by one of the major actors in the New Nordic Food movement. What is also interesting, however, is to look at the clusters of websites that their mutual interlinking generates.

 To the top and on the left are a clearly visible Norwegian (.no) and a clearly visible Swedish (.se) cluster. To the top right is a less clear but still discernible cluster of Finnish (.fi) and trans-Nordic websites (mostly.org). The rest of the map consists of three predominantly Danish clusters (.dk), with two of them clearly distinguishable in the bottom, and a third less clear on the right. It is the position of these clusters vis-à-vis one another, as well as their composition, that catches the eye. The language based clustering is no surprise on the Web and you can quite clearly see why if you take a look at the Norwegian cluster and notice how the Government website (regjeringen.no) acts like a national hub. That makes it interesting to find websites outside their language barrier and a case of this is observable in the bottom right corner of Figure 5.3. This cluster is indeed only Danish at a glance. The main hub of the cluster is the website of the San Pellegrino World's Best Restaurants list (theworlds50best.com), an annual award that has been instrumental in placing the New Nordic Cuisine on the throne of the international gastronomic scene and the cluster contains a number of international food bloggers as well. Besides Noma in Copenhagen, Swedish restaurants like Frantzén-Lindeberg, Fäviken Magasinet and Mathias Dahlgren belong in this world, rather than in their national cluster, and it attests to an important international dimension of the Nordic Food movement that is neither traceable on Gotland nor in the OPUS controversy.

The OPUS project itself (idégryden.dk, foodoflife.dk) can be found on the right side of figure 5.3 alongside several sites associated with Claus Meyer (meyersmadhus.dk, meyersmad.dk, meyerskoekken.dk, clausmeyer.dk). They are diametrically opposed, i.e. not very associated, to regional food sites in the Swedish cluster (regionalmat.se, eldrimner.se, skargardssmak.se), which is where you would eventually expect to find our informants on Öland and Gotland. The only connection appears to be with the Stockholm branch of Slow Food. It falls to other Danish sites to associate with Swedish regional food culture, namely those in the bottom left corner of the map. These sites are mainly about organic production, and in particular biodiversity in grain and seed cultivation (kulturplanter.dk, fuglebjerggaard.dk, aurion.dk, agrologica.dk, gl-estrup.dk), and the main hub that makes the connection possible is the Nordic Genetic Resource Center (nordgen. org). It becomes interesting now to compare this to the semantic map in figure 5.2 that had terms related to genetic resources and biodiversity appear alongside rural development, regional food and organic agriculture, typically cited by documents that mentioned New Nordic Food. Indeed, while we were on Gotland we were repeatedly told by informants that it was the rediscovery of a few seeds of old emmer, spelt and einkorn wheat varieties in a barn on the island that had enabled Danish grain enthusiasts to begin cultivating these species again, a cultivation that has since then become an integral part of the New Nordic repertoire. As already mentioned, few of the actors that we talked to on Öland had heard about the Öland wheat. What is interesting about this mapping is that it shows how the issue space in which old grain varieties acquire New Nordic properties is not driven by local actors.

This strategy of mapping based on hyperlink associations can of course be extended beyond the immediate neighborhood of the New Nordic Food program. There are other actors here that disserve the right to point out interesting sites for a research project on New Nordic Food, those of Claus Meyer or the OPUS project for example. Figure 5.4 thus shows what happens if you take this idea to its extreme and keep crawling, iteration after iteration, until there are no new websites showing up on your mapping that you would qualitatively deem to have something to do with the New Nordic Food phenomenon. It consists of 2007 websites but it is essentially a vastly expanded version of the kind of map shown in figure 5.3.

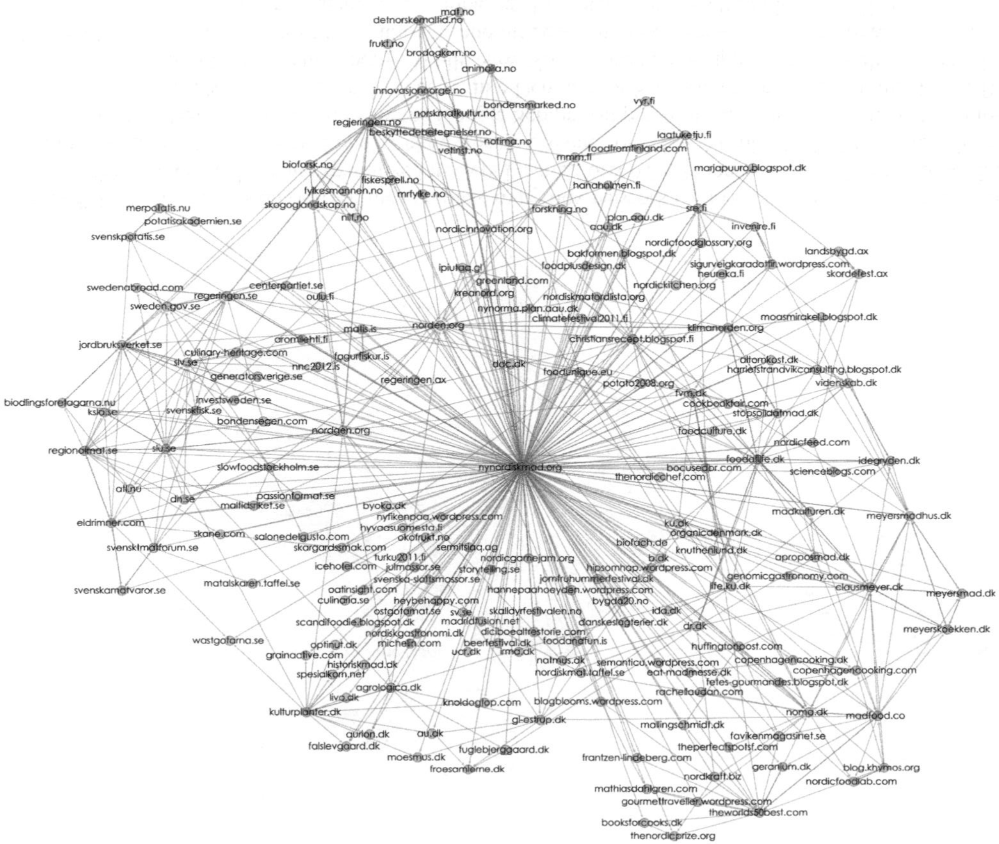

Figure 5.3 Hyperlink network around the website of the New Nordic Food program of the Nordic Council of Ministers (nynordiskmad.org). Links have been harvested using the Navicrawler (http://webatlas.fr/wp/navicrawler/) and spatialized in Gephi using ForceAtlas2.

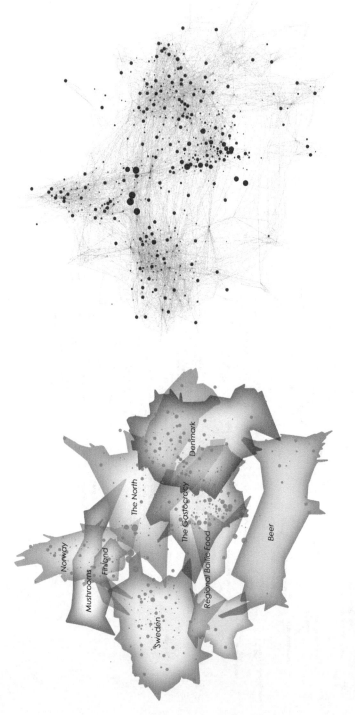

Figure 5.4 Stylized version (left) of the complete hyperlink network (right) consisting of 2007 websites crawled using the Navicrawler (http://webatlas.fr/wp/navicrawler/) and spatialized in Gephi using ForceAtlas2 (Jacomy, et al., 2014). Node size represents the degree to which a website mentions the terms "New Nordic Food", "New Nordic Cuisine" or "New Nordic Diet". Only sites with 1 mention or more are shown on the left. This information has been obtained using the Google Scraper (https://tools.digitalmethods.net/beta/scrapeGoogle/). The regions are derived from the main clusterings. Some are national in scope, like Denmark or Sweden, others are local, like Baltic Regional Food, and others are characterized by a practice, such as Beer or Mushrooms. While New Nordic issue terms appear extensively in the national clusters, and in the Gastocracy cluster which includes a large number of international food bloggers and fine dining sites, they are relatively absent from the more local and practice based clusters. A number of smaller local and practice-based clusters have been left out in the stylized version on the left.

At this zoom distance individual actors (websites) are not discernible. They can be reacquired by zooming back in, but it is the clustering rather than individual websites that is the most interesting result here. The language based clustering is retained with Sweden to the left, Norway at the top, Denmark to the right, and Finland and the trans-Nordic sites in the center of Figure 5.4. We have added a layer to the map generated by scraping each website for the occurrence of the terms New Nordic Food, New Nordic Cuisine and New Nordic Diet (in all the Scandinavian languages as well as English). The size of the nodes show you where, and to which degree, these terms appear, and it shows you where they are absent. It is quite noteworthy that websites from Gotland, Öland and other food regions in the Baltic, which are all found in the smaller clusters in the bottom left corner of Figure 5.4, do not mention these terms at all. Instead they talk about food culture, for instance, or terroir or local production, but never something New Nordic. We are thus in a situation where documents that talk about New Nordic Food and New Nordic Cuisine frequently mention Gotland, but actors that are actually on Gotland almost never return the favor. This corresponds well to our fieldwork experiences where most of our informants had heard about Claus Meyer and René Redzepi at Noma, but not much more than that, as well as to our experience of doing fieldwork in Copenhagen where produce like the Gotland Truffle, the Gotland Lamb or the Öland Wheat are hailed as the superstars of the New Nordic Cuisine.

Besides analyzing clusters and scraping the web-corpus for issue terms we also did a qualitative analysis of each website and tagged them according to the type of practice they were most engaged with. A microbrewery would be tagged 'beer' while a university would be tagged 'research', and so forth. This tagging combined with the scraped issue terms allowed for a different kind of visualization of the same dataset, and one where the potential navigational use becomes perhaps the most clear. In Figure 5.5 it is thus possible to compare the types of websites that are most frequently represented in the subsets of sites mentioning New Nordic Food, New Nordic Diet and New Nordic Cuisines, as well as the subset of sites not mentioning any of these terms. In principle you should be able to look at a map like this and get an indication of where to go and talk to people who, for instance, do something that is in principle very New Nordic but rarely talk about it in that way (such as people who make wine in Scandinavia).

The only type of site that is steadily reoccurring across all four subsets are the foodies, i.e. those who blog about their visit to a restaurant, their homegrown vegetables or their latest exploits in the kitchen. Besides that there are substantial differences to be observed. The most noticeable is perhaps the absence of Media, Research and Government sites in the top 10 types of websites not mentioning any of the issue terms. If you look at the total web corpus, which is not shown here, Research and Media sites are barely within the top 10, while Government sites are barely out of it. Their strong presence in the subsets mentioning the issue terms is thus telling us something about the type of actors driving the agenda. Along the same lines it is noteworthy that all the types occurring exclusively in the subset

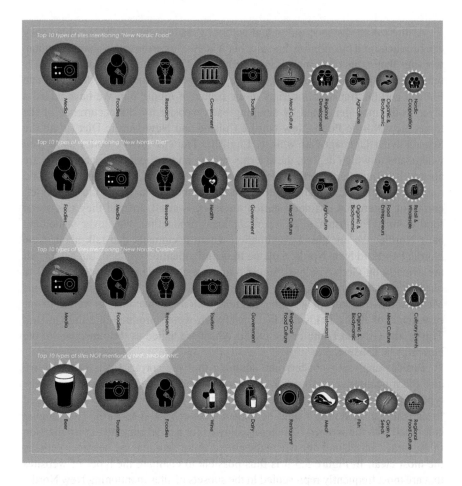

Figure 5.5   What are the top 10 types of websites that are talking about New Nordic Food, New Nordic Cuisine, New Nordic Diet, or not making use of the terms at all? Website types that are exclusively occurring in one of the top10s are marked with a star.

not mentioning the issue terms are producers or growers of one sort or another. Indeed the closest we get to production or growing in the subsets mentioning the issue terms is through types like Agriculture or Organic & Biodynamic, and they primarily contain interest organizations of different provenance. It suggests again that things tend to be articulated as New Nordic rather by a policymaking establishment than by growers and producers (see also Figure 5.4). Finally it is possible to corroborate some of the insights from the semantic mappings (Figure 5.1 and Figure 5.2): health is unique to New Nordic Diet, regional development and Nordic cooperation are unique to New Nordic Food, and tourism occurs at the interface between food and cuisine.

What the above mappings help us to do, then, is to navigate the overlapping issue spaces in which the New Nordic Food phenomenon is suspended. Quite literally: they can help us form hypothesis and decide how to proceed with the inquiry, where to go next, and who to ask which questions. They do not on their own provide the answers, but they are not supposed to either. What they are supposed to do is to provide navigational aids to a researcher trying to do fieldwork in a fractionally coherent world where it is never clear in which way and to what extent disparate situations may or may not have a purchase on one another. What is crucially important is that they do so without defaulting on the ambition to follow the actors themselves. Besides the typology of Figure 5.5 there is very little use of extraneous terminology in bringing these cartographic displays to life. They are based on the traces left by the associational work of the actors. There is thus no fundamental difference between the analytical level you would operate on as an actor-network scholar exploring the controversy qualitatively by moving from one online resource to the next, tracing each utterance and logging each connection, and the overview you see in Figure 5.4. The hyperlinks are the same. So are the terms collected from the websites. What these mappings allow us to do is to entertain the idea that there are different New Nordic issue spaces in which different practices can be located. To the field worker trying to answer questions about ongoing ontological politics it is both a rendering of the object of study and a way of making disparate practices matter to one other. It is an intervention that posits a necessary logic of association and suggests questions about translation and fractional coherence.

5.5 Conclusion

You might say that we have prematurely declared New Nordic Food a controversy. This would explain why we were having such trouble locating it as a matter of concern in the local context of regional development, tourism and organic food production on Gotland and Öland. But then you could equally argue that controversies are never *in* something (in tourism, for instance), which would somehow presume that they belonged within a well-defined ontological realm. Since the very thing that makes New Nordic Food interesting to study, from our point of view, is the way in which the movement is attempting to reorganize the delimitations of such realms and re-interest their inhabitants in one another, that presumption would be directly at odds with the kind of inquiry we were pursuing. The problem is perhaps that controversies, in order for them to be beyond reduction to mere disagreements, are never in something. On the contrary, it is the fact that they cut across different domains, upsetting them, creating moments of "ontological disturbance (...) in which", as Sarah Whatmore and Catharina Landström put it, "the things on which we rely as unexamined parts of the material fabric of our everyday lives become molten" (Whatmore, Landström, 2011, p.583), that sets them apart and makes them interesting. To deliberately label this complexity as a controversy opens up questions like: what happens when diffuse societal concerns are made palatable and manifest through the food we eat and the geographies from which we source it? When the Nordic landscapes and their flora and fauna become in this way the "stuff of politics" (Braun and Whatmore, 2010) it warrants an exploration of both their co-constitutive role in the formation of new publics and the ways in which they are themselves reconfigured as matters of concern in this process. It is, by definition, an interesting question to a social scientist, and especially to one who claims to be doing actor–network theory, when a group of practitioners propose to fundamentally reshape the terrain of a series of pertinent, contemporary issues through a concrete set of interventions.

If this is indeed the case, then it front stages the question of how to envision a space of research within which such an inquiry can take place. We have suggested that a first step could be to actively treat the phenomenon at hand as potentially controversial. To do so, at least, is to recognize its onto-political features and to keep the door open for the widest possible range of effects that it may or may not have across the social fabric, including those parts of it that we would label 'tourism'. But calling something a controversy is not without consequences either; it comes with a responsibility. The level of heterogeneity you consciously allow to flood your research design is liable to drown you, or at least throw you off course, if you are not equipped with the cartographic instruments to chart it and the navigational aids to keep your bearing. Ontological politics and its resulting fractional coherencies are what make complex social phenomena interesting, but they require a map. In this chapter we have presented a digital methods take on how to acquire it.[7]

References

Braun, B., Whatmore, S.J. and Stengers, I., 2010. *Political Matter: Technoscience, Democracy, and Public Life*. Minneapolis: University of Minnesota Press.
Callon, M., 1986. Some elements of a sociology of translation: Domestication of the scallops and the fishermen of Saint Brieuc Bay. In: J. Law (ed.) *Power, action and belief: A new sociology of knowledge?* London: Routledge, pp.196–233.
Callon, M., Lascoumes, P. and Barthe, Y., 2009. *Acting in an uncertain world: An essay on technical democracy*. Cambridge, MA: MIT Press.
Callon, M., Courtial, J., Turner, W.A. and Bauin, S., 1983. From translations to problematic networks: An introduction to co-word analysis. *Social Science Information*, 22(2), pp.191–235.
Collins, H., 2010. *Gravity's shadow: The search for gravitational waves*. Chicago: University of Chicago Press.
Collins, H.M., 1975. The seven sexes: A study in the sociology of a phenomenon, or the replication of experiments in physics. *Sociology*, 9(2), pp.205–24.

---

7   We would like to thank Tommaso Venturini, Audrey Baneyx, Kari de Pryck, Mathieu Jacomy and Bruno Laotur for their helpful comments on this text. We would also like to thank the edtiors of this book and an anonymous reviewer for their constructive responses.

Epstein, S., 1996. *Impure science: AIDS, activism, and the politics of knowledge.* Berkeley: University of California Press.

Epstein, S., 2009. Sick building syndrome and the problem of uncertainty: Environmental politics, technoscience and women workers. *Social Studies of Science*, 39(6), pp.953–6.

Garfinkel, H., 1964. Studies of the routine grounds of everyday activities. *Social problems*, 11(3), pp.225–50.

Horst, M. and Irwin, A., 2010. Nations at ease with radical knowledge: On concensus, consensusing and false consensusness. *Social Studies of Science*, 40(1), pp.105–26.

Hoyrup, J.F. and Munk, A.K., 2007. Translating terroir: Sociomaterial potentials in ethnography and wine-arowina. *Ethnologia scandinavica*, 37, pp.5–20.

Jacomy, M., Venturini, T., Heymann, S., and Bastian, M., 2014. ForceAtlas2, a Continuous Graph Layout Algorithm for Handy Network Visualization Designed for the Gephi Software. *PloS one*, 9(6), e98679.

Latour, B., 1988. *The pasteurization of France.* Cambridge, MA: Harvard University Press.

Latour, B., 1996. *Aramis, or, the love of technology.* Cambridge, MA: Harvard University Press.

Latour, B., 2004. A prologue in form of a dialog between a student and his (somewhat) socratic professor. In: C. Avgerou, C. Ciborra and F.F. Land (eds) *The social study of information and communication study.* Oxford: Oxford University Press, pp.62–76.

Latour, B., 2005a. From realpolitik to dingpolitik – or how to make things public. In: B. Latour and P. Weibel (eds) *Making things public – Atmospheres of democracy.* Cambridge, MA: MIT Press.

Latour, B., 2005b. *Reassembling the social – An introduction to Actor-Network-Theory.* Oxford: Oxford University Press.

Latour, B. and Woolgar, S., 1986. *Laboratory life – The construction of scientific facts.* Princeton, NJ: Princeton University Press.

Latour, B., Mauguin, P. and Teil, G., 1992. A note on socio-technical graphs. *Social Studies of Science*, 22(1), pp.33–57.

Law, J., 2006. Disaster in agriculture: Or foot and mouth mobilities. *Environment and Planning A*, 38, pp.227–39.

Leydesdorff, L., 1989. The relations between qualitative theory and scientometric methods in science and technology studies. *Scientometrics*, 15(5–6), pp.333–47.

Marcus, G.E., 1995. Ethnography in/of the world system: The emergence of multi-sited ethnography. *Annual Review of Anthropology*, 24, pp.95–117.

Marres, N., 2004. Tracing the trajectories of issues, and their democratic deficits, on the Web – The case of the Development Gateway and its doubles. *Information Technology & People*, 17(2), pp.124–50.

Marres, N., 2005. Issues spark a public into being: A key but often forgotten point of the Lippmann-Dewey debate. In: B. Latour and P. Weibel (eds) *Making things public – Atmospheres of democracy.* Cambridge, MA: MIT Press, pp.208–17.

Marres, N., 2012. On some uses and abuses of topology in the social analysis of technology (Or the problem with smart meters). *Theory, Culture & Society*, 29(4–5), pp.288–310.

Martin, B., 1988. Analyzing the fluoridation controversy: Resources and structures. *Social Studies of Science*, 18, pp.331–63.

Micheelsen, A., Holm, L. and O'Doherty Jensen, K., 2013. Consumer acceptance of the *New Nordic Diet*: An exploratory study. *Appetite*, 70, pp.14–21.

Mitchell, T., 2002. *Rule of experts – Egypt, technopolitics, modernity.* Berkeley, CA: University of California Press.

Mol, A., 1999. Ontological politics: A word and some questions. In: J. Law and J. Hassard (eds) *Actor Network Theory and After.* Oxford: Blackwell, pp.74–89.

Munk, A.K. and Abrahamsson, S., 2012. Empiricist interventions: Strategy and tactics on the ontopolitical battlefield. *Science Studies*, 25(1), pp.52–70.

Nowotny, H., Scott, P. and Gibbons, M., 2001. *Re-thinking science – Knowledge and the public in an age of uncertainty.* Cambridge: Polity Press.

Petersen, M.K. and Munk, A.K., 2013. I vælten: Kulturanalysens nye hverdag. *Kulturstudier*, 4(1), pp.102–17.

Pickering, A., 1984. *Constructing quarks – A sociological history of particle physics.* Edinburgh: Edinburgh University Press.

Pinch, T.J. and Bijker, W.E., 1987. The social construction of facts and artifacts: Or how the sociology of science and the sociology of technology might benefit each other. In: W.E. Bijker, T.P. Hughes and T.J. Pinch (eds) *The social construction of technological systems: New Directions in the sociology and history of technology.* Cambridge, MA: The MIT Press, pp. 17–50.

Rogers, R. and Marres, N., 2000. Landscaping climate change: A mapping technique for understanding science and technology debates on the World Wide Web. *Public Understanding of Science*, 9(2), pp.141–63.

Strathern, M., 1996. Cutting the network. *The Journal of the Royal Anthropological Institute*, 2(3), pp.517–35.

Tukey, J.W., 1977. Exploratory data analysis. Massachusetts: *Addison-Wesley.*

Teil, G. and Latour, B., 1995. The Hume machine: Can association networks do more than formal rules. *Stanford Humanities Review*, 4(2), pp.47–65.

Venturini, T., 2010. Diving in magma: How to explore controversies with Actor-Network Theory. *Public Understanding of Science*, 19(3), pp.258–73.

Venturini, T., 2012. Building on faults: How to represent controversies with digital methods. *Public Understanding of Science*, 21(7), pp.796–812.

Venturini, T. and Guido, D., 2012. Once upon a text: An ANT tale in text analysis. *Sociologica*, 3. doi:10.2383/72700.

Venturini, T. and Latour, B., 2010. The social fabric: Digital traces and quali-quantitative methods. *Proceedings of Future En Seine*, pp. 15–30.

Whatmore, S.J., 2009. Mapping knowledge controversies: Science, democracy and the redistribution of expertise. *Progress in Human Geography*, 33(5), pp.587–98.

Whatmore, S.J. and Landström, C., 2011. Flood apprentices: An exercise in making things public. *Economy and Society*, 1, pp.1–29.

Wynne, B., 1992. Misunderstood misunderstanding: Social identities and public uptake of science. *Public Understanding of Science*, 1(3), pp.281–304.

Yaneva, A., 2012. *Mapping controversies in architecture.* Farnham: Ashgate.

Chapter 6
Real Things, Tourist Things and Drawing the Line in the Ocean

Felicity Picken

6.1 Introduction

Western beliefs about reality are steeped in the idea of a single, pure or true reality that can be isolated from various substitute realities. Representations are early examples of these substitutions, fuelling scepticism towards art and photography (Kardaun, 2000; Jay, 1993) as well as tourism – a producer of contrived experiences and staged encounters. As a copyist *par excellence*, tourism creates these (falser) experiences of reality through technologies including photography and art, theme parks, museums and interpretation centres, and with tactics like miniaturisation, façadia and scripting (Cohen, 1988; Urry, 2002; Urry and Larson, 2011). The tourist gaze (Urry, 1990) itself follows Foucault's (1976) conceptualisation of the gaze as a technology that represents the world in a selective and particular way. In producing a partial view of reality, the creative potential of these technologies and strategies are often by-passed in favour of the dominant interpretation that, in re-presenting reality, tourism routinely *debases* it (Deleuze and Kraus, 1983, p.183). This distinction between reality and representation is traced to Plato's *ideal forms* and a long anxiety about what is "really real" that is evident through Descartes' *meditations* and in the epistemological sovereignty of modern science (Latour, 1999).

While this "model of reality" (Deleuze and Kraus, 1983) is particularly active in tourism scholarship, it is rarely made explicit. Instead, tourism is often implicitly tarnished insofar as it is receptive to the superficial, what MacCannell (1976) refers to as staged authenticity, where tourists are trapped in a 'circular structure of reference' (Van den Abbeele, 1980, p.9) and plagued by an industry described as deceptive (Turner, 1976 cited in Crick, 1989, p.306) and devious (Taylor, 2001, p.8). Since Plato, the nobler task has resided in the ability to distinguish essence from appearance, the original from the copy and the true from false reality (Caillois, 1984; Deleuze and Kraus, 1983; Golden, 1975). On the basis of this assumption the pilgrim, the traveller and the ethnographer have been well distinguished from tourists (Stronza, 2001; Bruner, 1989; 1994), as tourist sites are distinguishable from real ones.

This chapter engages with this inheritance by describing a tourist experience that is, in the traditional way of thinking, unapologetically designed to substitute "reality" – to be a typical tourist thing – but then fails to do this and ends up more like a real one. The biography of *The Museo Subaquático de Arte* (MUSA) troubles the waters that make visible any clear distinction between what is real or not and with this, the other ontological distinction between nature and culture. Few realities present as more self-evidently "non-substitutable" or "real" than wilderness areas do. Often these realities are regarded as "timeless", for which there is no substitution for visiting the wilderness proper. At the same time, visiting the wilderness "properly" risks compromising its existence since the very encounter performs a paradox of people being where they should not. In this case, tourism performs experiences designed to both facilitate proximity, while protecting the object wilderness from the threat this proximity brings. In *facilitating* proximity, tourism enacts an encounter but also interferes with the unadulterated immediacy of a real experience. Facilitation adds to an otherwise pristine, unadulterated encounter by its "interference" (Haraway, 1992) where boundaries like real and unreal, wilderness and artificial, begin to collapse or become destabilised. It is in this sense that tourism is regarded as enacting a poor substitute for the real thing.

Few realities present as more self-evidently *unreal* than those that are described as artificial. MUSA is an artificial reef in the Caribbean Sea off the coast of the holiday mecca of Cancún. It is also a new kind of tourist object in an undersea sculpture museum. Designed to protect the Meso-American Reef System from increasing numbers of tourists, the museum is comprised of more than 400 sunken, life-sized sculptures submerged near the second largest barrier coral reef in the world. What makes MUSA unique within the context of touristic encounter is that the requirements for substitution, of a clear distinction between original and copy, natural and artificial, are unable to be met. What MUSA does *not* do well is fit easily into existing taxonomies of artificial or real, nature or culture and this has implications for its representational validity. In other words, without this fit MUSA is not convincing as a poor copy of wilderness, but is instead a *performing-with* (Haraway, 2008) wilderness that privileges the view that realities are 'interactively determined in the production of alignments between them' (Pickering, 1995, p.2). MUSA troubles the primacy of "the real" and its subordinate representation by showing that real things and tourist things collapse into each other in the making of what passes for *real enough*.

6.2 Tourism and the Reality Principle

Modern tourism is most explicitly tied to questions of reality in two formidable ways. First, when it is perceived to be "exogenous" to the reality, or "ordinary life", of tourists (Cohen, 2008, p.33) and second, when it is claimed to offer a poor copy of reality (Boorstin, 1971). In both of these cases, what is often overlooked is that tourism *encounters the real* in important ways.

The first relationship has clear origins in the West and an interpretation of tourism as outside the everyday of tourist generating centres. The sense of tourism being outside the real is traceable to the tourist's own perception and the central role that they have been accorded in theorising tourism (Picken, 2006). This new possibility of becoming a tourist also marked tourism by its difference, separateness and marginality from what was at the same time discovered to be an ordinary, everyday reality. Explanations that posit tourism as an escape from, or even inversion of, "everyday life" conform to this, citing the apathy inspired by such a life as a formidable shaper of tourist becoming. At the other end, "tourism places" produce extraordinary experiences (Hollinshead, 1998) as those who do tourism, and equally those who sought to understand it, found that for them, reality was now more distinctly "two realities" (Picken, 2010). In the face of this potentially subversive phenomenon, and to reconcile what is *really real* (Latour, 1999), tourism realities were increasingly understood to be inauthentic ones – fantasia.

This modern anxiety about the authenticity of reality was fanned through the critique of capitalism, where tourism is claimed to *appropriate the real* to some commercial end (Davidson and Spearitt, 2000). Variously named Disneyfied reality (Judd and Fanstein, 1999) or commodity reality (Halewood and Hannam, 2001), none of these commercial ventures were found to be real enough, governed by the *un*natural laws of the market. This produced a bitter taste in the mouths of those with enough taste to know what *is* real, many of whom possessed a 'melancholy "aristocratic" disdain' for the 'manipulated mass who participate in an ersatz commodity culture' (Miller and Rose, 1997, p.2). This commodity culture, amidst which tourists were highly visible, was regarded as 'depreciative' and the commodifiers themselves as replacing God (Boorstin, 1971, p.252). Human-made novelty, as opposed to that which was serendipitous or naturally occurring, was less pure even if it did serve to treat the disillusionment that the realities of modernity itself wrought. In this compensatory form (Bruner, 1991), tourism became both the by-product of inauthentic modern life and its cure, as the *quest* for authenticity remained the only 'culturally approved motive for modern travel' (Cohen, 2008, p.331).

This anxiety about authenticity has a longer history that is connected to pre-modern concerns about distinguishing the real. Suspicion was placed upon modern phenomena found to be active in what Sontag identified through photography as *the creation of a duplicate world* (1977, p.53). When tourism attempts to duplicate reality, it performs the 'inevitable depreciation' (Crimp, 1980, p. 94) that this implies and consigns itself to a counterfeit existence (Deleuze and Kraus, 1983). As an industry, tourism is observed to be 'particularly adept at providing scripts and audiences that shape our choices' (Wood, 2005, p.325; Couldry, 1998). Supporting a morality of tourism based on a general 'repugnance for replications' (Cameron, 2007, p.50) tourism is endowed with 'low ontological status' (Kardaun, 2000, p.135). Bound to the 'history of the image and its reception' (Merrin, 2001, p.91), any attempt to re-present reality is an attempt to 'feign to have what one doesn't have' (Baudrillard, 1999, p.3). Through this legacy, and well before modern forms of anxiety about losing authentic reality, tourism was pre-ordained to signal a reality deficit.

While this has added to an appreciation of the 'productive' capacities of tourism, the experiences they produce lie in an asymmetrical relation to reality. Even the anti-tourist backpackers cannot escape what Shaffer (2004, p.150) refers to as the 'touristic rigor mortis [...] of perfect consumers'. If an escape from reality is an escape from the dominant order of reality, tourism is an escape *attempt*, remaining embedded in the safety of a model of reality that deems tourism impotent against it. Tourism's potential to disrupt this model is largely restrained to the 'constrained freedom from the everyday of the "non-travelling world" that is a 'strategy for the *deferral* of contradiction' (Sandland, 1996, p.391, emphasis added). This denies its other potential to be a 'strategy *of* the real' and this discourages seeing all that is 'simultaneously true', including the impossibility of rediscovering either the absolute real or the illusion (Baudrillard, 1999, p.7, 17–19).

Neither the modern tourist – anticipating prophets (but finding none), nor the post tourist (Feifer, 1985) – anticipating *false* prophets (and finding in these a prophecy), escapes this basic ordering of the real. Both are mired within the enduring belief that 'only in the name of a naïve realism can one see as realistic a representation of the real' (Bourdieu, 1990, p.77). This reality of the real continues to deliver stable ground and with it, a formidable *force of inertia* (Baudrillard, 1999, p.21) that is not often rendered visible in tourism research. While the reality principle is only an oblique reference in much tourism scholarship, it has had a powerful influence in decisions about what tourism does and how it occupies the world. In contrast to this purist ontology, a *relational ontology* (Pickering, 2000, p.308) recognises that there are 'parallel solutions for what passes as real' (Serres, 1982/1995, p.85). The benefit of this is that it is no longer certain that tourism 'reproduces', 'replaces' or 'ruins' a reality that is *outside* and *more real* and this begins a much wider conversation about what tourism is and does.

6.3   Artificial Wilderness

Nature tourism is a continuum (Orams, 1995) and the *very* natural end, known as wilderness or Eco-tourism, often involves tourism actively performing the role of *decontaminating* nature from humans. Human-nature interactions are controlled with implements like boardwalks to suspend humans above the ecosystem floor, with hard science to inform them of why this is important and with information centres, museums and guides to convey how to interact with nature, what to appreciate about it or how to be "mindful" (Wearing and Neil, 2009; Moscardo,1996; Cater and Lowerman, 1994). These ventures promote an intimate connection to nature, yet are notable for "no touching" or minimal touch and ultimately, to create in the wilderness tourist no *desire* to touch. The responsible solution from the tourism industry is to make the '"human interpretation of nature" stand-in for "nature"' wherever possible, and ultimately to replace as many dangerous human-nature interactions as it can. It follows that if tourism can perform in such a way that the human world (defined by its culture, language and interpretations) can stand in for nature (defined by the absence of these) their separateness is less in dispute.

If part of the modernist critique and solution was to break with monotony through excursions outside of the everyday, and that this tamed tourism to the dominant order of reality, then the paramount escape was to seek out modernity's absence in the romantic solitude afforded by wild places. "Wilderness" is authentic because it is defined as "other" than, and distant from, humans and their power to intervene and devastate its truth. A "true state of nature" describes a world of 'nature that is left to nature' (Williams, 1972, p.158), the purest form of ecosystem and now all important base-line from which to measure exactly what humans do when they impact the remainder. Just as tourism is posited as an escape from the 'everyday world' so wilderness tourism became an escape from 'our own too muchness' (Cronin, 1996, p.7). Both are reliant upon an ontological division in which they have won a claim to reality based on an appeal to foundational truths designed around structural binaries.

By virtue of these qualities, the ocean is a perfect wilderness. It is extremely foreign to humans, so much so that our relationship with it hinges 'precisely on its unfamiliarity' (Mentz, 2009, p.998) and confounded attempts to tame it (Sloan, 2002). The underexplored wilderness of the ocean extends almost so far as to render it 'unspeakable', existing 'just outside of discourse' (Veijola and Jokinen, 1994, p.138) and also 'the orderly world of land' (Mentz, 2009, p.1001). It is one of the least 'formatted, socialised or measured' places in the world (Latour, 2005, p.244) which is to say that undersea culture and social life is still an oblique reference.

Perhaps the first and most formidable characteristic of the oceanic wilderness is the literal and metaphorical scarcity of stable 'ground'. The absence of this ground performs a reality based upon impermanency due to the ocean's liquid form and the fact that only about 10 to 15 per cent of the seabed has a 'solid enough substratum' to allow marine life a settlement (Shani, Polak and Shashar, 2012, p.362). Natural reefs are the most common form of substratum providing habitats for marine life, hunting grounds for predators and fisheries and resources for marine tourism (Musa and Dimmock, 2013). In this way, reefs are technologies for enabling tourist experiences with oceanic wildlife that is otherwise highly mobile and distributed across marine environments. They are increasingly important for oceanic recreation, particularly among divers who constitute one of the global tourism industry's fastest growing markets (Kirkbride-Smith, Wheeler and Johnson, 2013).

Artificial reefs are considered important, yet always imperfect, substitutes for natural reefs. Widespread definitions are based on their capacity to replicate an oceanic substratum and its affordances (Shokry and Ammar, 2009; Jones, 2003). In this protective role, they are often regarded as 'sacrificial sites' by management (Kirkbride-Smith, Wheeler and Johnson, 2013, p.1). Shipwrecks were the first, accidental prototype of this kind of replication, followed by deliberate reef building, extending the old craft of marine engineering beyond the immediacy of the harbour. The success of early wrecks in acting like a reef, alongside improved salvage operations has led to artificial reefs installed as concrete slabs, balls, geotextile bags, rubble mound as well as deliberately scuttled vessels (Polak and Shashar, 2012). By design or accident, in securing a substratum on the ocean floor they aggregate or grow marine life, providing protection from extreme weather, security for fishing industries, defences for land and attractions for recreation.

Increasingly, the surplus value of these reefs are drawn into the tourism industry as attractions for diving, boating, angling and beach protection (Black, 2001; Antunes do Carmo, Ten Voorde and Neves, 2011; Shokry and Ammar, 2009). For the purposes of this chapter, since few terms sum up an authentic reality like 'wilderness' does, and few have come to describe the inauthentic reality so well as 'artificial', the artificial wilderness that is MUSA is a valuable site for examining how tourism performs within the dualistic model of reality and, equally, how it can disrupt this. This paper draws upon the findings of a fieldtrip to this artificial wilderness with the explicit purpose of understanding how these border realities are performed and whether and how they can be mobilised to promote the rethinking of established, and sometime hierarchically organised, dualities.

6.4   MUSA – Museo Subaquático de Arte

The Meso-American Barrier Reef is the largest natural reef system in the northern hemisphere and is second in size only to the Great Barrier Reef in the south. It is situated to the east of Mexico, Honduras and Belize in the Caribbean Sea and attracts almost 8 million visitors per year (The Nature Conservancy-Global Marine Initiative, 2013). Both barrier reefs are doubly attractive by virtue of being listed as World Heritage Areas mainly for their existing biodiversity and the importance attached to maintaining this. Consequently, both are under increasing pressure from tourism and recreation uses and these are also threatened by proximate industries that undermine the resilience of the reef and reef tourism (Coghlan and Prideaux, 2009). As a naturally occurring, long-time forming and complex resource, reefs constitute a reality with few alternative substitutes. It is this popularity and niche position that now threatens to destroy these minority structures that are so vital to marine life and marine tourism. Already 24 per cent of the world's reefs are under 'immanent risk of collapse' and a further 26 per cent face longer term destruction (Shokry and Ammar, 2009, p.37). The Meso-American reef system is a case in point and management has implemented a unique, and unapologetically artificial, solution for the problem.

When pioneer diver Jacques Cousteau described the Mediterranean as a 'sea girt with the oldest cultures, a museum in sun and spray' (1988, p.96), he was referring to the sunken artefacts of culture lost beneath the sea. MUSA applies this metaphor of 'underwater museum' quite deliberately and literally in the inauguration of an underwater spectacle in the sculptures of Jason deCaires Taylor. His first public instillation in Molinere Bay, Grenada involved the placement of 65 life-sized sculptures on the sea floor. These include *The lost correspondent* – a lonely typist sitting at a desk, *The Unstill Life* – mimicking the classical fruit bowl scene and *Vicissitudes* – a ring of children clasping hands. In 2009, the second and most ambitious project began in directing and producing MUSA as the largest underwater museum in the world (see Figure 6.1). Situated in the Caribbean Sea, between the coast of Cancún and Isla Mujeres in Mexico, MUSA began collaboratively with deCaires Taylor, Jaime Gonzalez, a biologist in the Cancún National Marine Park and Roberto Diaz, an entrepreneurial tourism operator in the area (Vance, 2013).

The explicit aim of MUSA is to protect the nearby Meso-American Reef by diverting tourists away from it. The idea followed a series of hurricanes that had intensified damage to the natural reef, requiring its temporary closure to recreational users (Archibald, 2012). Closure, in this sense, constituted a passive response to the rehabilitation needs of the reef and loss of tourists to the area, whereas the concept of MUSA became an active intervention that resulted in diversifying underwater leisure experiences. The main sculptural exhibit *Silent Evolution* is composed of 400 sculptures. It is silent by virtue of existing in the silent undersea world (Cousteau, 1988), and evolutionary by virtue of the way the sculptures are overtaken by a highly active ocean environment. *What Have We Done?* is an exhibition that includes *Inertia*, a sculpture of a man watching television on a lounge; *Void* a tall, contemplative woman and *Inheritance* showing a young boy sitting on an upturned waste-bin contemplating a pile of rubbish.

Figure 6.1   Silent Evolution – MUSA
Photo: Courtesy of deCaires Taylor

Described as one of the more pronouncedly despondent and ominous collections, these gesture towards social ills and environmental degradation in the isolated parts of a troubled nuclear family (Keltner, 2011). At the same time, many works embody a 'spirit of inspiration with roots in collective action' where, in deCaires Taylor's words, the museum acts as 'an icon of how we can live in a symbiotic relationship with nature' (in Keltner, 2011). The icon, in this sense, is not found in the stasis of an object or image in a representational space, but is embodied in the *symbiotic, living relationship* between culture and nature; an in-between that is radically open to ontological politics (Mol, 1999, p.77).

The sculptures are produced from silicon moulds of actual people – tourists and locals – weighing between one and two tonnes. They are made from marine grade cement that is engineered to attract coral and to provide an adhesive surface on which it can grow. The sculptures and their configuration are built to survive a category 4 hurricane and are positioned in such a way as to disperse the power of the current. Since its beginnings, MUSA has become a meeting ground for 1,000 different species of fish. It is described as a 'generative human intervention in the ecosystem' that goes against the 'land as commodity' mentality of capitalism while at the same time generating tourism revenue, and demonstrating how 'activists might be able to use the system's rapacious tendency against itself' (Keltner, 2011).

Some sculptures are implanted with fire coral before they are sunk at recreational depths between 8 to 20 metres below surface where visits are facilitated through scuba diving, skin diving, snorkelling and glass-bottom boats. Immersion is the condition of entry in the fullest sense and this itself marks the occasion as memorable and transformative (deCaires Taylor in Keltner, 2011). Being subject to floating without gravity, on the horizontal plane, with vastly altered acoustics, light and pressure performs what Westerdahl (2005, p.3) refers to as a 'paramount experience' for most. The museum website describes this experience as one of:

> Ephemeral encounters and fleeting glimmers of another world where art develops from the effects of nature on the efforts of man [*sic*] Subject to the abstract metamorphosis of the underwater environment [...] eventually this underwater society will be totally assimilated by marine life, transformed to another state – a challenging metaphor for the future of our own species (http://www.underwatersculpture.com).

In symbolic form, MUSA *represents* the natural reef and ideas about contemporary ecological ills. At the same time MUSA is *entangled* with the reef, expanding its range, performing an ecologically sustainable act as well as representing ideas about it. Signalling the 'significant impact humans have had on our planet's ecosystems and the subsequent effect to future generations' the museum confronts visitors with an undersea spectacle of themselves embedded in 'the origins of ecological trouble' where, 'in a twist of the usual relations, fish feed off people' (deCaires Taylor in Keltner, 2011). This inversion is important in what deCaires Taylor describes as a museum that takes 'things taken for granted and transposes them into different contexts [where] the relationship completely alters' (in Keltner, 2011). Following the logic of the 'cult of the real', MUSA was to create a substitutable experience by imitating a natural reef. However, instead of the usual materials that make up the staple of artificial reefs – as functional substrata – the reef is configured as an underwater sculpture museum that *also* acts like an artificial reef. Being more than substrata, and also more than a museum, MUSA begins to illustrate how tourism does not have to be consigned to one thing or another, real or artificial, nature or culture.

At MUSA, the gallery space is the Caribbean Sea and the sea is unlike any other gallery space. It is not contained in any real sense, and it is without the usual architecture that manifests a separation between nature and culture (Kallergi, 2008, p.2). deCaires Taylor describes this as a 'three dimensional world where all the laws have changed [including] gravity, light and refraction' (in Keltner, 2011). These 'natural laws' that nevertheless defy those familiar to land, are where oceanic nature steps in to alter the land-based conditions upon which the real has been defined – and in the absence of much elemental thinking (Irigaray, 1991; 1999; Baldacchino, 2010). The nature and laws of the ocean are unlike the nature and laws on land but neither can be called 'less real'. Flows of water, nutrients and sand regularly pass through the gallery and these flows are attended by deposits (of sand and organisms) that remain in the museum and begin to actively transform the exhibits by attaching to the sculptures and transforming them (see Figure 6.2). Giving form to the truth that 'tourism is teeming with things' (Franklin, 2003, p. 98), MUSA is a living exhibit in the fullest sense of the transformative oceanic environment making art *live* in an orchestration of nature and culture. What appears as traditional 'still life', the sculptures, reminiscent of the Classical artwork now associated with a period of cultural note, are destined to become 'indistinguishable from a vibrant and colourful coral reef' (http://www. underwatersculpture.com/pages/artist/overview.htm). And so, Atlantis resurfaces in the depths of the Caribbean Sea and the 'literal entry of history [and culture] into nature' (Serres, 1990/1995, p.7). The statues, evoking ancient civilisations and humanity's impermanence are not the fruits of marine archaeological discoveries but the creation of such material *as* that material.

6.5   Drawing a Line in the Ocean

In comparison to traditional gallery spaces, MUSA is a *blank* space upon which marine life collaborates as artist, medium, material and work. This blankness, like nakedness (Serres, 1982/1995) is a metaphor for describing an object that is underdetermined and therefore a quasi-object. It is simultaneously a *full* space that is lively and full of possibility given its potential for interference, with the instability of undersea migrations governed by autonomous transport systems. This is quite different to a fullness of space with meaning that comes from over-determining as with a museum that is designed with fixed objects in fixed locations

Figure 6.2   Transformation of Sculptures by the Sea

Photo: Courtesy of deCaires Taylor (2013)

to produce an already imagined or written experience. In this way MUSA *creates* nature as much as it is *in* nature and *re-presents* it. In a form of ultimate exchange, ecological life *doubles* as artistic practice and no 'body' finally executes it. Algae begin to bloom within one week, two to three years realises coral and within an estimate of six years the coral will completely overtake the sculptures, 'leaving only suggestive shapes' (Archibald, 2012). Like the porous borders of the oceanic space itself, the artist's work, or 'culture', is always incomplete and destined to remain so since, once situated at MUSA, it will be added to by oceanic life. As the artist shifts to spectator, he yields to witnessing the will of the sea in determining the sculptures form. This follows an increasing tendency towards a 'politics of connective aesthetics' and its related rejection of the 'myths of neutrality and autonomy' supposed of, and romanticised by, artists (Gablik, 1992, p.6). At MUSA, exhibiting becomes secondary to the use of art as a 'means for creating and recreating new relations' (Doherty, 2004 in Bishop, 2006, p.180). The other worldliness of undersea collapses the nature/culture binary insofar as the sculptures are assimilated to, and become indistinct from, the reef.

MUSA is not wilderness, since traditionally museums and wilderness have mutually exclusive roles as, respectively, custodians of culture and nature. MUSA contains parts of the wilderness, and in diverting estimates of 40 per cent of visitors away from the natural reef, can substitute in part or in full for wilderness, despite being a bad copy of it. Rather than always falling foul of the diabolical link between recognition and representation (Serres in Latour, 1990/1995, p.78), this encounter assembles and redistributes some elements of the wilderness proper, while also gathering together a lot of very 'un-Wilderness' things like cement, sculpture and photography for visibility on land. Substituting, without copying, the object of 'wilderness', it makes instead a translation or 'other version' of it that may act as equivalent or partial equivalent without a pretence of being 'the same'. The interesting question then becomes *how* this assembly of heterogeneous materials substitutes another by enrolling at some points the very material it decontaminates and re-ordering it differently with others.

In this space there is a disturbance of the traditional model of reality and representation, and radical reorientation of the relations between architecture and art where the gallery is fluid and the art is immovable, yet both are very much alive. This sets up a commensurate radical reorientation of the separation between nature and culture through a somewhat 'unnatural' collaboration where once the sculptures enter their gallery space beneath the sea, nature intervenes in the production of culture or art. Through this intervention, representing reality becomes a luxury of a certain kind of space; it is a situated circumstance and not a condition that precedes all situations. In undersea, these sculptures instead 'enact a visceral aesthetic that refuses more of the same' (Dixon, 2008, p.671) and their placement on the seabed is an 'imminent arrival' that allows for the consideration of 'new modes of being and doing' (p.672). After Clark (2011, p.11), MUSA demonstrates that there is 'no functionally intact nature enduring beyond, beneath, amidst or after this assimilation'.

While the notion of 'version of reality' is not new to tourism research it has tended to live implicitly in the criticism that tourism adds another incomplete or false version of an object, place, event or people (Hollinshead, 1998; 2004). While this has added to our understanding of the 'productive' capacities of tourism, these are not symmetrically derived versions of reality since each version is code for a substitute or a "less real" version than the real one. On the other hand, to understand tourism as an ordering of reality (Franklin, 2004) or as a 'radical ontology' (Ren, 2011) is a symmetrical scholarly stance that recognises in tourism various *performances* of versions of reality that are real "enough". This frees tourism from any claim to *re-present* a reality "badly or well" since it does not automatically follow that by adding another version tourism "reproduces", "replaces" or "ruins" an otherwise authentic one. To believe so is to ignore the possibility of co-existing versions of reality (Mol, 1999) and what Serres' (1982/1995, p.22) refers to as a 'metaphysics of multiplicity'.

In Boorstin's (1964) 'pseudo event' and MacCannell's (1976) "staged authenticity" through to the most recent edition of *The Tourist Gaze* (Urry and Larsen, 2011) is evidence of tourism's competing roles in decisions that are made about reality. These include getting back to it; escaping it; being duped by it; or being wary of it and the delinquency of false prophets (Deleuze and Kraus, 1983). Analysing tourist attractions in terms of how well they re-present means they will always fail the test of copy(ing)-right and always provide an inferior substitution for 'the real thing'. This simultaneously dismisses tourists who participate in these substitutions as poor copies of real people. Perhaps instead, the interesting work is not to be found in making fun of tourists, who enjoy these experiences, and to play into the hands of the inadequate 'cultural dupe' thesis that is no less pronounced in tourism research, and neither is it to be found in denigrating the object world if it is not arranged according to an ancient regime of the real. Rather, tourism can be taken more seriously, as a phenomenon that seriously mixes things together in new forms.

Cutting across the orderly reality that specifies the true from the false, lies the radical potential of action that is uncooperative with the model upon which the "real" is always privileged (Deleuze and Kraus, 1983). Such potential has been accorded only limited utility in its application to tourism, except in somewhat nihilistic accounts of hyperreality (Belk, 1996), supporting a despair that is also born of the inability of tourism to deliver authentic versions of reality. Instead of offering a poor copy of the wilderness 'proper', and therefore a poor copy of 'reality', MUSA blurs the distinction altogether. This in turn opens the possibility that tourism is more than representation since it is an experiential mode of being that is enacted through the deployment of images, bodies, technologies, discourses, nature and objects that are, with varying degrees of success, assembled in the performance of making, or indeed faking, an alternative. In casting doubt upon 'the very notion of the copy', MUSA threatens the difference between 'true' and 'false' (Deleuze and Kraus, 1983, p.47) as 'the sign is liberated to be what it will' (Sandland, 1996, p.387). When this happens, and 'value radiates in all directions', it brings with it the production of 'new categories of experience' that are without an original (Merrin, 2001, pp.91–6). The absence of an 'original' dislodges this dominant order of reality and the 'ontological and epistemological traditions' (Merrin, 2001, p.88) that have held in place the 'perilous opposition between the organism and the milieu' (Caillois, 1984, p.30).

MUSA creates *nature* as much it reflects upon it and as much as it creates or reflects upon culture, art and tourism. According to Dixon (2008, pp.671–3), such 'designer life forms' always manifest in "a range of spatial strategies [and] rhetorical geographies" and these cannot continue to be measured against a solid 'reality' that exists outside of this. Instead these are restless objects and spaces (Rendell in Potter, 2009, p.2) and this is exemplified through MUSA in the performative properties of the ocean. If the museum was the cathedral of the twentieth century (Newhouse, 1998, p.49), then MUSA is a cathedral of the twenty-first and it is a cathedral that testifies to the co-production of life in nature-culture (after Haraway, 1992). As a living art exhibit it does not represent anything well since it is always becoming in the highly mobile, material relations (Law and Mol, 1995) of undersea. Rather than poorly substituting one 'real' reality of wilderness with another false reality of artificial reef, tourism 'connects' these disparate entities (Ren, 2011, p.878). The gallery performs an aesthetic of evolution and of transformation not unlike that befalling Ariel's father's 'sea-change' in Shakespeare's (1610) *The Tempest*. Beneath the sea is a reality that will always test, or at least highlight, traditional land-based notions of reality and the land bias that theories about tourism are based upon. Without such solid ground is an absence also of foundational truths and a reality-in-the-making that is perhaps a little kinder to the creative potential of tourism.

References

Antunes do Carmo, J., Ten Voorde, M and Neves, M., 2011. Enhancing submerged coastal constructions by incorporating multifunctional purposes. *Journal of Coastal Conservation*, 15, pp.531–46.

Archibald, R., 2012. Trying to protect a reef with otherworldly diversion. *New York Times*, [online] 13 Aug. Available at: <http://www.nytimes.com/2012/08/14/world/americas/in-cancun-trying-to-protect-reef-with-underwater-statues.html?pagewanted=all&_r=0> [Accessed 27 March 2013].

Baldacchino, G., 2010. Re-placing materiality: A Western anthropology of sand. *Annals of Tourism Research*, 37(3), pp.763–78.

Baudrillard, J., 1999. *Simulacra and Simulation.* Translated by S. Glaser. City? Michigan: University of Michigan Press.

Belk, R., 1996. Hyperreality and globalisation. *Journal of International Consumer Marketing,* 8(3), pp.23–37.

Bishop, C., 2006. The social turn: Collaboration and its discontents. *Artforum*, 44(6), pp.178–84.

Black, K., 2001. Artificial surfing reefs for erosion control and amenity: Theory and application. *Journal of Coastal Research*, 34, pp.1–14.

Boorstin, D., 1964. *The image: A guide to pseudo-events in America.* New York: Atheneum.

Boorstin, D., 1971. From news-gathering to news-making: A flood of pseudo-events. *The process and effects of mass communication*: 116–150.

Bourdieu, P., 1990. *Photography: A middle-brow art.* Stanford: Stanford University Press.

Bruner, E., 1989. Review of cannibals, tourists and ethnographers. *Cultural Anthropology*, 4(4), pp.438–45.

Bruner, E., 1991. Transformation of self in tourism. *Annals of Tourism Research*, 18(2), pp.238–50.

Bruner, E., 1994. Abraham Lincoln as authentic reproduction: A critique of postmodernism. *American Anthropologist*, 96(2), pp.397–415.

Caillois, R., 1984. Mimicry and legendary psychasthenia. Translated by J. Shepley. *October*, 31(Winter), pp.16–32.

Cameron, F., 2007. Beyond the cult of the replicant – Museums and historical digital objects: Traditional concerns, new discourses. In: F. Cameron and S. Kenderdine (eds) *Theorizing digital cultural heritage.* Cambridge, MA: MIT Press, pp.49–76.

Cater, E. and Lowerman, G., 1994. *Ecotourism: A sustainable option?* Sussex: John Wiley and Sons.

Clark, N., 2011. *Inhuman nature: Sociable life on a dynamic planet.* London: Sage.

Coghlan, A. and Prideaux, B., 2009. Welcome to the wet tropics: The importance of weather in reef tourism resilience. *Current Issues in Tourism*, 12(2), pp.89–104.

Cohen, E., 1988. Authenticity and commoditization in tourism. *Annals of Tourism Research*, 15(3), pp.371–86.

Cohen, E., 2008. The changing faces of contemporary tourism. *Society*, 45, pp.330–33.

Couldry, N., 1998. The view from inside the 'simulacrum': Visitors' tales from the set of Coronation Street. *Leisure Studies*, 17(2), pp.94–107.

Cousteau, J., 1988. *The silent world.* London: Penguin.

Crick, M., 1989. Representations of international tourism in the social sciences: Sun, sex, sights, savings and servility. *Annual Review of Anthropology*, 18, pp.307–44.

Crimp, D., 1980. The photographic activity of postmodernism. *October*, 15(Winter), pp.91–101.

Cronin, W., 1996. The trouble with wilderness: Or, getting back to the wrong nature. *Environmental History*, 1(1), pp.7–28.

Davidson, J. and Spearritt, P., 2000. *Holiday business: Tourism in Australia since 1870.* Melbourne: Melbourne University Press.

Deleuze, G. and Krauss, R., 1983. Plato and the Simulacrum. *October*, 27(Winter), pp.45–56.

Dixon, D., 2008. The blade and the claw: Science, art and the creation of the lab-borne monster. *Social and Cultural Geography*, 9(6), pp.671–92.

Feifer, M., 1985. *Going places: The ways of the tourist from imperial Rome to the present day.* London: MacMillan.

Foucault, M., 1976. *The birth of the clinic: An archaeology of medical perception.* Translated by A. Sheridan. London: Tavistock.

Franklin, A., 2003. *Tourism.* London: Sage.

Franklin, A., 2004. Tourism as an ordering: Towards a new ontology of tourism. *Tourist Studies*, 4(2), pp.277–301.

Gablik, S., 1992. Connective aesthetics. *American Art*, 6(2), pp.2–7.

Golden, L., 1975. Plato's concept of mimesis. *The British Journal of Aesthetics*, 15(2), pp.118–31.

Halewood, C. and Hannam, K. 2001. Viking heritage tourism: Authenticity and commodification. *Annals of Tourism Research*, 28(3), pp.565–80.

Haraway, D., 1992. The promise of monsters: A regenerative politics for inappropriate/d others. In: L. Grossberg, C. Nelson and P. Treichler (eds) *Cultural studies.* New York: Routledge, pp.295–337.

Haraway, D., 2008. *When species meet.* Minneapolis: University of Minnesota Press.

Hollinshead, K., 1998. Tourism, hybridity and ambiguity: The relevance of Bhabha's 'third space' cultures. *Journal of Leisure Research*, 30(1), pp.121–56.

Hollinshead, K., 2004. Ontological craft in tourism: The productive mapping of identity and image in tourism settings. In: J. Phillimore and L. Goodson (eds) *Qualitative research in tourism: Ontologies, epistemologies and methodologies.* London: Routledge, pp.83–101.

Irigaray, L., 1991. *Marine lover of Friedrich Nietzsche.* Translated by G. Gill. New York: Columbia University Press.

Irigaray, L., 1999. *The forgetting of air in Martin Heideggar.* Translated by M. Mader. Austin: University of Texas Press.

Jay, M., 1993. *Downcast eyes: The denigration of vision in twentieth-century French thought.* London: University of California Press.

Jones, K., 2003. What is an affordance? *Ecological Psychology*, 15(2), pp.107–14.

Judd, D. and Fanstein, S., 1999. *The tourist city.* Boston: Yale University Press.

Kallergi, A., 2008. Bioart on display – Challenges and opportunities of exhibiting bioart. [online] Available at: <http://www.kallergia.com/bioart/kallergi_bioartondisplay.pdf> [Accessed 14 May 2013].

Kardaun, M., 2000. Platonic art theory: A reconsideration. In: M. Kardaun and J. Spruyt (eds) *The winged chariot: Collected essays on Plato and Platonism in honour of L.M. de Rijk.* Leiden: Brill, pp.135–64.

Keltner, D., 2011. Dredging our eco inheritance: New work by Jason deCaires Taylor. *Newfound: An Inquiry of Place*, 2(2). [online] Available at: <http://www.newfoundjournal.org/archives/volume-2/issue-2/sculpture-taylor/> [Accessed 12 August 2013].

Kirkbride-Smith, A., Wheeler, P. and Johnson, M., 2013. The relationship between diver experience levels and perceptions of artificial reefs – Examination of a potential management tool. *PLoS one*, 8(7): e68899.

Latour, B., 1990/1995. *Michel Serres with Bruno Latour: Conversations on science, culture and time.* Translated by R. Lapidus. Michigan: University of Michigan Press.

Latour, B., 1999. *Pandora's hope: Essays on the reality of science studies.* Cambridge, MA: Harvard University Press.

Latour B., 2005. *Reassembling the social: An introduction to Actor-Network Theory.* New York: Oxford University Press.

Law, J. and Mol, A., 1995. Notes on materiality and sociality. *Sociological Review*, 43(2), pp.274–94.

MacCannell, D., 1976. *The tourist: A new theory of the leisure class.* New York: Schocken Books.

Mentz, S., 2009. Toward a blue cultural studies: The sea, maritime culture and early modern English literature. *Literature Compass*, 6(5), pp.997–1013.

Merrin, W., 2001. To play with phantoms: Jean Baudrillard and the evil demon of simulacrum. *Economy and Society*, 30(1), pp.85–111.

Miller, P. and Rose, N., 1997. Mobilizing the consumer: Assembling the subject of consumption. *Theory, Culture and Society*, 14(1), pp.1–36.

Mol, A., 1999. Ontological politics: A word and some questions. In: J. Law and J. Hassard (eds) *Actor Network and after.* Oxford: Blackwell, pp.74–89.

Moscardo, G., 1996. Mindful visitors: Heritage and tourism. *Annals of Tourism Research*, 23(2), pp.376–97.

Musa, G. and Dimmock, K. (eds), 2013. *Scuba diving tourism*. New York: Routledge.

Newhouse, V., 1998. *Towards a new museum*. Singapore: The Monacelli Press.

Orams, B., 1995. Towards a more desirable form of ecotourism. *Tourism Management*, 16(1), pp.3–8.

Picken, F., 2006. From tourist looking-glass to analytical carousels: Navigating tourism through relations and context. *Current Issues in Tourism*, 9(2), pp.158–70.

Picken, F., 2010. Tourism, design and controversy: Calling non-humans to explain ourselves. *Tourist Studies: An International Journal*, 10(3), pp.245–63.

Pickering, A., 1995. Cyborg history and the World War II regime. *Perspectives in Science*, 3, pp.1–48.

Pickering, A., 2000. The objects of sociology: A response to Breslau's "Sociology After Humanism". *Sociological Theory*, 18(2), pp.308–16.

Polak, O. and Shashar, N., 2012. Can a small artificial reef reduce diving pressure from a natural coral reef? Lessons learned from Eilat, Red Sea. *Ocean and Coastal Management*, 55, pp.94–100.

Potter, E., 2009. Environmental art and the production of publics: Responding to environmental change. *The International Journal of the Arts in Society*, 3, pp.1–6.

Ren, C., 2011. Non-human agency, radical ontology and tourism realities. *Annals of Tourism Research*, 38(3), pp.858–81.

Sandland, R., 1996. The real, the simulacrum and the construction of 'gypsy' in law. *Journal of Law and Society*, 23(3), pp.383–405.

Serres, M., 1982/1995. *Genesis*. Translated by G. James and J. Nielson. Michigan: University of Michigan Press.

Serres, M., 1990/1995. *The natural contract*. TransLated by E. MacArthur and W. Paulson. Michigan: University of Michigan Press.

Shaffer, T., 2004. Performing backpacking: Constructing 'authenticity' every step of the way. *Text and Performance Quarterly*, 24(2), pp.139–60.

Shani, A., Polak, O. and Shashar, N., 2012. Artificial reefs and mass marine ecotourism. *Tourism Geographies: An international Journal of Tourism, Space, Place and the Environment*, 14(3), pp.361–82.

Shokry, M. and Ammar, A., 2009. Coral reef restoration and artificial reef management, future and economic. *The Open Environmental Engineering Journal*, 2, pp.37–49.

Sloan, N., 2002. History and application of the wilderness concept in marine conservation. *Conservation Biology*, 16(2), pp.294–305.

Sontag, S., 1977. *On photography*. Ontario: Penguin.

Stronza, A., 2001. Anthropology of tourism: Forging new ground for ecotourism and other alternatives. *Annual Review of Anthropology*, 30, pp.261–183.

Taylor, J., 2001. Authenticity and sincerity in tourism. *Annals of Tourism Research*, 28(1), pp.7–26.

The Nature Conservancy-Global Marine Initiative, 2013. Reef resilience: Building resilience into coral reef building. [online] Available at: <http://www.reefresilience.org/index.html> [Accessed 17 July 2013].

Urry, J., 1990. *The tourist gaze.* London: Sage.

Urry, J., 2002. *Consuming places.* London: Routledge.

Urry, J. and Larsen, J., 2011. *The tourist gaze.* 3rd ed. London: Sage.

Van den Abbeele, G., 1980. Sightseers: The tourist as theorist. *Diacritics*, 10, pp.2–14.

Vance, E., 2013. Birth of the world's first underwater museum. [online] Availabe at: <http://www.lastwordonnothing.com/2013/09/16/birth-of-the-worlds-first-underwater-museum/> [Accessed 16 September 2013].

Veijola, S. and Jokinen, E., 1994. The body in tourism. *Theory, Culture and Society*, 11(3), pp.125–51.

Wearing, S. and Neil, J., 2009. *Ecotourism: Impacts, potentials and possibilities.* 2nd ed. Oxford: Butterworth-Heinemann.

Westerdahl, C., 2005. Seal on land, elk at sea: Notes on and applications of the ritual landscape at the seaboard. *International Journal of Nautical Archaeology*, 34(1), pp.2–23.

Williams, R., 1972. Ideas of nature. In: J. Benthall (ed.) *The shaping enquiry.* London: Longman.

Wood, A., 2005. What happens [in Vegas]: Performing the post-tourist flaneur in New York and Paris. *Text and Performance Quarterly*, 25(4), pp.315–33.

Chapter 7

Conflicts Forever. The Path Dependencies of Tourism Conflicts; the Case of Anabeb Conservancy, Namibia

Arjaan Pellis, Martijn Duineveld and Lauren Wagner

7.1 Introduction

In tourism studies attention is paid in a plethora of books and articles to a wide variety of conflicts: human-wildlife conflicts, conflicts between tourists and hosts, conflicts related to destination management, conflicts on stewardship over tourism related resources, value conflicts, or conflicts over inequalities of economic development through tourism (e.g. Dahlberg, 2005; Hitchcock and Darma Putra, 2005; Okello, 2005; Porter and Salazar, 2005). A great deal of this literature has aimed to problematize conflicts and to find solutions for them, based on the taken for granted idea that conflicts ought to be dealt with in order to make sure they do not delay development or produce inefficiency for an industry with such a high net worth (Von Ruschkowski and Mayer, 2011; Bennett, et al., 2001; Hitchcock and Darma Putra, 2005). Conflicts are deemed to be in need of management solutions through 'joint collaborative arrangements between public-private partnerships', 'consensus making', 'local involvement', 'participatory community practices', 'good governance' and 'compensation deals' (cf. Bramwell and Cox, 2009; Douglas and Lubbe, 2006; Porter and Salazar, 2005; Uddhammar, 2006).

Within tourism studies' work on conflicts, conflicts are conceptualised in a large variety of ways, yet there seem to be some recurring features. First, conflicts are often seen as entities that exist between two or more actors, like people, classes, organizations or institutions (Robinson and Boniface, 1999; Ramsbotham, Woodhouse and Miall, 2011). Second, conflicts are thought to result from differences between actors and these actors are often presented as fixed entities, pre-existing the conflict. Conflicts are conceptualised as the result of actors' distinctive and somehow oppositional ideas, world views, claims on their environment, ideas for the future, intentions, plans and so on (Dredge, 2010; Domingo and Beunen, 2013). Third, except from literatures (mostly outside the field of tourism studies) in which conflicts are conceptualised as productive (Putnam, 1994; Van Assche and Duineveld, 2013; Bernshausen and Bonacker, 2011), many works on conflicts in tourism studies frame them as problematic. Conflicts then should be avoided, resolved or overcome (Eagles, McCool and Haynes, 2002; Marshall, White and

Fischer, 2007). Related to the latter, there are tourism scholars highlighting the persistent character of conflicts (Lee, Riley and Hampton, 2010) and scholars that consider conflicts to be mouldable, resolvable or manageable (Bennett, et al., 2001).

Based on insights from Actor-Network Theory (ANT) and systems theory (Van Assche, Beunen and Duineveld, 2014a; 2014b), we seek to get beyond these actor-centred approaches. We understand conflicts as self-referential modes of ordering. Like any mode of ordering, conflicts can disappear or get resolved, yet they have a tendency to endure (Luhmann, 1995). If they endure, they can become (temporarily) stabilised. We will argue that conflicts can only be understood if one takes into account the history of their emergence, understanding them as subject to path dependencies (Van Assche, Beunen and Duineveld, 2014a; Duineveld, Van Assche and Beunen, 2013). To study these dependencies in more detail we will focus on technologies that shape and maintain conflict, namely: reification, solidification, codification, naturalization, objectification and institutionalization. Furthermore, through our understanding of conflicts, we stress that we paradoxically become part of ongoing path dependencies of conflict.

To further develop our analytical framework we will mine several (ethnographic) studies of conflict in Anabeb Conservancy in north-west Namibia (Lipinge, 2010; Pellis, 2011a; Sullivan, 2003). The findings we present are based on a triangulation of: 1) fieldwork performed in and around Anabeb Conservancy (Pellis, 2011a; 2011b) 2) ethnographic findings of Sullivan (2003) who observed related developments in the larger region of Sesfontein between 1992 and 2000, and 3) different scientific, professional and historical accounts (see for example Corbett and Daniels, 1996; IRDNC, 2011; Lipinge, 2010; MET, 2011; NACSO, 2013). Field notes were taken, 37 in-depth interviews conducted, and participant observations aid in reconstructing how conflict in Anabeb has become manifested before and after the introduction of the prestigious policy model of Namibian community conservation.

We will first present the basic premises of our theoretical framework and related concepts. Then we will return to the case of Anabeb Conservancy to demonstrate the importance of often-underestimated path dependencies occurring at the background of tourism developments projects. Based on our analysis we will further develop our conceptual framework and critically discuss to what extent it is conceptually useful to consider and observe conflicts as self-referential entities.

7.2 Conflicts Forever: Theoretical Framework

7.2.1 *Self-referential Conflicts*

We compose our conceptual framework using inspiration from actor network theory (Latour and Woolgar, 1986; Latour, 2004; Mol, 2002; Law, 2004) and Niklas Luhmann's systems theory (Luhmann, 2000; Luhmann, 1987). The coalescence of ANT and systems theory, as beautifully demonstrated by (Fuchs, 2001; see also Teubner, 2006; Bryant, 2011), provides us with theoretical and conceptual formulations of conflicts as entities with their own history of emergence. Conflicts have a life of their own, marked by different dependencies and different technologies that co-constitute them. Contrary to the latent assumption or overt hope that conflicts can be resolved – that they are temporary, non-static events – we argue that they have a propensity to endure (Luhmann, 1995) because they are self-referential modes of ordering. To mine these different theoretical foundations and construct a compatible theory we will first explicitly present our theoretical argument.

7.2.2 Self-referential Modes of Ordering

We align with ANT as a radical constructivist theory, in the sense that every element in a network (or in a mode of ordering) is constituted within that network (Law, 2009). A priori the observation of a mode of ordering, we cannot presume persons, objects, concepts or any 'thing' else to be fixed entities, waiting patiently 'out there' for their discovery. They are the contingent outcome of particular mode of orderings.

According to ANT, some of the capacities of humans and non-humans should be treated equally: agency for example cannot be presumed for humans only; non-humans can have agency too (Sayes, 2014). For Luhmann humans and non-humans are also treated more or less equally, because agency is *absent* for both. They exist in the environment of a mode of ordering or they are constituted within it. They can 'irritate' a mode of ordering, but lack the agency to steer or control it. For Luhmann, a social system consists of communications and only communications communicate, not humans, artifices, things, individuals, washing machines, animals or rocks.

These communicative modes of ordering, furthermore, are autopoietic or self-productive (Luhmann, 1995). The elements constituted within a mode of ordering are reproduced through a self-referential network of communications communicating with each other. Van Assche and Verschraegen illustrate the theory of autopoietic systems with the following example:

> For in order to circumscribe a particular class of systems, such as organic, psychic or social systems, one has to distinguish the recursive (or 'repeated') self-referential operation that ensures the production and reproduction of all the basic elements. Operations of this kind are, for example, thoughts, produced from previous thoughts and generating further thoughts: from their connection results the psychic system, that is, consciousness. There is no production of thoughts outside consciousness, and consciousness exists if and as long as it is able to continuously produce new thoughts that are only its thoughts. These thoughts are indissolubly linked to the chain of operations that produced it and cannot be exported into other consciousness; in other words: one cannot enter 'the head' of another individual (Van Assche and Verschraegen, 2008, p.267).

For Luhmann not only is the brain operationally closed, but all modes of ordering are. A mode of ordering produces itself and thereby delineates itself from its environment. Modes of ordering appear in each other's environment and observe each other based on their own internal dynamics. This implies that although they can influence each other, they never directly communicate, nor do they determine each other's reproduction (Luhmann, 1995). A scientific mode of ordering, for example, cannot determine or steer a political mode of ordering and vice versa. Likewise, labelling tourism entrepreneurs as sustainable does not necessarily imply any change within the economy related to tourism, and the chances are very limited it will directly affect the environment (Moeller, 2006). Although there are interdependencies between different modes of ordering, one mode of ordering can never communicate with another mode of ordering, or with an event in the environment of a mode of ordering. Observations of other modes of orderings, of events in the environment of one mode of ordering, are always mediated by the internal dynamics of that mode of ordering. That is, modes of ordering in a Luhmannian perspective are ontologically distinct from their environment. If we add these insights of Luhmann to ANT, we can say that modes of ordering are self-referential and operationally closed.

But what about conflicts? Instead of observing conflicts as something in between actors, we follow Bernshausen and Bonacker (2011, p. 24) who, following Luhmann, claim that:

> As opposed to actor-centric approaches, systemic approaches – and especially approaches founded on systems theory – direct considerable attention to the self-selectivity and self-referentiality of conflicts. Based on this perspective, conflicts tend to escalate due to cumulative effects that the participants can often neither control nor fully understand.

Conflicts, then, do not exist between modes of ordering. Difference between them can exist but conflicts are not the explicit and contested difference or contradiction between different actors or between modes of ordering (Luhmann, 1995). Different modes of ordering may be observed to have totally different interests, yet this only implies that there are differences, not conflicts. A conflict is a conflict when it is an operationalized contradiction, not a latent one (Luhmann, 1995). Conflicts as self-referential modes of ordering exist parasitically, meaning that they have the tendency to draw all the attention and resources to the conflict (Luhmann, 1995). They also occur daily and randomly. They can emerge everywhere; any time and can easily disappear, yet often they can also make a 'greater social career'. (Luhmann, 1995, p.392) In the words of Luhmann:

> As social systems, conflicts are autopoietic, self-reproducing unities. Once they are established, one can expect them to continue rather than to end. Their end cannot ensue from autopoiesis, but only from the system's environment as when one party in the conflict kills the other, who then cannot continue the social system of conflict. (Luhmann, 1995, p.394)

Seemingly stable conflicts, embedded in and sustained by a variety of networks, discourses or institutions, are subject to constant change, whatever the perceived eternal meaning at any given point (Duineveld, Van Assche and Beunen, 2013). The historical and contextual contingency of conflicts becomes visible when some observers (e.g. a scientific mode of ordering) start to observe how other modes of ordering observe conflicts (Fuchs, 2001), or how they embody conflicts.

7.2.3 Conflict Formation

After coming into existence, conflicts are constantly evolving and although this is not determined by the context (the environment) in which they evolve, they cannot escape the impact of their history of emergence (Callon, 1991). Conflicts are therefore marked by path dependencies that enable and constrain their evolution (Van Assche, Beunen and Duineveld, 2014a). Here, one could think of the early formation of conflicts, laying grounds for the formal and informal institutions that naturalise an opposition (Van Assche, Beunen and Duineveld, 2014a; Van Assche, et al., 2011; North, 2005). Path dependency is shaping the course of a conflict at each step, marked by interdependence: the evolving relationship between involved actors. Path dependency creates limited possible progressions in the evolution of conflicts.

A path is a series of events and decisions within which a conflict is formed that can relate different sites (or contexts). Settings like conversations in the corridor or at parties can be sites; NGOs, bureaucratic organizations and academic contexts can be sites too. In different societies, times and contexts, different sites function as 'authorities', like universities in some or NGOs in others (Duineveld, et al., 2013). These sites can be more influential to the formation and stabilisation of a conflict than others: they can formalise what is informal in other sites, make the conflict known to a wider audience, or put it under theoretical scrutiny (Foucault, 1972). Each site can have unique knowledge/power relations, influencing the formation of conflicts (Law, 2004). With each step on the path and within each site through which the conflict travels, the irreversibility of a conflict can be increased or decreased – it can stop or be fortified, with each subsequent decision, depending on the sequence that preceded it (Duineveld, Van Assche and Beunen, 2013). *Reification, solidification* and *codification* (Duineveld, Van Assche and Beunen, 2013; Van Assche, Beunen and Duineveld, 2014a) are techniques that enable us to understand the emergence of a conflict. These techniques can be supplemented by three techniques of conflict stabilisation that increase the likelihood of a conflict to persist: *naturalisation, objectification* and *institutionalisation*. Before detailing how these techniques might be realized, we turn towards the example at hand: the life of a particular conflict in Namibian community conservation.

7.3 The Case of Namibian Community Conservation

Namibian community-based conservation has an international reputation for its success, a success that is at odds given the general low success rate and critique of Community Based Natural Resource Management (CBNRM) projects around the world (Brockington, 2004; Büscher and Dietz, 2005; Dressler, et al., 2010). According to the Namibian Ministry of Environment and Tourism (MET), its policy provides communities with 'unprecedented incentives to manage and conserve their areas and wildlife' (MET, 2011). Such incentives, they claim, are enacted through local, regional and national property right arrangements that prescribe the management of unique wildlife resources on communal land (MET, 2011). Resources are managed by local custodians, supported by local organizations, and embedded in (inter)national community conservation frameworks. As the Namibian Association of Community Based Natural Resource Management Support Organizations (NACSO) states, these frameworks ought to enable rural communities to earn benefits from wildlife roaming over their land (NACSO, 2013). Where land formally remains in the hands of the Namibian state, registered communities are given formal rights to benefit from what is claimed to be sustainable natural resource management.

A dominant philosophy within this Namibian conservancy discourse is the ideal of CBNRM that emphasizes a decentralized management of land use. A coalition of rural communities is said to be capable of managing common resources whereby both nature conservation and economic development are enhanced (Boudreaux and Nelson, 2011; MET, 1995):

> Conservancies are self-selecting social units or communities of people that choose to work together and become registered with the Ministry of Environment and Tourism (MET). In order to meet the conditions for registration a conservancy must have a legal constitution, and have clearly defined boundaries that are not in dispute with neighbouring communities. They must also have a defined membership and a committee representative of community members. Conservancies are also required to draw up a clear plan for the equitable distribution of conservancy benefits to members. (NACSO, 2013, p.11)

Over the past twenty years Namibian conservancies have irrefutably become a showcase for community conservation in southern Africa, with solid numbers indicating growing wildlife populations and economic benefits for the rural poor (Boudreaux and Nelson, 2011; NACSO, 2009, 2010, 2011, 2013; Weaver and Skyer, 2003). Conservancies are presented as unique in that they allow rural communities almost full ownership and management of local natural resources (Hulme and Murphree, 1999), making the Namibian CBNRM system 'one of the most successful examples of legal empowerment of the poor of the past decade' (Boudreaux and Nelson, 2011, p.17). Recently, NACSO (2013) reported that around 79 conservancies make about 50 million Namibian dollars per year for over 250,000 rural communities on nearly 150,000 square metres of land. Figure 7.1 illustrates how north-western (Kunene) and parts of eastern Namibia (the Caprivi strip) have particularly embraced conservancy management. Much of Namibia's tourism itineraries are organised within these areas.

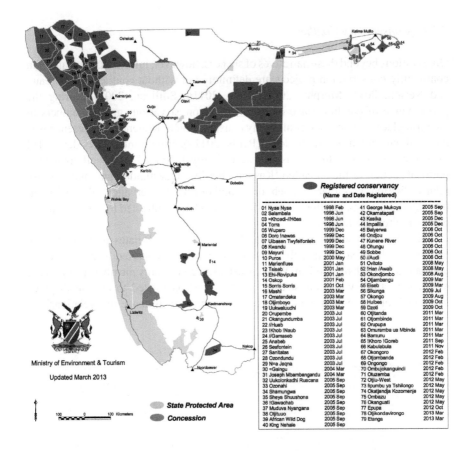

Registered conservancy (Name and Date Registered)			
01 Nyae Nyae	1998 Feb	41 George Mukoya	2005 Sep
02 Salambala	1998 Jun	42 Okamatapati	2005 Sep
03 =Khoadi-//Hôas	1998 Jun	43 Kasika	2005 Dec
04 Torra	1998 Jun	44 Impalila	2005 Dec
05 Wuparo	1999 Dec	45 Balyerwa	2006 Oct
06 Doro !nawas	1999 Dec	46 Ondjou	2006 Oct
07 Uibasen Twyfelfontein	1999 Dec	47 Kunene River	2006 Oct
08 Kwandu	1999 Dec	48 Ohungu	2006 Oct
09 Mayuni	1999 Dec	49 Sobbe	2006 Oct
10 Puros	2000 May	50 //Audi	2006 Oct
11 Marienfluss	2001 Jan	51 Ovitoto	2008 May
12 Tsiseb	2001 Jan	52 !Han /Awab	2008 May
13 Ehi-Rovipuka	2001 Jan	53 Okondjombo	2008 Aug
14 Oskop	2001 Feb	54 Otjambangu	2009 Mar
15 Sorris Sorris	2001 Oct	55 Eiseb	2009 Mar
16 Mashi	2003 Mar	56 Sikunga	2009 Jul
17 Omatendeka	2003 Mar	57 Okongo	2009 Aug
18 Otjimboyo	2003 Mar	58 Huibes	2009 Oct
19 Uukwaluudhi	2003 Mar	59 Dzoti	2009 Oct
20 Orupembe	2003 Jul	60 Otjitanda	2011 Mar
21 Okangundumba	2003 Jul	61 Otjombinde	2011 Mar
22 //Huab	2003 Jul	62 Orupupa	2011 Mar
23 !Khob !Naub	2003 Jul	63 Omuramba ua Mbinda	2011 Mar
24 //Gamaseb	2003 Jul	64 Bamunu	2011 Mar
25 Anabeb	2003 Jul	65 !Khoro !Goreb	2011 Sep
26 Sesfontein	2003 Jul	66 Kabulabula	2011 Nov
27 Sanitatas	2003 Jul	67 Okongoro	2012 Feb
28 Ozondundu	2003 Jul	68 Otjombande	2012 Feb
29 N≠a Jaqna	2003 Jul	69 Ongongo	2012 Feb
30 =Gaingu	2004 Mar	70 Ombujokanguindi	2012 Feb
31 Joseph Mbambangandu	2004 Mar	71 Otuzemba	2012 Feb
32 Uukolonkadhi Ruacana	2005 Sep	72 Otjiu-West	2012 May
33 Ozonahi	2005 Sep	73 Iipumbu ya Tshilongo	2012 May
34 Shamungwa	2005 Sep	74 Okatjandja Kozomenje	2012 May
35 Sheya Shuushona	2005 Sep	75 Ombazu	2012 May
36 !Gawachab	2005 Sep	76 Okanguati	2012 May
37 Muduva Nyangana	2005 Sep	77 Epupa	2012 Oct
38 Otjituuo	2005 Sep	78 Otjikondavirongo	2013 Mar
39 African Wild Dog	2005 Sep	79 Etanga	2013 Mar
40 King Nehale	2005 Sep		

Ministry of Environment & Tourism
Updated March 2013

State Protected Area
Concession

Figure 7.1 Registered communal conservancies in Namibia
Source: MET, 2013 cited in NACSO, 2013

NACSO attributes the positive economic returns from rural community efforts mostly to gains derived from trophy hunting and joint venture tourism (NACSO, 2010; 2013). The functioning of community conservancies are, as such, a vital partner for the Namibian tourism industry, one of Namibia's priority sectors (Novelli and Gebhardt, 2007; WTTC, 2006).

Tracing a path dependency for this success, conservancy discourses attribute the source of the Namibian model to early developments in the north-western region of Kunene since the 1980s (IRDNC, 2011; Murphy, 2003). Informal community conservation was taking place well before conservationist discourses became popular in many parts of Africa. It was only after independence (since the 1990s) that an international discourse on community conservation started to reflect a more utilitarian use of wilderness that was increasingly promoted by international networks in nature conservation and natural heritage protection (cf. Barrow and Murphree, 2001).

7.3.1   Conservancy Conflict

Observations beyond these narratives of success, however, inform us that Namibian community conservation projects are definitely not without conflicts (Boudreaux and Nelson, 2011; Murphy, 2003; Pellis, 2011a; Sullivan, 2003). During the performance of our first stage of fieldwork amongst various group members in the birth place of Namibian community conservation in Kunene, our presence was met with suspicion to say the least (Pellis, 2011a). Where interviews demanded local translation, our first translator accordingly belonged to a well-connected political faction of the so-called 'Kasaona family'. Questioning any other family related faction in either Anabeb or neighbouring conservancy of Sesfontein (see figure 7.2) required the use of different translators entrusted by respondents to represent their interests well.

Initially, we researchers were branded as Kasaona affiliates by other family factions in the area of Anabeb. This changed when we started to hire different translators for each respondent. We were asked by community members to approach different factions with utmost care, as any question related to current disputes in Anabeb or Sesfontein would possible surface already tense interrelationships

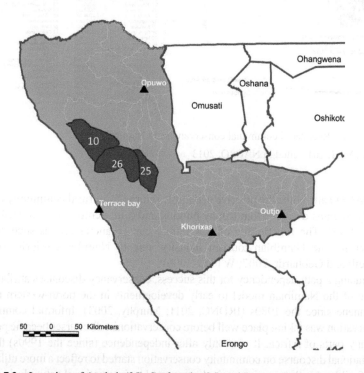

Figure 7.2   Location of Anabeb (25), Sesfontein (26) and Puros (10) conservancies in North-Western Namibia (based on IRDNC, 2014)

between factions. We experienced a multiplicity of tensions that seemed to have become established into an ever-present and unquestionable conflict to insiders in Anabeb. Controversially, this nebulous conflict was observed by external (public and private) networks as ever-present and ineradicable in 'communities': there has, according to proponents of Namibian CBNRM, always been conflict in communities, yet this has, in their observation, nothing to do with the business of community conservation.

One frequently repeated complaint by community members of conservancies throughout Kunene concerned the mysterious disappearance of earnings from conservancy accounts. According to some community members the 'money was eaten' by powerful people with access to conservancy accounts. Others argued income was lost due to inefficient daily management of conservancy personnel. Often mentioned conflicts in the larger region of Kunene concerned the overall distribution of jobs, the lack of transparency in communication and the unequal use of conservancy assets (Murphy, 2003; Pellis, 2011a; Sullivan, 2003). Other conservancy tensions concerned the undermining of the autonomy of traditional leaders. Before the introduction of conservancies they had had an informal role in allocating land use. Hence for them conservancies competed with their traditional authority (Corbett and Daniels, 1996). These everyday events might be observed as ephemeral, but are often 'anchored in more stable conflicts and dilemmas which help to characterize the texture of a more enduring political context' (Meadowcroft, 2002, p.172).

How can we explain the stark contrast observed between Namibian CBNRM as an international success story and the many controversies occurring on the ground? In order to more fully understand the discrepancy between the success stories and conflicts observed, we expand our case study to neighborhood levels, to trace the emergence and endurance of conflict(s) within the context of Anabeb Conservancy.

7.3.2 The Emergence of a Conflict

Until 2000, Anabeb was embedded within Sesfontein conservancy. Various (escalating) conflicts dating back to early community conservation efforts in the 1980s resulted eventually in fracturing Sesfontein into three autonomous conservancies (see earlier figure 7.2): 1) *Puros conservancy* in the west of Sesfontein constituency (registered in 2000), 2) *Sesfontein conservancy* in central Sesfontein constituency (registered in 2003), and 3) *Anabeb conservancy* south-east of the Sesfontein constituency (registered in 2003).

To exemplify how conflicts play a central role in these developments, we will continue to provide a brief version of historical context of recurring conflicts in this specific region of Kunene, eventually reflecting upon specific developments taking place in present-day Anabeb conservancy. One particular regional conflict is of major importance: originally enacted by two dominant Herero families, this conflict is affecting and affected by discursive alliances in this region that includes connections to locally based NGOs funded by international donors.

Due to past ethnic migrations and displacements, Anabeb conservancy currently contains seven traditional groups: four Herero (Kasaona, Kangombe, Uakazapi, Mbomboro) and three Damara (Uises, Taniseb, Ganaseb) family lines. These groups and relative coalitions are outlined in figure 7.3.

To constitute conservancy management, two regionally based conservation and development NGOs within Kunene (co-funded by international donors) have actively been organizing support with traditional leaders since the 1980s. Their formal aim was to protect highly valued wilderness resources such as desert lions, rhinoceros, desert adapted elephants, and other animals (Blaikie, 2006; Jones, 2006; Novelli and Gebhardt, 2007). Western managing partners of both NGOs previously worked for one conservation organization in Kunene. Due to personal differences that we were unable to reconstruct, one of these Western partners decided to establish a second organization, which became active through a Community Game Guard programme in 1982 (Jones, 2001). The newly established NGO, that we call Integrating Conservation with Development in Namibia (ICDN; cf. Sullivan, 2003) was increasingly perceived by (marginalized) community members as a political force with strong ties to one particular Herero family: the Kasaona. It was the ICDN who formally introduced community

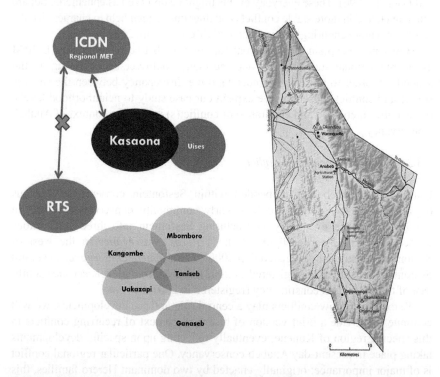

Figure 7.3 Communal factions in Anabeb and a detailed map of Anabeb Conservancy
Source: NACSO, 2013

conservation in cooperation with different village headmen in Kunene (personal correspondence with local game guard in Warmquelle). '*The ICDN is the mother of the conservancy*', and when its Western managing partner transferred management to one of the local Kasaona employees, '*the ICDN became Kasaona*' (headman in Warmquelle). In the contemporary organizational structure of the ICDN, we still find foremost Herero staff members named, or closely connected to, Kasaona (Pellis, 2011b).

Local reconstructed memories of first conservancy-related conflict date back to 1999/2000, when a former treasurer of Sesfontein conservancy was publicly accused of fraud related to missing financial accounts reserved for conservancy salaries. Not long after these accusations, the conservancy office in Sesfontein, interviewees reported, was shut down by armed Herero guards. A heated protest march organised by leaders of various communal groups feeling excluded from conservancy affairs followed shortly after. On 23 February 2000, at a community meeting in Sesfontein, protestors claimed that A) the accused treasurer should be given back his job, that B) armed Herero guards 'must leave so that [Damara] gardens [situated near the conservancy office in Sesfontein] can be used in peace', and that C) it is difficult for people 'to participate [in conservancy affairs] without access to NGO vehicles'. According to a representative of the ICDN, this community meeting 'was controlled by an aggressive and unrepresentative faction concerned to bolster their privileged access to resources' (all quoted in Sullivan, 2003, p.75).

Another observation by Sullivan (2003) depicts former treasurer of Sesfontein conservancy as frequently communicating with a competing regional conservation NGO – which we will call RTS here – to establish tourism enterprises in the region. RTS and the ICDN were seen by community members as competitors for donor income, as both organizations had comparable developmental aims for Kunene. The role of both the ICDN and the RTS is well acknowledged by respondents as an important factor in establishing rivalry between different community factions in the larger Sesfontein constituency.

> If an elephant and an elephant fight, then the grass is suffering. The NGOs in the area are fighting. The grassroots, the poor members, are suffering from that because people who can reach media, who can disperse information easily, are turning things to their wishes. The communities were fighting [in the larger region of Sesfontein]. One group was saying; conservancy from Puros to Palmwag [a concession area south of Anabeb]? We don't want such a conservancy, we want three different conservancies. (Sesfontein councillor)

Those factions in favour of three separate conservancies, including the RTS and the Damara councillor of Sesfontein himself, argued that the region was too large for one conservancy to be managed. One popular argument against the idea of a single conservancy was the wide dispersal of homes throughout the area, making access to central infrastructure – necessary to meet on a regular basis – a practical challenge. This discourse of distance is cited as the official reason why Puros conservancy was the first to split from Sesfontein in 2000 to continue operating as an independent conservancy.

In the end, two political camps emerged from these tensions in the larger area: 1) a resisting (and self-identified underrepresented) set of community groups (both Damara and Herero), and 2) a dominant alliance between the Kasaona and the ICDN. The ICDN and Kasaona are seen by the first camp as the 'evil' of all conservancy related conflict in Kunene. These accusations and reactions have resulted into repeating blame games played out by different camps:

> ... there is always a problem [...] we were from other traditional leaders, traditional set up, I mean other traditional community, and we were the people who mostly involve with the [ICDN] [...] [other leaders] were never informed what was happening in the conservancy, the committee does not inform them well or involve them into decision making. So [these leaders] complain here and then. (headman Kasaona in Warmquelle)

> The problem comes from the people that work for [ICDN], the regional representatives of the Ministry of Environment and Tourism and the Kasaona group. These three groups are together, and that is just where the whole problem comes from. (headman Kangombe in Warmquelle)

The heated escalation of 1999/2000 can hardly be explained as a simple fight between two regional NGOs. Instead, local observers dedicate its existence to old quarrel in the region. The Kangombe and Kasaona, both well-represented Herero families in Kunene, have been in dispute since time remembered. Sullivan argues that the 1999/2000 conflict '[plays] out their own dispute' (2003, p.81). Asking diverse community members in Sesfontein/Anabeb why these two families are engaged in a vendetta, only vague memories, if any, are brought forth. For some it can be explained as religious (different families practice different religions in and around their homesteads), for some as an old problem that started during apartheid:

> Can you see that big tree? Initially, the old people were getting money from the government. The [government] car was initially standing at the tree, and people would come there to collect. This was before independence, before 1990. It was the South African government who came to provide the elderly. The other headmen didn't want to collect money from this tree, since this tree is owned by me ... There are seven headmen, but the issue was initially just against one here. It was Goliath *Kasaona* [former Kasaona headman]. [...]. The whole issue started in the 1980s. Because the government people said that we initially agreed to meet under this tree, and those people who do not want to come ... we [the government] don't care, we just give out to those who come. (headman *Kangombe* based in Warmquelle)

For others the conflict between these two fronts is simply the way things have always been, persistently recurring on various occasions, in diverse appearances. There has always been conflict, it is a fact of life, and it is expected that it will endure forever. 'Why would you even bother researching it?'

7.3.3   Present-day Conflict in Anabeb

In 2010, similar tensions between Kangombe and Kasaona materialised, this time developing into slightly different alliances between communal groups in the south-eastern region of former Sesfontein conservancy (cf. Pellis, 2011b). During elections in the village of Warmquelle, new committee members of the conservancy board (the main governing body) were to be elected in August 2010. This time the conservancy in question was Anabeb that once belonged to the larger Sesfontein conservancy.

During elections in Warmquelle, two alliances in Anabeb conservancy emerged in disagreement over the correct sequence of events that day. One group, an alliance related to the Kangombe, wanted to learn more about the functioning of the previous conservancy board before they could decide upon electing new board members. The other group, an alliance related to the Kasaona, held the opinion that the requested report should be due after the elections, since the presentation of last term's performance was not yet ready for public disclosure. Regional election facilitators from the Ministry of Environment and Tourism (MET) and the ICDN were present during the election process, and decided that the elections had to continue in line with the Kasaona argumentation. Facilitators stressed the importance of continuation for the sake of time (more elections were already planned that day) and democratic principles: 'if the majority votes to continue, we continue'. The complete opposition, under leadership of Joseph Kangombe, was furious with this process and decided to withdraw entirely from the election, leaving only Kasaona members to vote for the future committee of the conservancy.

> People could not agree upon how the election process should be. And eventually like any other election you will agree upon the process, but at the end of the day if you lose, you start complaining, complaining, complaining ... about the other party of breaking the election ... . this and this and this ... people know that you are part of the whole election process. (headman Kasaona in Warmquelle)

When present day conflict takes place within the context of an election event, it stages the typical recurrence of recognizable old quarrel between earlier mentioned families. This time, the oppositional Kangombe group disappeared from the election process believing that the previous conservancy committee had something to hide. Not addressing this issue became reason enough for this group to block local elections for the conservancy committee, consequently necessitating external interference by the national Ministry of Environment and Tourism

(Lipinge, 2010). The Kasaona group argued in complete contrast, promoting democratic procedures and efficient time management. Nevertheless, this conflict is once again seen by all involved parties to frustrate conservancy (and tourism) affairs in the region – developments that, despite all controversy, are still valued as crucial for nature conservation and poverty alleviation to happen (cf. Pellis, 2011b).

7.3.4   Understanding and Managing Conflicts

Conversations with policy makers and involved actors on regional, national or international levels revealed different conceptions about conflict in Anabeb Conservancy. These perspectives generally formulate local conflicts as, by definition, local. A spokesperson of a regional supporting NGO illustrates that conservancy conflict circles around trifling self-interest or envy:

> Most conservancies [are] about fighting who is going to be a manager, about
> income, why the money was spent in this way … .[…] people here seem to
> mix politics with conservancy business … the real problem lies with the fact that
> there are too many headmen, and all of them want to be represented equally in
> the management of the conservancy.

Communal differences were also mentioned, especially by politicians on a national level. They argue that these differences were recognized and dealt with in post-apartheid Namibia. After Namibia's independence, a dominant discourse of black empowerment led to popular community participation to make up for past wrong-doings towards ethnic groups under apartheid (Büscher and Dietz, 2005). One would argue that today only Namibians are living in Namibia, as all people are considered equal in terms of rights; disregarding race, colour, or political position. The Namibian Traditional Authorities Act however creates a contradictory role for 'recognition' of post-apartheid communities and communal leadership structures. Homogeneity of distinct communities is formally required to get conservancies and related communities recognized under contemporary Namibian law. The Traditional Authorities Act (2000) states that a traditional community is:

> an indigenous, homogeneous, endogamous social grouping of persons comprising
> of families deriving from […] clans which share a common ancestry, language,
> cultural heritage, customs and traditions, recognizes a common traditional
> authority and inhabits a common communal area.

Although traditional leaders are recognized in Namibia, they are occasionally remembered as former representatives of apartheid who 'administer[ed] native areas' on behalf of the state (Werner, 1993). There is no longer formal space for traditional authorities to manage 'their' land which used to be a self-proclaimed task of local chiefs who after independence had to re-register themselves (Corbett and Daniels, 1996):

> I think that the chiefs see the conservancy as a person that is taking over their role. [...] The chiefs want to be the one allocating the land, and the one who is getting all the benefits. But the conservancies say no, we are having the right over land, and we are going to allocate this land. We in turn will give you the benefits, like we give to anybody else that is a member of the conservancy. (spokesperson international conservation NGO)

To deal with the fuzziness of local leadership, conservancies are seen by support organizations as solutions to problems coming from communal conservation: 'When the conservancy was coming in, they said let us stop this [conflict]. Let the conservancy take over [...] and we let somebody take over the management because of this conflict' (spokesperson international conservation NGO). The conservancy policy's mode of ordering does not typically recognize a role for local divisions in these conflicts, as illustrated by the approach of supporting organizations: 'we didn't really work with groups, but rather on the products. Whoever was there, we were not interested in politics, we are not a political organization'. (spokesperson NACSO). Nevertheless, some analysts repeat that strong local governance measures (e.g. clear tenure rights) are instrumental to ensure effective working relations with communities in order to keep developing profitable tourism enterprises (Boudreaux and Nelson, 2011; Murphy, 2003).

One proposed solution to deal with traditional community conflict led to an ongoing experiment to institutionalize the position of traditional authority (TA) representatives into formal conservancy committees. In Anabeb, the conservancy committee consists of ten elected community members (with voting power), and seven traditional authority representatives (without voting power). 'Traditional Authorities complain here and there ... if that is the case we decide [that] traditional authorities select their representative that is going to represent them on the management board' (ICDN officer).

Related more specifically to the Anabeb election in 2010, mediating officers from the Ministry of Environment and Tourism (MET) observed that most of the issues in Anabeb were related to differences between traditional authorities and more widespread political affiliations. The MET concluded that it is the continued influence of traditional authorities that need 'to be clarified in the conservancy constitution' (Lipinge, 2010, p.7). Traditional divides, in their view, existed already before the election process (cf. Murphy, 2003). 'You should be careful in arguing that a conservancy creates conflicts in community lands. If you look at the historical development, you see that these conflicts already existed in the past, the conservancy is merely surfacing them to the foreground' (NACSO representative).

In retrospect, the Namibian Ministry of Environment and Tourism explains the entire Anabeb situation as follows: 'It is observed that, the root cause of the conflict is a vague Conservancy Constitution with regards to the process of election of the Conservancy Committee' (Lipinge, 2010, p.12). For the MET it is therefore a matter of improving the implementation of policies and streamlining democratic processes for conflicts to be resolved within the ongoing development of conservancies as a successful policy model.

7.3.5 Enacting Conflicts, Forever?

Our re-mining of a history of decision-making in Sesfontein and Anabeb has shown traces of interdependent conflicts. Old conflicts are partly reproduced in new conflicts. At different sites and at different stages in the development of conflict, old conflict was recalculated in various ways. Pre-conservancy history has illustrated particular mobilizations of communal actors into distinct spatial configurations that, after independence, are simultaneously hidden ('we are all Namibians in one democratic nation') and brought back to the fore (traditional structures and conflict are irrefutably connected to the development of modern communal conservation).

Unrepresented factions within Anabeb/Sesfontein conservancy, especially traditional authorities, cannot fully grasp the idea that 'their' access to land management, to a large extent, is taken over by an 'apolitical' actor: the conservancy. Simultaneously, there seems to be a general blind trust by community members in the 'goodness' of community conservation as a historical correction for past oppression under apartheid law which would not allow communities to 'rightfully' take decisions on natural resource management (Pellis, 2011a). As a consequence, community members, as well as support organizations, continue to search for experimental solutions to 'local' conflicts, and thereby co-construct an ideal and internationally appraised future for Namibian CBNRM. These so-called solutions, such as the re-introduction of traditional authority in conservancy committees or the homogenisation of communities in democratic conservancy policies, do not necessarily solve old and new conflicts, but rather allow old conflict to become manifest. Every proposed change in the conservancy, no matter how good the proposal, is closely observed by opposing factions to a point where it no longer seems to matter what individuals have to say. What truly counts is affiliation to particular modes of ordering; the rest is irrelevant in the eyes of local observers.

7.4 Conflict Formation and Stabilisation

We return now to our theoretical approach towards conflict, to explore how the different techniques of conflict formation and stabilization can help us approach this scenario where conflict can be understood through its path dependency. The first of three techniques that increase the likelihood of conflict to endure is *naturalisation*, the process in which the conflict becomes part of the natural order of things (Foucault, 2006; Fuchs, 2001; Barthes, 1957), it becomes impossible to imagine a world without it. In this process the constructed character of the conflict is hidden, masked or forgotten (Latour and Woolgar, 1986). In this process of masking, conflicts solidify gradually and take up their final shape, becoming part of the 'warehouse of unquestioned commonplaces' (Duineveld, 2011, p.82). In Anabeb/Sesfontein conservancy, an old vendetta between two families has been around as long as people can remember. Members of two renowned families claim not to remember why they actually are in conflict. Over time it has slowly become a *natural* characteristic of this region. One of our translators illustrated this by asking: 'why are you interested to learn about this conflict? We all know here that it exists, why bother to look further into it?'

Naturalisation is sometimes highly entangled with the process of *objectification*, which is the processes in which a conflict is constructed as an objective truth, as a fact, as something that seemingly exists independent of observation (Foucault, 1998; Foucault, 1972). Science, law and bureaucracy are in many societies the dominant sites and sources of objectification. Different alliances in Sesfontein and Anabeb demonstrate how interrelations of conflict have become exceptionally complicated over time. Encounters between NGO alliances, relationships with other traditional authorities or intermarriages, but also our own scientific inquiry, have contributed to sharpened distinctions between coalitions. We are not claiming that these distinctions are automatically leading to conflict; rather they are a mere result of it, perpetuated as an irreversible effect of already established conflict. Whatever 'solution' is brought in to resolve the situation, the central and historical conflict keeps re-emerging as a strong local immobilizer to desired communal development. We as outsiders might think that such hindrance is negative, and as such we keep on looking for ways to understand conflicts, in order to deal with them.

When conflict is recognised as a distinctive, 'natural kind', by a growing number of institutions, we can speak of *institutionalisation*. The cementing of conflict into organizations, policies, politics, regulations, techniques and plans (cf. Foucault, 1979; Foucault, 2007; North, 1990) increases its path dependency. This enables an increased irreversibility of conflict in a specific practice or discourse. Conservancies are known for their instrumentality to devolve decision making and resolve conflicts through locally established rules. It is within a complex web of national and local regulations that various contradictory traditional and modern practices are to be regulated; e.g. recognizing traditional authorities while ensuring decisive roles for democratically elected community conservancies. Allowing traditional representatives to attend communal conservancy committee meetings symbolises how past conflict between factions have become institutionalised. It might have temporarily satisfied traditional leaders, yet allows old conflict settings to endure.

Reification is the process in which a conflict emerges as more than just a couple of unrelated misunderstandings, utterances or loose assemblages of parts. It becomes a unity, more or less coherent and observable as 'this conflict, not that one'. In time this can lead to a process of solidification where internal connections within a conflict become so tight that they can delineate an existence of their own.

Involved community members in Kunene, as well as support organizations, are all too well aware of locally manifested conflict. The fact that it exists, and that it hinders effective community conservation, is disputed by no one. And where conflict in Anabeb/Sesfontein increasingly became distinguishable as a separate entity, it has repeatedly been understood as a local vendetta. Furthermore, conflict was framed particularly in relation to discourses of inequality in benefit distribution coming from the conservancy, not in terms of ethnic or religious differences, which touches upon another (apartheid like) discussion that has not been addressed in this study.

Finally, *codification* is the simplification of conflict boundaries. It comes with the simple applicability of codes to decide on conceptual inclusion/exclusion: 'a conflict about the land not the water resources', or 'an ideological conflict not a religious one'. Dominant local factions and national policy makers see conflict in Anabeb as a long-lived *local* issue inherent to rural communities, and not as a *national* problem.

7.5 Conclusion

Much has been written about conflicts in tourism studies, in terms of how they could be managed and overcome. Yet the structural and persistent character of conflicts is often overlooked and the possibility to steer, manage and understand them overstated. We have argued and illustrated that conflicts can only be understood if one takes into account their histories of emergence and ways by which they become solidified, decreasing their possible pathways. When we understand conflicts as self-referential modes of ordering we should be able to observe conflicts through dependencies in conflict formation and stabilisation.

This approach to conflicts enables us to be more critical about the hope implied in the management approaches to tourism conflict. Not only do we argue that it is difficult to expect conflict management to resolve conflicts, we also argue that conflict management can have many other effects. It can temporarily tuck away conflicts, or spuriously stabilise a conflict by making it an object of managerial procedures. By institutionalising factions as oppositional, 'homogenous' groups, they can even perpetuate a state of conflict, making it part of official, institutionalised modes of ordering, which may then be reproduced by international voices that make conflict travel far beyond its local context.

References

Barrow, E. and Murphree, M., 2001. Community conservation: From concept to practice. In: D. Hulme and M. Murphree, eds. 2001. *African wildlife & livelihoods: The promise & performance of community conservation.* Oxford: Marston Book Services Limited. pp.24–37.

Barthes, R., 1957. *Mythologies*. Paris: Éditions du Seuil.

Bennett, E., Neiland, A., Anang, E., Bannerman, P., Atiq Rahman, A., Huq, S., Bhuiya, S., Day, M., Fulford-Gardiner, M and Clerveaux, W., 2001. Towards a better understanding of conflict management in tropical fisheries: Evidence from Ghana, Bangladesh and the Caribbean. *Marine Policy*, 25(5), pp.365–376.

Bernshausen, S. and Bonacker, T., 2011. A constructivist perspective on systemic conflict transformation. In: D. Körppen, N. Ropers and H. J. Gießmann, eds. 2011. *The non-linearity of peace processes – Theory and practice of systemic conflict transformation*. Opladen/Farmington Hills: Barbara Budrich Verlag. pp.23–38.

Blaikie, P., 2006. Is small really beautiful? Community based natural resource management in Malawi and Botswana. *World Development*, 34(11), pp.1942–1957.

Boudreaux, K. and Nelson, F., 2011. Community conservation in Namibia: Empowering the poor with property rights. *Economic Affairs*, 31(2), pp.17–24.

Bramwell, B. and Cox, V., 2009. Stage and path dependence approaches to the evolution of a national park tourism partnership. *Journal of Sustainable Tourism*, 17(2), pp.191–206.

Brockington, D., 2004. Community conservation, inequality and injustice: Myths of power in protected area management. *Conservation and Society*, 2(2), pp.411–432.

Bryant, L.R., 2011. *The cemocracy of objects*. City in Michigan state or is Michigan a UK city?, Michigan: Open Humanities Press.

Büscher, B. and Dietz, T., 2005. Conjunctions of governance: The state and the conservation-development nexus in southern Africa. *The Journal of Transdisciplinary Environmental Studies*, 4(2), pp.2–15.

Callon, M., 1991. Techno-economic networks and irreversibility. In: J. Law, ed. 1991. *A sociology of monsters: Essays on power, technology and domination*. London: Routledge. pp.132–165.

Corbett, A. and Daniels, C., 1996. Legislation and policy affecting community-based natural resource management in Namibia. *SSD Research Report 26*. Windhoek: University of Namibia (MDRC).

Dahlberg, A., 2005. Local resource use, nature conservation and tourism in Mkuze wetlands, South Africa: A complex weave of dependence and conflict. *Geografisk Tidsskrift-Danish Journal of Geography*, 105(1), pp.43–55.

Domingo, I. and Beunen, R., 2013. Regional planning in the Catalan Pyrenees: Strategies to deal with actors' expectations, perceived uncertainties and conflicts. *European Planning Studies*, 21(2), pp.187–203.

Douglas, A. and Lubbe, B.A., 2006. Identifying value conflicts between stakeholders in corporate travel management by applying the soft value management model: A survey in South Africa. *Tourism Management*, 27(6), pp.1130–1140.

Dredge, D., 2010. Place change and tourism development conflict: Evaluating public interest. *Tourism Management*, 31(1), pp.104–112.

Dressler, W., Büscher, B., Schoon, M., Brockington, D., Hayes, T., Kull, C. A., McCarthy, J. and Shrestha, K., 2010. From hope to crisis and back again? A critical history of the global CBNRM narrative. *Environmental Conservation*, 37(01), pp.5–15.

Duineveld, M. and Van Assche, K., 2011. The power of tulips: constructing nature and heritage in a contested landscape. *Journal of Environmental Policy & Planning*, 13(2), pp.79–98.

Duineveld, M., Van Assche, K. and Beunen, R., 2013. Making things irreversible. Object stabilization in urban planning and design. *Geoforum*, 46, pp.16–24.

Eagles, P.F.J., McCool, S.F. and Haynes, C.D., 2002. *Sustainable tourism in protected areas: Guidelines for planning and management*. City of publication?: IUCN.

Foucault, M., 1972. *The archaeology of knowledge & the discourse on language*. New York: Pantheon Books.

Foucault, M., 1979. *Discipline and punish: The birth of the prison*. Harmondsworth: Penguin Books.

Foucault, M., 1998. *The will to knowledge. The history of sexuality: 1*. London: Penguin Books.

Foucault, M., 2006. *History of madness*. London and New York: Routledge.

Foucault, M., 2007. *Security, territory, population: Lectures at the College de France, 1977–78*. Basingstoke: Palgrave Macmillan.

Fuchs, S., 2001. *Against essentialism: A theory of culture and society*. Cambridge: Harvard University Press.

Hitchcock, M. and Darma Putra, I.N., 2005. The Bali bombings: Tourism crisis management and conflict avoidance. *Current Issues in Tourism*, 8(1), pp.62–76.

Hulme, D. and Murphree, M., 1999. Communities, wildlife and the 'new conservation' in Africa. *Journal of International Development*, 11(2), pp.277–285.

IRDNC, 2011. An IRDNC summary: Doing African conservation the sustainable way. Available at: <http://www.irdnc.org.na/> [Accessed 7 June 2011].

IRDNC, 2014. Kunene location. Available at: <http://www.irdnc.org.na/map_locationkunene.htm> [Accessed 21 January 2014].

Jones, B., 2001. The evolution of a community-based approach to wildlife management at Kunene, Namibia. In: D. Hulme and M. Murphree, eds. 2001. *African wildlife and livelihoods: The promise and performance of community conservation*. Oxford: Marston Book Services Limited. pp.160–176.

Jones, S., 2006. A political ecology of wildlife conservation in Africa. *Review of African Political Economy*, 33(109), pp.483–495.

Latour, B., 2004. *Politics of nature. How to bring the sciences into democracy*. Cambridge: Harvard University Press.

Latour, B., 2005. *Reassembling the social: An introduction to actor-network theory*. Oxford: Oxford University Press.

Latour, B. and Woolgar, S., 1986. *Laboratory life: The construction of scientific facts*. Princeton, N.J.: Princeton University Press.

Law, J., 2004. *After method: Mess in social science research*. London: Routledge.

Law, J., 2009. Actor network theory and material semiotics. In: B.S. Turner, ed. 2009. *The new blackwell companion to social theory*. Oxford: Blackwell. pp.141–158.

Lee, T. J., Riley, M. and Hampton, M. P., 2010. Conflict and progress: Tourism development in Korea. *Annals of Tourism Research*, 37(2), pp.355–376.

Lipinge, J., 2010. Report on the investigations with regard to the allegations made on the election process of conservancy committee – Anabeb Conservancy. Windhoek: Ministry of Environment and Tourism.

Luhmann, N., 1987. *Soziale Systeme: Grundriss einer allgemeinen Theorie*. Frankfurt am Main: Suhrkamp.

Luhmann, N., 1995. *Social systems*. Stanford: Stanford University Press.

Luhmann, N., 2000. *Art as a social system*. Stanford: Stanford University Press.

Marshall, K., White, R. and Fischer, A., 2007. Conflicts between humans over wildlife management: On the diversity of stakeholder attitudes and implications for conflict management. *Biodiversity and Conservation*, 16(11), pp.3129–3146.

Meadowcroft, J., 2002. Politics and scale: some implications for environmental governance. *Landscape and urban planning*, 61(2), pp.169–179.

MET, 1995. *Wildlife management, utilisation and tourism on communal land: Using conservancies and wildlife councils to enable communal area residents to use and benefit from wildlife and tourism on their land*. Windhoek: METMET, 2011. Conservancies. Available at: <http://www.met.gov.na/Directorates/Parks/Pages/Conservancies.aspx> [Accessed 2 November 2011].

Moeller, H.-G., 2006. *Luhmann explained: From souls to systems*. Chicago, IL: Open Court.

Mol, A., 2002. *The body multiple: Ontology in medical practice*. Durham: Duke University Press.

Murphy, C., 2003. *Community tourism in Kunene: A review of five case studies for the WILD Project*. Directorate of Environmental Affairs, Ministry of Environment and Tourism.

NACSO, 2009. Namibia's communal conservancies. Windhoek: NACSO.

NACSO, 2010. Namibia's communal conservancies – A review of progress and challenges in 2009. Windhoek: NACSO.

NACSO, 2011. Summary of conservancies. Available at: <http://www.nacso.org.na/SOC_profiles/conservancysummary.php> [Accessed 20 September 2011].

NACSO, 2013. Namibia's communal conservancies: A review of progress in 2011. Windhoek: NACSO.

North, D.C., 1990. *Institutions, institutional change and economic performance*. Cambridge: Cambridge University Press.

North, D.C., 2005. *Understanding the process of economic change*. Princeton: Princeton University Press.

Novelli, M. and Gebhardt, K., 2007. Community based tourism in Namibia: 'Reality show' or 'window dressing'? *Current Issues in Tourism*, 10(5), pp.443–479.

Okello, M.M., 2005. Land use changes and human–wildlife conflicts in the Amboseli Area, Kenya. *Human Dimensions of Wildlife*, 10(1), pp.19–28.

Pellis, A., 2011a. *Access to benefits from community based tourism: A discursive ethnography of conflict over benefits in Anabeb Conservancy, Namibia.* MSc. Wageningen University.

Pellis, A., 2011b. Modern and traditional arrangements in community-based tourism: Exploring an election conflict in the Anabeb Conservancy, Namibia. In: V.R. Van der Duim, D. Meyer, J. Saarinen and K. Zellmer, eds. 2011. *New alliances for tourism, conservation and development in eastern and southern Africa.* Delft: Eburon.pp.127–145

Porter, B.W. and Salazar, N.B., 2005. Heritage tourism, conflict, and the public interest: An introduction. *International Journal of Heritage Studies*, 11(5), pp.361–370.

Putnam, L.L., 1994. Productive conflict: Negotiation as implicit coordination. *International Journal of Conflict Management*, 5(3), pp.284–298.

Ramsbotham, O., Woodhouse, T. and Miall, H., 2011. *Contemporary conflict resolution.* Cambridge: Polity Press.

Robinson, M. and Boniface, P., 1999. *Tourism and Cultural Conflicts*, Wallingford: CAB International.

Sayes, E., 2014. Actor–network theory and methodology: Just what does it mean to say that nonhumans have agency? *Social Studies of Science*, 44(1), pp.134–149.

Sullivan, S., 2003. Protest, conflict and litigation: Dissent or libel in resistance to a conservancy in north-west Namibia. In: D.G. Anderson and E.K. Berglund, eds. 2003. *Ethnographies of conservation.* New York: Berghahn Books. pp.69–86.

Teubner, G., 2006. Rights of non-humans? Electronic agents and animals as new actors in politics and law. *Journal of Law and Society*, 33(4), pp.497–521.

Traditional Authorities Act 2000.Windhoek (moet hier geen ministry of iets dergelijks bij? is dit voldoende zo?)

Uddhammar, E., 2006. Development, conservation and tourism: Conflict or symbiosis? *Review of International Political Economy*, 13(4), pp.656–678.

Van Assche, K. and Verschraegen, G., 2008. The limits of planning: Niklas Luhmann's Systems Theory and the analysis of planning and planning ambitions. *Planning Theory*, 7(3), pp.263–283.

Van Assche, K., Beunen, R., Jacobs, J. and Teampau, P., 2011. Crossing trails in the marshes: Rigidity and flexibility in the governance of the Danube Delta. *Journal of Environmental Planning and Management*, 54(8), pp.997–1018.

Van Assche, K. and Duineveld, M., 2013. The good, the bad and the self-referential: Heritage planning and the productivity of difference. *International Journal of Heritage Studies*, 19(1), pp.1–15.

Van Assche, K.,Beunen, R. and Duineveld, M., 2014a. *Evolutionary Governance Theory. An Introduction.* Heidelberg: Springer.

Van Assche, K., Beunen, R. and Duineveld, M., 2014b. Governance Paths and Reality Effects *Evolutionary Governance Theory.* Dordrecht: Springer International Publishing. pp.55–62.

Von Ruschkowski, E. and Mayer, M., 2011. From conflict to partnership? Interactions between protected areas, local communities and operators of tourism enterprises in two German national park regions. *Journal of Tourism and Leisure Studies*, 17(2), pp.147–181.

Weaver, L.C. and Skyer, P., 2003. Conservancies: Integrating wildlife land-use options into the livelihood, development and conservation strategies of Namibian communities. In: (organisation?), *The 5th world parks conference.* Durban, South Africa, 8–17 September 2003. Windhoek: US Agency for International Development.

Werner, W., 1993. A brief history of land dispossession in Namibia. *Journal of Southern African Studies*, 19(1), pp.135–146.

WTTC, 2006. Namibia – The impact of travel and tourism on jobs and the economy. London: World Travel and Tourism Council.

Chapter 8
The Tourist-Vampire and the Citizen as Ontological Figures: Human and Nonhuman Encounters in the Postpolitical

Richard Ek

8.1 Introduction

In tourism theory the tourist is often understood as a postmodern figure, particularly connected to tourism as a postmodern phenomenon during the second half of the 20th century. But the understanding of the tourist as a genuinely modern figure is also well established in tourism studies. Tourism is in this understanding something that cannot be separated out from the development of an industrial and capitalist society during the 19th century. This chapter however, is based on the idea that the tourist, as an *ontological* figure (the metaphysical imagination of the nature of different faces and functions of the human in Western thought), is not a postmodern or modern creature, but a figure that has been a companion to the central ontological figure in Western metaphysics – the citizen – since the establishment of *polis* as an ordering principle of society (Ek and Tesfahuney, submitted). The tourist has literally been a paradigmatic figure, a figure that "shows itself beside" (from the Greek *para* meaning "beside" and *deiknynai*, "to show"). The tourist can thus be seen as a part, a fragment of society that has been separated out, has been excluded from the *polis* through the orderings of ontological politics, through performative distinctions that creates a topographical dichotomy of tourist and citizen as separated that simultaneously masks the topological relation between the two ontological figures (Agamben, 2009, see also the introduction).

This reasoning echoes and relies to a significant degree on Giorgio Agamben's thesis on the relational tension between the city/*polis* and the camp (Agamben, 1998). The camp has been a part of *polis* since the very beginning, but more or less invisible or not taken seriously in Western political thought, particularly due the dominance of the state (with territorial sovereignty based on the idea of community) in political philosophy. The 20th century was for Agamben, however, the century the camp started to rival the dominance of *polis*, not the least due to the Holocaust: 'Today it is not the city but rather the camp that is the fundamental biopolitical paradigm of the West' (Agamben, 1998, p.181). In a similar way we could argue that the tourist as the political citizen's ontological *doppelganger*, (a mostly silent figure, i.e. for the most part forgotten or not taken seriously but nevertheless an inherent part of the citizen of *polis*) is the fundamental paradigmatic figure of the West. The very idea that "tourism" is something non-political, something unworthy of consideration in political thought, and something that is an outcome of economic development (the rise of industrialism or the rise of a society of mass consumerism) are all indications of the traditional negligence of the tourist as a figure of political nature. However, increasingly in tourism studies the political character of tourism performativity are admitted, mainly in an empirical or ontic way but still not that much as a figure of political nature metaphysically or ontologically speaking.

As often, new attempts of theoretical claims have usually already been elaborated upon in literary fiction. We could turn to Fyodor Dostoyevsky's *Dvoynik* (*The Double*), first published in 1846. In the novel, the government clerk Yakov Petrovich Golyadkin suddenly encounters his own identical double in appearance but not in behaviour. The double, Golyadkin jr., is charming, extrovert and social, while Golyadkin sr. is anxious, shy and inward-oriented. Starting out as friends they soon become enemies as the double through opposite behaviour, being both aggressive and likable, takes over the social sphere of Golyadkin sr. Is it possible that we could see the same tendency today as in the Dostoyevsky novel; that the *doppelganger*, the tourist, attempts to take over the life and the societal position of the citizen? Could we connect this argument to the idea that we now live in postpolitical times rather than political? Do we live in the condition where societal questions are not recognized and treated as political questions that need collective solutions on a societal level but rather as for instance economic or individual questions with the result that the current liberal-democratic and capitalistic power structure is naturalized and framed as politically taken for granted?

Working schematically with these two ideal figures; the citizen as the archetype of the political and the tourist as the archetype of the postpolitical, the idea in this chapter is that the contemporary political citizen is challenged by the postpolitical tourist, a paradigmatic figure that has, as discussed above, been a constant companion to the figure of *polis*. The reasoning thus parallel critical accounts on tourism encounters and controversies, of tourists as invaders in different regards, destroying destinations, cultures and nature through the creation of serial tourist districts without place specific characteristics (Augé, 1995; MacCannell, 1976; Turner and Ash, 1976) as well as accounts on the "tourist syndrome" and other attempts to argue that tourism is a cipher to understand the contemporary world in all its diversity and heterogeneousness (Franklin, 2003; 2004). These are all however sociological, mainly ontic or empirical accounts based on critical social theory. This chapter relies on an ontological and relational reasoning in political philosophy with a topological reasoning, vocabulary and set of concepts, in order to give further food for thoughts. While there is a tendency in sociological accounts to try to prove the empirical validity of theoretical ideas by showing their realist correspondence, the argumentative strategy in this chapter is of another kind – pushing lateral thinking to its (imaginative) limits through suggesting topologically outstretched relations between concepts and phenomenon. This is done through lateral thinking, a grip which mobilises and juxtaposes thematically speaking very different sociological ideas and ideas from philosophies of inquiry. In a fashion that may seem reductionist from a naturalistic point of view, I hope to engage (and in some sense provoke) the reader and challenge his or hers ontological horizon.

How is this lateral thinking executed or operationalized? How to epistemologically approach this ontological encounter between the political citizen and the postpolitical tourist, how to flesh-out this ontological reasoning in order to make it graspable and illustrative? The approach chosen here is to play with the idea that in the collective cultural imaginary (i.e. popular culture), the postpolitical tourist can be envisioned as an inhuman but increasingly humanized figure – the vampire. Following Diken and Laustsen (2008), popular culture is considered not as a representative of the social (the actual society) but as an indicator of the virtual (the coming society) that persists alongside the actual society. Human vampires do not exist (literary at least) but vampire movies nevertheless are real phenomenon, social facts. Consequently, the tension between the political citizen and the postpolitical tourist (as a humanized vampire) is unfolded through the discussion of vampire movies – here the popular *Twilight Saga* movie series (*Twilight* [2008], *New Moon* [2009], *Eclipse* [2010], *Breaking Dawn part I* [2011] and *Breaking Dawn part II* [2012]). In these movies the political citizen Bella becomes romantically involved with the vampire Edward. Edward is however not a ruthless beast of the night. Edward is a hunk, but an inhuman hunk – a humanized vampire.

The *Twilight Saga* is a part of the current increase of vampire movies in which vampires are humanized but still inhuman. The movie series and the vampire renaissance in general also address a wider topic of political philosophy of interest here – the tension between the human and the inhuman. Is the interest in inhuman or monstrous figures stemming from an increased awareness in the cultural imaginary (and unfolded in contemporary popular culture) that the human will not suffice (physiologically, mentally, and cognitively) in an extrapolated postpolitical capitalism? Is it not like this, after all, that hovering about outside *polis*, the nonhuman figures keep reminding us that the walls of *polis* in no way are eternal barriers. *Polis* is a topological spatiality (Agamben, 1998) – a threshold on which humans and nonhumans are placed upon, side by side – and whenever the sovereign power of contemporary capitalist societal order finds it suitable, human and nonhumans may very well change positions?

After all, is not the zombie the perfect consumer, the superhero, the perfect defender of *status quo*, and the robot, the perfect service worker? The humanized but still inhuman vampire, we could argue, is the perfect sophisticated experience seeking tourist. The vampire thus becomes the figure of the postpolitical proper, a tourist-vampire that with a passive nihilistic (hedonistic) take on the world without political or civil attachments to the local communities it passes through, dependent on the energy/blood of others, like the tourist is dependent on the comforts of (ever new) tourist destinations. In this reasoning, the vampire figure thus symbolises a figure that gives in to the imperative of the contemporary capitalist system: to consume without limits and enjoy it! This does not mean that tourists are easily lured into such behaviour or lack the potential to engage in local communities and the politics that takes place there, or that they do not engage or give back anything. My point is that the current capitalistic, commercial society encourages the tourists to behave in a certain way, as tourists we confront a plethora of imperatives, but perhaps primarily two (interlinked): "consume" and "enjoy" (enjoy through consumption) (Kingsbury, 2005; Malone, McCabe and Smith, 2014). Naturally, the tourist is not necessarily a one-dimensional dupe that just does what is expected of him or her without reflection or contemplation. But at the same time, tourism is mobilized consumption (that also the very self-aware tourist is a part of, also the critical scholar having a beer at the Copenhagen airport before take-off) arranged so that it is increasingly difficult to not consume excessively, particularly products of hedonistic legal, semi-legal and illegal character (sugar, tobacco, heroin): 'So places of excess are often places where significant numbers of people come to be addicted. Places of excess are places of significant addiction' (Elliot and Urry, 2010, p.123). So if we concur with Franklin's remark (2004) that tourism is an ordering force in the world, perhaps *the* ordering force, then the contemporary vampire as an ideal postpolitical figure, a tourist-vampire, deserves more consideration.

This chapter contains three subparts, besides introduction and conclusion. In the next section (8.2) the postpolitical contemporary is introduced and discussed. What is the postpolitical and how does it connect to the tourist-vampire as a mobile figure increasingly trapped in an economy of *jouissance*? This reasoning is illustrated in section 8.3 "through the projector" (Diken and Laustsen, 2008), through the *Twilight Saga*. Section 8.4 discusses the tourist encounter (controversies, alternatives and orderings) in the postpolitical condition. In the conclusion (8.5) the need for a political-philosophical turn in tourism theory is addressed.

8.2   The Postpolitical Tourist[1]

The position and vitality of politics in contemporary society and to what degree the world is still democratic after the claim of the "end of history" (Fukuyama, 1992) is an ongoing discussion in political theory (Swyngedouw, 2009; 2010; 2011a; 2011b; for a critical comment, see McCarthy, 2013). The theoretical starting point is Rancière's writings (1998) on the ontology of politics and his ambition to update Aristotle's political theory. Rancière outlines a distinction between "the political", "politics" and "the police". "The political" is the unfolding space, the actualized arena in which political demands and disagreement of the marginalized ("politics")

---

1   Parts of this subsection are rewritten and shortened texts of a similar section in Ek and Tesfahuney (submitted).

is formulated so that the order of and in society ("the police") is challenged. The postpolitical catches the claim that in the society today, politics in its general sense has become increasingly synonymous with "the police" (an upholding of a certain societal order) while politics as a radical questioning of the current societal order and an urgent call for societal change is not seen, recognized or related to as political in nature. "Politics" in this postpolitical shape is thus quite synonymous to managerial-like principles of distribution, allocation and administration of and in society not as a distribution or allocation that fundamentally challenges the societal order or asymmetrical relations of power or even admits the existence of an existing disagreement (Dikeç, 2005; Swyngedouw, 2009). Critical thinking that challenges the liberal, consumer-materialist capitalistic world order, is foreclosed and isolated, conceptualized as something else than politics and thus out-defined. To Žižek (and also Mouffe, 2005) the postpolitical is the out-definition of the presence of ideology in politics, especially the rejection of ideological distinctions and the claims of universal, metaphysical, political demands. In other words, the centre of political ontology has been emptied out and replaced with postpolitical mechanisms and practices (Žižek, 1999). Postpolitics expresses a managerial approach to government: governing societies is considered as a technological, administrative and expert-bound craft rather than a conduct anchored in ontological, metaphysical and ideological commitments (Žižek, 2002).

What used to be considered to be topics of political nature is more and more defined as of no political character but instead of, primarily, economic character (and thus something that should be solved by market mechanisms and not through political decisions on a societal level), or of individual, moral, nature (and something for each person to handle and be responsible for). Topics and issues that are not recognized as political also become difficult to address as topics of societal matter, or problems that preferably is handled on a societal, collective level. The postpolitical thus enhances the neoliberal dogma that there is no "society" (in the shape of collective solidarity based on class consciousness for instance) but rather that the societal is only an accumulation of individuals.

But in what sense is the postpolitical an inhuman societal condition, what is postpolitical monstrosity? Taking departure from Marxian contemporary analysis (McNally, 2011), capitalism is monstrous in its systematic alienation, its creative destruction, its commodification of abstract labour, colonization, exploitation and unlimited expansion of nature and its opening up of markets of whatever kind. Capitalism self-referentially exists only for itself, has become its own final destination (Cederström and Fleming, 2012). But so normalized and naturalized has capitalism become through its colonization of the everyday life that an arsenal of de-familiarizing approaches within critical social theory have to be mobilized, and through estrangement effects unfold the bizarre and the monstrous of everyday capitalism (McNally, 2011, p.2–6).

What is the place of the tourist in the monstrous postpolitical contemporary? The postpolitical tourist bears several of the attributes that Simmel ascribed to the figure of the stranger: 'If wandering considered as a state of detachment from every given point in space, is the conceptual opposite of attachment to any point, then the sociological form of "the stranger" presents a synthesis, as it were, of both these forms' (Simmel, 1971, p.143). As Simmel's stranger, the postpolitical tourist embodies the topological synthesis of proximity and distance, the familiar and alien. Key here is mobility as the relations of the postpolitical tourist with the places and people visited are usually if not always transient and fleeting as there is no explicit imperative directed towards the typical tourist to engage in the situation of homeless people. There is rather an imperative directed towards the destination to get rid of homeless people on places where tourists abound, like railway stations. The postpolitical tourist is thus not bound up organically with the goings of the polity, the *polis*. The postpolitical tourist may physically be in a place, but not of it, that is not a part of the local society of the places visited (Bauman, 1993). The postpolitical tourist is not like the wanderer who comes today and goes tomorrow, but one who comes today and stays tomorrow, an absent-but-still-present anomaly, not really one of "us" or one of "them" (Andersson Cederholm, 1999, p.106).

As such, the postpolitical tourist has a status of being immune; exempt from commitments and liabilities (Derrida, 2005), more precisely exempt from the *munis,* communal burdens, responsibilities, tasks. The postpolitical tourist is similar to the sovereign subject that decides the house rule, but from a privileged position outside the *polis*. The postpolitical tourist is a sometimes visible, sometimes invisible agent spurring various destination branding and city marketing strategies. Perhaps we could use another literary example, The Cheshire Cat with its mischievous grin in Lewis Carroll's *Alice's Adventures in Wonderland*: 'The Cat only grinned when it saw Alice. It looked good-natured, she thought: still it had *very* long claws and a great many teeth, so she felt that it ought to be treated with respect' (Carroll, 2000, p.64, original emphasis). When the Cat disappears the last thing to be visible is its grin, and if it is a malevolent or benevolent grin is impossible to say. The tourist also smiles, saying "what a lovely place", but the tourist developers do still not know if they are going to return, or stay for a longer time than planned. Still, places are turned into touristic places in order to attract the postpolitical tourists. Perhaps post-industrial cities should rather be seen as touristic cities as whole cityscapes are laid out and arranged to satisfy the pleasures and preferences of the tourist? The tourist is in practice at the heart of spectacle society (Debord, 1994), a society in which hedonism is no longer a choice, but an imperative (Žižek, 2000).

As conventions, norms and values are suspended, the hedonistic imperative is even enforced, because for the postpolitical tourist, 'a change in place becomes a justification for the change in morals' (Littlewood, 2002, p.37). The absence of binding commitments is characteristic for the economy of *jouissance* and as thematic commercial spaces of experience and enjoyment are staged to suit the pleasure-economy, the hedonistic drives are enhanced even further. Crucial here is Simmel's remark (1971, p.143) that 'spatial relations not only are determining conditions of relationships among men (*sic*), but are also symbolic of those relationships'. Personal principles and social proscriptions are encouraged to be thrown out with the consequence that the economy of *jouissance* de-humanizes both the postpolitical tourist and the objects of his or her enjoyment. Events and experiences which are not included in the predetermined supply of carefully controlled market forces are removed and/or banished, like street musicians or beggars. The result is a postpolitical tourist that wanders around in "secure" touristic places of circulation, in the bubble of connected hedonistic enclaves, eventually with a nagging feeling of being trapped. The all-inclusive resort tourism is one ample example of a tourist space in which pleasure is reduced to a lifestyle hospitality protocol that efficiently suffocates all kind of alterity (MacCannell, 2000), gluttony (Koc, 2013) and psychological sublimation (Kingsbury, 2011). The imperative to enjoy that is the cornerstone of the hedonistic spirit is thus emptied-out, as pleasure is arranged and unfolded in predestined places. So besides being a dehumanized creature of the market (while the political citizen is a creature of the *polis*), the postpolitical tourist is essentially an empty person, hollowed-out by the economy of *jouissance* that simultaneously nurtures him or her.

The postpolitical societal order makes it possible for the tourist to give full expression to hedonistic desires as a living dead within the scope of mass consumption. The hedonistic drive implies that postpolitical tourist – like a herd of living dead – wanders in predestined paths from one touristic place to another, consuming stylised pleasures offered by the tourist industry. Rather than appeasing the hunger of the postpolitical tourist, the touristic consumption culture increases it (Žižek, 1996). Since the postpolitical tourist is a privileged figure when it comes to mobility s/he is free to roam for whatever it desires, wherever (new opening and development of "new" destinations is another rationality that plays a prominent role in the pleasure economy). In that sense the tourist is a new cosmopolitan ideal subject, a global subject that the time-space compression mobility machine has created through territorialisation and touristification of the world. There is thus no coincidence that the postpolitical security doctrine, the "war on terror", is increasingly about securing events and the peace in cities (so the inflow of tourists remains) and securing the mobility of tourists all over the world.

8.3 The Tourist-Vampire and the Citizen

Using metaphorical tropes and inhuman figures to illustrate and sharpen a theoretical critique of the contemporary society is a well-established course of action in the social sciences. The future of the human, the human city (*polis*) and the possibility of an actual apocalypse is a topic that is well illustrated through science fiction (Shaw, 2013). Monstrous and undead figures (May, 2010; Shildrick, 2002; Waller, 1986) have been invoked in order to shed light on human (Western) culture in order to present a cultural critique (Parker, 2005). The two most prominent monstrous figures are probably the zombie and the vampire. Some scholars have used the zombie metaphor to characterise neoliberalism and neoliberal politics, with no new ideas about how to handle the 2007–2008 economic crisis but still dominant ideologically (Giroux, 2011; Smith, 2008; Peck, 2010; Quiggin, 2010). The zombie has also been acknowledged as a metaphor for a sedated state of mind and an overflow of consumption in advanced capitalism (Horne, 1992; Lauro and Embry, 2008). Also, it has been seen as the embodiment of different cultural and geopolitical anxieties after 9/11 (Bishop, 2010; Dendle, 2007; Saunders, 2012) as the political anxiousness regarding the bare life of "displaced" humans (Schinkel, 2009; Stratton, 2011).

In critical social theory the vampire however is the most well-known figure due to Marx's invocation of the vampire in his ambition to reveal the nature of capital: 'Capital is dead labour, that, vampire-like, only lives by sucking living labour, and lives the more, the more labour it sucks. The time during which the labourer works, is the time during which the capitalist consumes the labour-power he has purchased of him' (Marx, 1867/1976, p.342, see also MacLellan, 2013; Neocleous, 2003; 2005). The vampire has also been addressed as a figure that expresses a cultural anxiety, a threat towards conservative values like heterosexuality and ethical purity (Heidenreich, 2012). But at the same time, vampire screen works like *Buffy the Vampire Slayer*, *Angel*, *True Blood* and *Twilight* have focused on the (female) erotic attraction of the vampire (as a hunk) rather than the fear of the vampire (as a despicable monster) (Backstein, 2009; Beck, 2011; Clements, 2011).

In tourism however, the vampire or other inhuman figures have not so far been invoked in order to enrich tourism studies (An exception is the growing and very interesting research field of "pop-culture tourism") (see further Crowe, 2013 and Larson, Lundberg and Lexhagen, 2013). In this section, the two archetypes of the citizen and the tourist-vampire are thus juxtaposed in order to illustrate the encounter between the political and the postpolitical.

8.3.1 Citizen Bella Swan meets Tourist-Vampire Edward Cullen

The *Twilight Saga* movies is based on four books by Stephanie Meyer (2005; 2006; 2007; 2008) in which the love story of Bella and Edward is unfolded. In the first movie, *Twilight*, Bella has just moved from Phoenix to Forks, a small community of 3,120 inhabitants in the state of Washington in the northwest corner of the US. Leaving her mum and stepdad, she has come to live with her dad, the chief of police in the community. In her new school, she meets Edward Cullen; one of five foster children living with the city doctor Carlisle and his wife Esme. They immediately feel attraction even if it does not run that smoothly right away. Bella eventually finds out that the Cullens are vampires, but only living on animal blood. This does not diminish their feelings, even if it does complicate things. For once, Edward must constantly stop himself from sucking blood from Bella, killing her in the process (a bit of a detail!). Further, the family's secret is threatened to be revealed, something that would force them to leave the geographical area. During a family baseball game, three nomadic vampires show up, and one of them, James, finds out about Bella being a human and feels an irresistible urge to suck her dry of blood. The rest of the first movie is then about the Cullen family protecting Bella from James, eventually killing him in a violent showdown.

In the second movie, *New Moon*, Edward makes the decision to leave Bella in order not to risk her life again. The whole Cullen family moves to an unknown destination. Bella is heartbroken for several months but eventually finds comfort in the childhood friend Jacob Black, a Native American of the Quileute tribe in La Push, near Forks. New complications arrive as Jacob, reaching a certain maturity, finds out he is a werewolf. The werewolves and the vampires are mortal enemies, and the werewolves see it as their task to protect humans from the vampires. One of the surviving nomadic vampires from the first movie, Laurent, shows up with the intention of killing Bella in order to revenge James' death on the behalf of Victoria, James' former lover. Bella is saved by the werewolves, but Edward is misinformed, believing Bella is dead. Edward travels to the city of Volterra in Italy, in grief in order to end his life through the hands of the Volturi, the most ancient (more than 3,000 years) and powerful vampire coven. Bella follows Edward in order to stop his suicide and the two lovers are eventually reunited.

The third movie, *Eclipse*, starts with Edward trying to persuade Bella to marry him while Bella wants Edward to make her into a vampire. Edward is very hesitant towards her idea but eventually agrees, but only after the wedding. Old threats rise on the horizon, however, as Victoria is orchestrating an army of new-born vampires in Seattle. Due to the fact that blood still runs in their veins, new-born vampires are more fierce and stronger than "established" vampires like the Cullens. Simultaneously, Jacob falls deeper in love with Bella and wants her to choose him instead of Edward. Even if Bella is attracted to Jacob, her heart still belongs to Edward. In the final face-off against Victoria's army of new-born, the Cullens form a fragile alliance with the werewolves in order to protect Bella. The new-born army is defeated, and Victoria is killed, but the Volturi show up at the battlefield, ordering the Cullens to turn Bella into a vampire in order to protect the secret of the vampires' existence.

Breaking Dawn Part One, the fourth movie, begins with the declaration of the wedding between Edward and Bella, making Jacob furious. The problem is that Edward could easily kill Bella in the expected sexual act in connection to the wedding due to his inhuman strength. The wedding still takes place, followed by a honeymoon on the Isle Esme, Cullen's private island. The marriage is consummated as planned. What comes as a surprise, however, is Bella's pregnancy, as vampires are not supposed to be able to conceive a child. The foetus is growing unnaturally fast literally draining the life out of Bella. Carlisle the doctor is helpless as the medical situation is unique. It seems like the birth will kill Bella as she refuses to be turned into a vampire with the child still in her womb. The plan is however to deliver the child and then turn Bella into a vampire even if the chance that she will live is small. New complications arrive however, as the werewolf pack becomes aware of the child. As a child with unknown capacities and urges it poses a threat to the whole community of Forks, guarded by the werewolves. The werewolves decide to kill the baby, even if some of them, as Jacob, decide to protect the newborn half-vampire half-human child. The confrontation between werewolves and vampires is however stopped before any causalities rise, as Jacob is imprinted on the child (a werewolf thing, to fall unconditionally in agapic love, a heavenly love in contrast to an erotic love (Kokkola, 2011)) making her untouchable by werewolf rules. And Bella wakes up, as a vampire.

Breaking Dawn Part Two is the fifth and last movie. Now Bella experiences her senses enormously enhanced being a vampire. The tension between her and Jacob is gone now when Jacob is imprinted on her daughter, Renesmee, who grows more quickly than a human child. New dark skies rises on the horizon however, as a former lover of Laurent and a cousin to the Cullen's foster kids, Irina, reveals Renesmee's existence to the Volturi. Immortal vampire children cannot be restrained and have destroyed whole villages back in history and are thus a serious threat to the secrets of the existence of vampires. Volturi arrives at Forks in full number and is met by the Cullens and allied vampire and coven clans. Volturi is showed that Renesmee is not a vampire child but a half-vampire and thus mortal. Aro, the head of the Volturi is however a greedy person and is looking for a fight in order to increase the Volturi's power. The fight is however avoided, as Alice Cullen, with the ability to foresee the future, shows Aro how the fight would end – Aro himself being one of the many killed vampires in the eventual fight. The Volturi leave and the family can finally be united in peace and harmony.

The *Twilight* franchise has received much attention in academic studies, especially through feminist accounts of the different gender stereotypes that can be found in both the novels and the movies (Happel and Esposito, 2010; Kokkola, 2011; Lindén, 2013; Silver, 2010; Taylor, 2011). In the next section, I instead focus on the encounters between the human and inhuman figures of the drama and the physical settings for these encounters.

8.3.2   The Polis, the Forest, the Beach and the Open

The events depicted in the saga take place in several different locations that can be related to the spatial grammar of *polis* (spaces of the *polis* and spaces outside the *polis*). The different figures (human and non-human) are also related to certain places. The small community of Forks represents *polis*-Gemeinschaft, the traditional notion of a small community with strong ties, where everyone knows everyone. Bella arrives to Forks but remains a bit estranged. Her father is the chief of the police and according to its slogan, her school; Forks High School is "Home of the Spartans". Her friends (with different ethnic origins) welcome her but there is something missing.

The forest is the place of Edward and his foster family. The Cullens are living in the forest in a larger, luxurious, seemingly architect design house. The vampires reign in this state of nature as they are free to hunt animals for their blood. The forest is the place in which Bella confronts Edward about him being a vampire and it is also the place in which he reveals his supernatural powers to her. It is also in the forest that Edward in *Full Moon* abandons Bella (in order to not risk her life any longer); Bella gets lost, falls asleep but is eventually saved by the leader of the werewolves, Sam. In contrast to the forest, the beach is the place where Bella gets involved with

Jacob. On the beach, Jacob informs Bella about the legend of the "cold one" (a lead that makes her eventually find out about the inhuman nature of Edward), that he is a werewolf and that he loves her. The beach becomes the limit between life and death. In *Full Moon* Bella cliff dives (as a part of her mourning and self-destructive behaviour) and is about to drown when Jacob rescues her from drowning.

As the saga unfolds, the open increasingly becomes the central place of events. In the opening of *Eclipse* Bella and Edwards claim the open as their space. On a meadow they persuade each other, as Edward wants to marry Bella and Bella wishes Edward to turn her into a vampire. The open is repeatedly a terrain that needs to be defended against different threats coming out of the forest. In the beginning of *Full Moon* Bella dreams that she is on a meadow and an old lady walks out of the forest. At first, she thinks it is her grandma, but she then realises that it is her, as an old lady, and at the same time Edward shows up in the dream, still looking like he is seventeen. The open is also a battlefield in *Eclipse* and *Breaking Dawn Part II* as the Cullens, in alliance with the werewolves, first confront Victoria's new-born army of vampires and later in the saga the Volturi, dramatically entering the open from the misty dark forest. The last movie also ends out in the open, with the happy postpolitical community/family (see next section) finally at rest, looking forward to a long "life" together.

The Open could here be understood as a postpolitical space that is unfolded or created, a space in-between the *polis* and the state of nature or perhaps a caesura (break/cut) between the human and the animal. The anthropological machine (set of discourses that decide what is to be considered being human, see further Agamben, 2004) opens up this metaphysical space of the non-human creature, outside both the forest and the village, outside *polis* and the state of nature.

8.3.3   The Citizen, the Tourist-Vampire and the Werewolf

Bella the citizen meets and falls in love with a humanized vampire. The Cullens are living only on animals, seeing themselves as "vegetarians". But this way of life comes at a cost: '*It's like a human only living on tofu*' (*Twilight*), a sacrifice but a price worth it: '*I don't want to be a monster*' (*Twilight*). But it is not that easy; in *Breaking Dawn Part I* Edward confesses to Bella '*All the men I killed were monsters ... and so was I*'. For some time Edward killed and sucked out the blood of murderers, but even if they were "monsters" they were still humans. His body is also inhumanely cold, a fact that is several times contrasted to Jacob's inhumanely warm body, as Bella notices in *New Moon*; '*You're just warm, you're like your own sun.* Hiding out in the mountain the night before the showdown in *Eclipse*, Jacob's warm body literally saves Bella's life as she is about to freeze to death. The werewolf Jacob is the contrast to the vampire Edward (warm/hot, mortal/ immortal, an inhuman out of heritage/an inhuman turned) but still they have similarities; they are both aggressive and territorial by nature even if the vampires move back and forth between territories while the werewolves are stationary.

Bella is the human who wants to be inhuman; '*I am nothing, I am human, I am nothing*'(*New Moon*) she says to Edward, as well as '*death is simple, life is harder*'

(*Twilight*). That this is more than infatuation or because of her love to Edward is eventually revealed, with Edward she feels; '*more real, more myself, because it's my world too, it's where I belong*'. She confesses that for her whole life she has been and felt detached and desynchronised with the world on an existential level. When she finally enters the scene as an inhuman, in the beginning of *Breaking Dawn Part II* she declares: '*My time as a human was over ... but I never felt so alive ... I was born to be a vampire*'. She meets her father, now as a vampire. He, still human, confesses '*My daughter looks like my daughter ... but doesn't*'. The perhaps key scene of the saga is when he hugs his daughter, sensing her coldness but without comment upon it. She now has the same temperature as Edward and with her new powers she exploits the forest with inhuman speed and strength as well as with inhuman senses of vision and hearing.

She now also belongs to a family of strangers or passers-by, as the Cullens move around. Since they do not age they have to move in order to not reveal their true nature. They do not feel totally placeless but neither do they develop deeper relations to the communities they live close-by. Carlisle works as a doctor and thus contributes to the well-being of the society. But also, medicinal practice is an easy way to supply the family with donated human blood (convenient when Bella's foster needs human blood still inside the womb in *Breaking Dawn Part I*). They are constantly aware that they will move on, in contrast to the werewolves who are stationary with a clear existential mission; to protect the humans against vampires. Bella and Edward discuss this shortly in *Breaking Dawn Part II* when Bella exclaims '*I am gonna miss this place*' and Edward replies '*We'll come back, we always do*'.

Belonging to the family of inhuman tourist-vampires rather than to the community of humans is stressed again and again in the two last movies, implying the shift from a political agonistic tension between humans, werewolves and vampires to a postpolitical consensus between humans, werewolves and vampires. The consensus is however a chimera as it is a postpolitical condition in which the vampires reign, spelled out in the open when Edward claims to Jacob in *Breaking Dawn Part I*: '*Bella is part of the family now*' and Jacob replies '*Yeah, I can see that. It really is a family ... as strong as the one I was born into*'. The love triangle between Bella, Edward and Jacob is dissolved (and at the same time the postpolitical consensus disclosed) when Renesmee imprints Jacob. In the last movie, the postpolitical order is defended against the Volturi. The very last scene of the last movie shows the postpolitical family smiling towards each other, bathing in a religious illumination, indicating that there is nothing outside the light.

8.4   The Tourist Encounter in the Postpolitical

It does not end well for Yakov Petrovich Golyadkin as he is declared insane by his doctor, and put in an asylum. His double, probably a figure of his schizophrenic imagination, seemingly triumphs. It ends better for Bella, as she joins her new postpolitical family of undead vampires as an undead herself. Golyadkin comes out of his encounter with his "tourist/double" as mad, apparently, as he is unable to adapt to the contradictory and different behaviour of his friend-become antagonist. Bella on the other hand adapts by letting herself be transformed into a tourist, thus mentally "surviving" her encounter with the vampire-tourist Edward. Ontologically, the tourist encounter that takes place in *The Twilight Saga* results in the disclosure of the human and the triumph of the unfolded inhuman (presented as more alive than the disclosed human in the movies). Bella abandons *polis*, and finds her place in the postpolitical consensus (a consensus that is invoked by force and violent measures) and in a family based on the household (*oikos*) rather than a community principle. As strangers to the *polis* and to humans, the family of vampire-tourists has opened up an ontological and postpolitical space between Commonwealth and the state of nature – a state of exception in which they reign as sovereigns.

Thus, ontologically speaking, the citizen is eradicated in the tourist encounter; either as the citizen abandons *polis* or *polis* abandons the citizen (puts him in the asylum). In both cases a caesura is created between the citizen and *polis*. Can we find any empirical indications of this caesura and is the caesura completely total, is the isolation complete? In order to say something about the empirical indications, we need to address the messiness of the world, and see the ontic or empirical as socio-material assemblages in a relentless state of becoming, appearance and disappearance (and different social topologies of disappearance of appearances and appearance of disappearances). One ontic phenomenon or empirical trajectory that, in my understanding, enhances the caesura between the citizen-cum-tourist and *polis* is the increased use of mobile technologies, digital media and technological artefacts. Through mobile technology, our understanding of space becomes based on other topological understandings than the topographical (Cartesian, Newtonian), as the distance variable's importance changes, not necessarily is diminished or reduced even if that is often the case, but intertwined with distances based on other spatialities than the topographical. The tourist goes through processes of ontological renegotiations with an altered understanding of space and place as a result. The tourist, as a privileged figure when it comes to being mobile, is distanced from the binary logic of topography, a process that also weakens the political sense of belonging since *polis* is based on such a topographical logic of inside/outside (Ek, 2012).

Another factor that separates the tourist from the *polis* more directly is the growth of digital tourism social media. The interactive potential that is unfolded through the internet and particularly social media 2.0 is usually regarded as a community beneficial practice and a technological setting that eventually enriches democracy and public participation. But this interpretation is too optimistic. Social media is very much anchored in a commercial electronic infrastructure (commercial platforms like Trip Advisor and Facebook) in which user-generated content is integrated and turned into corporate profit. Online communities are weak in accountability and responsibility and the social media practice per se encourages digital narcissism and consumer centricity (Munar and Ek, submitted). Again, it is not that political, community-based engagement or a questioning of the postpolitical consensus is not possible through social media, or that the tourist is not capable of engaging in the politics of a destination using mobile technology and digital media. It is just something that is not encouraged. The most prominent imperatives are economic and commercial: 'enjoy, and let your friends know you are enjoying yourself through social media' and 'increase and expose your cultural capital (tourist capital?) through pointing out the countries you have visited on a visited countries world map'. Tourism social media nurtures the passive nihilism (hedonism) of the postpolitical tourist rather than the political activism of the citizen.

Is there no escape, is the caesura an abyss impossible to transgress? The understanding of space in this chapter as well as in the anthology in its entirety has been that spaces (and power) are relational and can be approached topologically. As relations and interaction between humans, actualized in socio-material assemblages in general, are always subject to change, no absolute ontological or empirical divisions or distinctions exist. Bella's father still hugs his then unhuman daughter, and even if he feels her unnaturalness (her cold body) he does not pass remark on it. The Cullen family, even if they have to move around in order to preserve their secret, still seems to feel something for Forks, if not for the community than at least for the geographical area in itself. Perhaps they are, after all, not immune to politics, a politics of propinquity of sorts, even if it requires new entanglements of identities and responsibilities (Amin, 2004; Massey, 2004)? Change is then a question of probability rather than potentiality, change is always possible, the question is how probable this change is.

8.5 Conclusion

Taking tourism seriously obliges an ambition to seek out all its shapes and characteristics, all its encounters and im/material implications not only when and where tourism is expected to appear and unfold but also – perhaps especially also – when and where it is not expected to appear and unfold. This implies that the contact surfaces between tourism studies and other research fields or academic disciplines need to increase still more than is the case today. Tourism studies or tourism theory needs to address how tourism, tourism practices and the tourism industry are part of the postpolitical trajectory and condition, an inherent part of forced capitalism-driven *jouissance*, obligatory consumption and forceful biopolitical hospitality. Now, tourism theory is no stranger to philosophical accounts of biopolitics and power (see particularly Minca, 2009; 2012 and Chapter 9 this volume) but there is more to do here, a need in a political-philosophical way to address the ontological encounter between the citizen and the tourist. This encounter takes place "everywhere" in the sense that it can (or will) unfold wherever people are, humans that are engaging the materiality and agency of the world (Gren and Huijbens, 2012) and engaging each other, often through increasingly small, mobile technological artefacts that not only enhance the world-picture but increase the postpolitical trajectory as well (Munar and Ek, submitted).

Taking tourism seriously implies thus that ontological figures like the vampire and the citizen are discussed in different ways, not only as a certain approach towards or engagement in the world, not only as an encounter between the human and the world, but also as an encounter of humans and thus a biopolitical topic. The citizen as a figure and *polis* as a mode of organization of society expresses a certain sociality, a societal situation that in different ways is challenged and undermined in the encounter with the tourist as a figure of a postpolitical mode of order. In the end the question pivots on the topic of community and how people encounter each other as subjects of a capitalistic regime that encourage individualistic passive nihilistic consumerist society in which each human interaction is a value-based transaction. Thus, we need to be more human and to a lesser degree fulfil the role of the floating experience-seeker travelling through hospitality landscapes of sight-seeing and leisure consumption. Travelling requires an engagement *in* the world, not a floating movement *through* the world.

References

Agamben, G., 1998. *Homo Sacer: Sovereign power and bare life*. Stanford: Stanford University Press.

Agamben, G., 2004. *The open: Man and animal*. Stanford: Stanford University Press.

Agamben, G., 2009. *What is an apparatus? And other essays*. Stanford: Stanford University Press.

Amin, A., 2004. Regions unbound: Towards a new politics of place. *Geografiska Annaler B: Human Geography*, 86(1), pp.33–44.

Andersson Cederholm, E., 1999. *Det extraordinäras lockelse: Luffarturistens bilder och upplevelser*. Lund: Arkiv.

Augé, M., 1995. *Non-places: Introduction to an anthropology of supermodernity*. London: Verso.

Backstein, K., 2009. (Un)safe sex: Romancing the vampire. *Cineaste*, 38(Winter), pp.38–41.

Bauman, Z., 1993. *Postmodern ethics*. Oxford: Blackwell.

Beck, B., 2011. Fearless vampire kissers: Bloodsuckers we love in Twilight, True Blood and others. *Multicultural Perspectives*, 13(2), pp.90–92.

Bishop, K.W., 2010. *American zombie gothic. The rise and fall (and rise) of the walking dead in popular culture*. Jefferson, NC and London: McFarland & Company.

Carroll, L., 2000. *The annotated Alice: The definitive edition. Introduction and notes by Martin Gardner*. New York: W.W. Norton & Company.

Cederström, C. and Fleming, P., 2012. *Dead man working*. Winchester: Zero Books.

Clements, S., 2011. *The vampire defanged: How the embodiment of evil became a romantic hero*. Ada, MI: Brazos Press.

Crowe, J., 2013. The Twilight of Forks? The effect of social infrastructure on film tourism and community development in Forks, WA. *Journal of Rural Social Sciences*, 28(1), pp.1–25.

Debord, G., 1994. *The society of the spectacle*. New York: Zone Books.

Dendle, P., 2007. The zombie as barometer of cultural anxiety. In: N. Scott, ed. *Monsters and the monstrous. Myths and metaphors of enduring evil*. Amsterdam and New York: Rodopi.

Derrida, J., 2005. *Lagens kraft: Auktoritetens mystiska fundament*. Eslöv: Östlings Bokförlag Symposion.

Dikeç, M., 2005. Space, politics and the political. *Environment and Planning D: Society and Space*, 23(2), pp.171–188.

Diken, B. and Laustsen, C.B., 2008. *Sociology through the projector*. London: Routledge.

Ek, R., 2012. Topologies of human-mobile assemblages. In: R. Wilken and G. Goggin eds. *Mobile technology and place*. New York: Routledge.

Ek, R. and Tesfahuney, M., (submitted) The paradigmatic tourist. In: T.B. Jamal and A.M. Munar, eds. *Tourism research paradigms*. Bingley: Emerald.

Elliot, A. and Urry, J., 2010. *Mobile lives*. Abingdon: Routledge.

Franklin, A., 2003. The tourism syndrome: An interview with Zygmunt Bauman. *Tourism Studies*, 3(2), pp.205–217.

Franklin, A., 2004. Tourism as an ordering: Towards a new ontology of tourism. *Tourist Studies,* 4(3), pp.277–303.

Fukuyama, F., 1992. *The end of history and the last man*. New York: The Free Press.

Giroux, H.A., 2011. *Zombie politics and culture in the age of casino capitalism*. New York: Peter Lang.

Gren, M. and Huijbens, E.H., 2012. Tourism theory and the Earth. *Annals of Tourism Research*, 39(1), pp.155–170.

Happel, A. and Esposito, J., 2010. Vampires, vixens and feminists: An analysis of Twilight. *Educational Studies*, 46(5), pp.524–531.

Heidenreich, L., 2012. Vampires among us. *Peach Review: A Journal of Social Justice*, 24(1), pp.92–101.

Horne, P., 1992. I shopped with a zombie. *Critical Quarterly*, 34(4), pp.97–110.

Kingsbury, P., 2005. Jamaican tourism and the politics of enjoyment. *Geoforum*, 36(1), pp.113–132.

Kingsbury, P., 2011. Sociospatial sublimation: The human resources of love in Sandals Resorts International, Jamaica. *Annals of the American Geographers*, 101(3), pp.650–669.

Koc, E., 2013. Inversionary and liminoidal consumption: Gluttony on holidays and obesity. *Journal of Travel & Tourism Marketing*, 30(8), pp.825–838.

Kokkola, L., 2011. Virtuous vampires and voluptuous vamps: Romance conventions reconsidered in Stephanie Meyer's "Twilight" Series. *Children's Literature in Education*, 42(2), pp.165–179.

Larson, M., Lundberg, C. and Lexhagen, M., 2013. Thirsting for vampire tourism: Developing pop culture destinations. *Journal of Destination Marketing & Management*, 2(2), pp.74–84.

Lauro, S.J. and Embry, K., 2008. A zombie manifesto: The nonhuman condition in the era of advanced capitalism. *Boundary 2*, 35(1), pp.85–108.

Lindén, C., 2013. Virtue as adventure and excess: Intertextuality, masculinity, and desire in the Twilight Series. *Culture Unbound: Journal of Current Cultural Research*, 5, pp.213–237.

Littlewood, I., 2002. *Sultry climates: Travel and sex since the Grand Tour*. Cambridge, MA: Da Capo Press.

MacCannell, D., 1976. *The tourist: A new theory of the leisure class*. New York: Schocken Books.

MacCannell, J.F., 2000. Urban perversions. *Third Text*, 14(51), pp.65–74.

MacLellan, M., 2013. Marx's vampires: An Althusserian critique. *Rethinking Marxism*, 25(4), pp.549–565.

Malone, S., McCabe, S. and Smith, A.P., 2014. The role of hedonism in ethical tourism. *Annals of Tourism Research*, 24, pp.241–254.

Marx, K., 1867/1976. *Capital: A critique of political economy, volume 1*. Harmondsworth: Penguin.

Massey, D., 2004. Geographies of responsibility. *Geografiska Annaler B: Human Geography*, 86(1), pp.5–18.

May, J., 2010. Zombie geographies and the undead city. *Social & Cultural Geography*, 11(3), pp.285–298.

McCarthy, J., 2013. We have never been "post-political". *Capitalism, Nature, Socialism*, 24(1), pp.19–25.

McNally, D., 2011. *Monsters of the market. Zombies, vampires and global capitalism*. Boston and Leiden: Brill.

Meyer, S., 2005. *Twilight*. London: Atom.

Meyer, S., 2006. *New moon*. London: Atom.

Meyer, S., 2007. *Eclipse*. London: Atom.

Meyer, S., 2008. *Breaking dawn*. London: Atom.

Minca, C., 2009. The island: Work, tourism and the biopolitical. *Tourism studies*, 9(2), pp.88–108.

Minca, C., 2012. No country for old men. In: C. Minca and T. Oakes, eds. *Real tourism: Practice, care and politics in contemporary travel culture*. Abingdon: Routledge.

Mouffe, C., 2005. *On the political*. London: Routledge.

Munar, A.M. and Ek, R., Tourism social media.

Neocleous, M., 2003. The political economy of the dead: Marx's vampires. *History of Political Thought*, 24(4), pp.668–684.

Neocleous, M., 2005. *The monstrous and the dead: Burke, Marx, Fascism*. Cardiff: University of Wales Press.

Parker, M., 2005. Organisational gothic. *Culture and Organization*, 11(3), pp.153–166.

Peck, J., 2010. Zombie neoliberalism and the ambidextrous state. *Theoretical Criminology*, 14(1), pp.104–110.

Quiggin, J., 2010. *Zombie economics. How dead ideas still walk among us.* Princeton and Oxford: Princeton University Press.

Rancière, J., 1998. *Disagreement: Politics and philosophy* Minneapolis: The University of Minnesota Press.

Saunders, R.A., 2012. Undead spaces: Fear, globalisation and the popular geopolitics of zombies. *Geopolitics*, 17(1), pp.80–104.

Schinkel, W., 2009. "Illegal aliens" and the state, or: Bare bodies vs. the zombie. *International Sociology*, 24(6), pp.779–806.

Shaw, D.B., 2013. Strange zones: Science fiction, fantasy and the posthuman. *City*, 17(6), pp.778–791.

Shildrick, M., 2002. *Embodying the monster. Encounters with the vulnerable self.* London: Sage Publications.

Silver, A., 2010. *Twilight* is not good for maidens: Gender, sexuality and the family in Stephanie Meyer's *Twilight* Series. *Studies in the Novel*, 42(1–2), pp.121–138.

Simmel, G., 1971. *On individuality and social forms: Selected writings*. Chicago: The University of Chicago Press.

Smith, N., 2008. Neo-liberalism: Dominant but dead. *Focaal – European Journal of Anthropology*, 51, summer edition, pp.155–157.

Stratton, J., 2011. Zombie trouble: Zombie texts, bare life and displaced people. *European Journal of Cultural Studies*, 14(3), pp.265–281.

Swyngedouw, E., 2009. The antinomies of the postpolitical city: In search of a democratic politics of environmental production. *International Journal of Urban and Regional Research*, 33(3), pp.601–620.

Swyngedouw, E., 2010. Apocalypse forever? Post-political populism and the spectre of climate change. *Theory, Culture & Society*, 27(2–3), pp.213–232.

Swyngedouw, E., 2011a. Interrogating post-democratization: Reclaiming egalitarian political spaces. *Political Geography*, 30(7), pp.370–380.

Swyngedouw, E., 2011b. Whose environment? The end of nature, climate change and the process of post-democratization. *Ambiente & Sociedade*, 14(2), pp.69–87.

Taylor, A., 2011. The urge towards love is an urge towards (un)death: Romance, masochistic desire and postfeminism in the Twilight novels. *International Journal of Cultural Studies*, 15(1), pp.31–46.

Turner, L. and Ash, L., 1976. *The golden hordes: International tourism and the pleasure periphery*. New York: St. Martin's Press.

Waller, G.A., 1986. *The living and the undead. From Stoker's Dracula to Romero's Dawn of the Dead*. Urbana and Chicago: University of Chicago Press.

Žižek, S., 1996. *For they know not what they do: Enjoyment as a political factor*. London: Verso.

Žižek, S., 1999. *The ticklish subject – The absent centre of political ontology*. London: Verso.

Žižek, S., 2000. *The fragile absolute: Or, why is the Christian legacy worth fighting for?* London: Verso.

Žižek, S., 2002. *Revolution at the gates – Žižek on Lenin – The 1917 writings.* London: Verso.

Chapter 9

Hotel California: Biopowering Tourism, from New Economy Singapore to Post-Mao China

Claudio Minca and Chin Ee Ong

This chapter focuses on care, custody and tourism and on how their associated spatial arrangements are often controlled, stewarded and monitored by the state. The title's reference to famous rock band The Eagles' 1977 song is meant to suggest the arguably contentious and biopolitical nature of some tourist spaces (Diken and Laustsen, 2004; Minca, 2009). Written by Don Felder, Don Henly and Glenn Frey, the lyrics paint a surrealistic portrait of a luxury hotel which initially appears as inviting and alluring, but turns out to be a hedonistic prison where 'you can check out anytime you like, but you can never leave' and 'where we are all just prisoners here, of our own device'. The reference to this passage intends to suggest a deliberately provocative parallel between Hotel California and many spaces that are conceived to host leisurely activities and that promise to provide care and well-being (at time even happiness and a temporary new persona), in other words, to "re-create" their willingly guests[1]. Contemporary tourism is indeed an industry often concerned with care and "custody", protection and segregation, always with "re-creation". From spa-treatments at seaside resorts to trekking in the woods, much focus is placed on recreation-as-rejuvenation of minds and bodies, and/or the realisation of more resilient individuals (Minca, 2012).

While these forms of tourism are often marketed using tropes of freedom and escape, such practices are in some cases, rather ironically, endorsed by or even regulated by the state (see, for example, Semmens' 2005 study on Nazi tourism). From the creation of specialised state-backed travel companies (see, amongst others, Grandits and Taylor, 2010; also Baranowski, 2004; 2005), to the shaping of policies conducive to travels, the state has been and often continues to be involved in the production of certain modalities of tourism, especially if aimed at governing the body politic through the incentive of varying forms of individual and collective care as part of the tourist experience (see Minca and Oakes, 2012; 2014). This chapter, thus, seeks to interrogate the extent and the ways in which this involvement represents a deliberate attempt on the part of the state to biopolitically intervene in the lives of their citizenry through tourism. Accordingly, it also investigates how some state-endorsed tourism practices may be indeed bound up with control, surveillance and restrain, despite their appearance as potential fields of freedom

---

1   On enclavic tourism see Edensor, 2000.

and individual self-realisation. In this sense, we suggest that 'Hotel California' is a useful, potentially controversial, metaphor for state-sponsored tourist spaces and experiences, sometimes implemented in the form of facilitating consumerist practices presumably related to happiness, health and well-being of its indulgent citizen-consumers; these spaces, we claim, may be realms of relaxation and re-creation, but also sites where the bartender and concierge, there to serve you, also keep a close watch on you, and from where it is never too easy checking (completely) out.[2]

This discussion is facilitated through the reference to two tourism encounters in Asia: (1) Singapore-state endorsed adventure tourism in the "New Economy" years of the late 1990s and at the start of the new millennium; and (2) Chinese casino-based mass tourism to and in Macao in the post-handover years between 1999 and 2013. These two cases have relevant similarities and differences. In the first exemplary case, we discuss how a neo-liberal "new economy" discourse has shaped the Singapore state's preoccupation with adventure ideals and workplace ethics. In previous work, Ong (2005) has examined how the Singapore state, through its community-outreach organisation – *The People's Association* – has endorsed and promoted adventure training at the time of emergence of the so-called "post-Tiger Economy" – a period of social uncertainty following rapid double digit economic growth phases powered by rampant Japanese investment and subcontracting in Singapore and the other "Tiger Economies" (Lall and Albaladejo, 2004). Such a deployment of adventure tourism was indeed very much framed within the "New Economy" thinking circulating in Singapore in those days, but which was in turn shaped by a broader neoliberal regime championing flexible and adaptable workers capable of navigating and surviving treacherous economic conditions (with minimal state welfare support). Building upon Ong's (2005) earlier efforts to analyse those discursive formations, here we reflect on how such manifestations of state sponsored care and re-creation of citizen-workers may produce leisurely regimes of (self)discipline.

In the second example, we instead look at how the post-Mao Chinese state endeavours to regulate and contain middle-class aspirations and hyper-consumerism within specified spatial boundaries (Pow, 2009; Pow and Kong, 2007). More specifically, we examine how the Chinese state, through its *Individual Visit Scheme*, has tried to govern and control mass consumption (often involving indulgent experiences) at Macao's large casino resorts. Macao is thus provocatively presented here as China's Hotel California. Such a deployment of casino-based tourism, often promoted as a form of care and happiness for the travelling citizen, was indeed very much framed within discourses of mass consumption and 'middle-class' consumer culture, in particular by emphasizing the creation and/ or re-creation of a new middle-class of indulgent bodies and subjects. In both Singapore adventure tourism and Chinese mass tourism to Macao, politically-backed care took place in specific 'Hotel Californias' – alluring regulated spaces

---

2   On tourism work and biopower see, again, Minca, 2009; also Veijola, 2009.

based on pleasure-seeking and re-creation, together with the announced and promised realisation of specific idealised minds and bodies.

This chapter thus intends to show how state-sponsored tourism may indeed be a controversial field, where indirect provision of well-being is often matched by forms of control, and, moreover, by the influence of discursive formations aimed at shaping a specific kind of subjectivities, at incorporating the (for the state) qualities of the citizen turned into a docile worker/consumer. These deliberately provocative arguments are thus presented by first briefly reviewing some key literature on controversy in tourism, especially in relation to biopower, care and custody and to how these may be linked to Singapore adventure and Chinese mass tourism. Following that, we discuss the two cases, reflecting on their differing disciplinary qualities: in the case of Singapore adventure tourism, participants seem subjected to perpetual self-internalisation of adventure ideals and an 'addiction' to sublime adventure landscapes; in the Chinese casino tourism case, the whole of Macao becomes a 'hotel' some gamblers and hedonistic tourists find difficult in 'checking out'. We conclude with a few considerations on the arguments made and their wider implications for a biopolitical understanding of controversy in some late modern tourism encounters.

9.1 Tourism Controversies, Care and Custody

From Bruner's (1989) review of O'Rourke's *Cannibal Tours* to Britton's (1991) analysis of enclavic tourism in the "peripheries", tourism research has for long revealed the existence of controversial and conflicting tendencies in tourist practice: Bruner by showing the problematic nature of tourism imaginaries in projecting the desires and fantasies of the tourists on the people toured; Britton by highlighting the scalar and spatial dimensions of exploitation in tourism. Such an attention to controversy and conflict in tourism is also found in more recent research (see for example, Bianchi, 2004; Hing, 2005; Minca, 2012; Oakes, 2006; Suntikul, 2013). Drawing largely on post-structural approaches, much of these interventions have argued tourism practice and experience to be the result of existing travel epistemologies and subject formations, and the consequent contestation over such framings (Minca and Oakes, 2006a; 2012; Ong and du Cros, 2012b; Van der Duim, Ren and Jóhannesson, 2012; 2013).

In this chapter, we thus discuss the biopolitical in state-sponsored forms of tourism and some of its related controversies. In particular, we focus on the promised fulfilment of happiness, health and well-being for some specific groups of citizen-tourists. To do this, we draw upon Foucault's conceptualisation of the ways in which power began to be exercised over life, or biopower, in modern human history. One dimension of this concerned the implementation of disciplinary techniques and methods of biopower on individual bodies, which effectively fine-tuned their productive potential and abilities, simultaneously expanding their economic efficacy and maintaining their political docility (Foucault, 1990a, p.145). A second dimension was the exercise of biopower over the collective body politic – for example, by measuring and governing issues of health, reproduction, mortality – and hence the government and regulation of the population (Foucault, 1990a.; see also Philo, 2001; 2005). The use of a caring and "pastoral" power over life broadly conceived (populations), and in specific (the individual subject), is presented by Foucault as the defining characteristic and the prerequisite for the circulation of capitalistic economic relations throughout modern social life. In his *History of Sexuality* trilogy (1990a; 1990b; 1990c) Foucault explains that the deployment of power over life, the "birth" and expansion of biopower is:

> ... without question an indispensable element in the development of capitalism; the later would not have been possible without the controlled insertion of bodies into the machinery of production and the adjustment of the phenomena of population to economic process (1990a, p.140–141).

Such concerns over biopower have seen recent resonances in tourism studies (Diken and Laustsen, 2004; Minca, 2009; Minca and Oakes, 2012; Ong, Minca and Felder, forthcoming). The study of the biopolitical in tourism, on the one hand, responds to the emergence of several mainstream debates in the social sciences concerning the politicisation of life in all its forms, including its incorporation in questions of contemporary travel; on the other, despite being relatively recent, this interest in the biopolitical somehow resonates with earlier attempts at theorising the broader socio-political implications of tourism as envisaged first by MacCannell's path breaking intervention (1976), and in particular his focus on the management of labour and on the production of docile subjectivities in tourism in late capitalist societies (see, among others, the special issue on "Work in Tourism" published by *Tourist Studies* in 2009; and in particular Veijola's intervention), but also by the work on the ordering power of tourism (see, for example, Franklin, 2004; also Minca and Oakes, 2006a; 2006b) and its influence in the production of specifically gendered and/or racialised bodies (see, on the tourist body, Veijola and Jokinen's 1994 influential essay; but also Kirshenblatt-Gimblet, 1998).

Using the metaphor of "the island", Minca has thus recently examined the biopolitical and the exercise of power over life in capitalistic societies and what they entail for tourists and tourism worker. Specifically, drawing from Agamben's work, Minca (2009) identified secluded holiday and tourist resorts as spaces where Foucault's "caring" and "pastoral" powers operate, for both the tourist and the tourism worker. Often-expertly crafted as pseudo-paradises, such holiday spaces draw the tourists in with promises of rest, rejuvenation and re-creation (see also Minca, 2012). The workings of such tourism enclaves, Minca contends, were built on the twin architectures of perpetual segregation and in keeping people in place (see also, Law, Bunnell and Ong, 2007; Teo and Leong, 2006; Wilson and Richards, 2008). Such socio-spatial design entails the double suspension of disbelief on part of the tourist and the suspension of many of the outside world's rules (Edensor, 2000; Wilson and Richards, 2008). More in general, he claimed some tourism spaces to approximate Agamben's "regimes of exception" (2005), regimes supported and made possible by an array of walls and fences, and enforced and policed by private and public security forces (Minca, 2007; 2009).

In casino and adventure tourism, gamblers and adventurers too are subjected to regimes of exception of the rule that normally apply to their places of origin. The liminal, suspended and contingent nature of some of these spatialities have indeed led tourism researchers to argue that tourism spaces may sometimes be good examples of Foucault's hypothesised "heterotopias" (Foucault, 1986): from Bangkok hospitals (Bochaton and Lefebvre, 2009), to English Cathedrals (Shackley, 2002), to tour guiding life/work-spaces in Macao (Ong, 2011; Ong, Ryan and McIntosh, 2014), the creation and maintenance of such exceptional spatialities illustrate the operations of specific spatio-temporal power regimes (Salanha, 2008). However, the production of such contingent conditions requires biopolitical interventions and might indeed be related to the governmentality of the body politic. Tourism research has also contended that much of tourism is constituted of the regulation of the Self and internalisation of societal ideals at both destination and home (Bruner, 1991; Elsrud, 2001; Galani-Moutafi, 2000; Nyiri, 2009; Oakes, 1998; Sin and Minca, 2014), as much as being made up of culturally-coded escapes (Cohen, 1979; Edensor, 2000). This can take the form of tourists internalising the societal or workplace norms and values when supposedly on holiday, of tourists transforming themselves through the experience or adopting destination norms even after leaving the sites (Loker-Murphy and Pearce, 1995; Maoz, 2004; Noy and Cohen, 2005; Ong, 2005) and of tourists repeating their visits. Biopolitics may thus be inherently involved in the enactments of tourism, especially when the driving ideology behind the promotion of collective and individual leisure is about the realisation of a specific kind of citizenry. Tourism and biopolitics may thus be intertwined in the production of certain forms of leisure, of a liminal, but nonetheless highly political, nature. The bodies of the tourists may therefore become the central stage where these strategies are implemented, including forms of self-disciplining on which biopowers very often operate and thrive if successful.

9.2 Biopowering through Adventurescapes: Singapore Adventure Training and Tours

The Singapore state's investment in the care (and the inherent custody) of its people has been persistent in the past decades and is now considered a well-established fact in the lives of citizens (George, 2000). Speaking about the highly-publicised revamp of Singapore's basic healthcare insurance, the Medishield, Prime Minister Lee Hsien Loong has recently reiterated the salience of individually (but with the help of the community and the state) maintaining healthy and fit bodies:

> What I have talked about on healthcare so far is what the Government is doing,
> but there is always that aspect which the individual must do. We each have to
> take personal responsibility for ourselves, both financing and also just looking
> after our health ... But the *best way for us generally to keep healthcare costs
> down is to stay healthy and especially for older people, because for older people
> exercise is not just keeping fit or keeping well but also making friends, having the
> social contacts, the networks, the mutual support* (in Channelnewsasia, 2013).

Although Prime Minister Lee is here referring to the elder more specifically, the
quote does reveal the overarching ideology of care and custody the Singapore
government has envisaged for its citizens – driven in particular by an emphasis on
self-reliance. As illustrated in Lee's speech to the Economics Society of Singapore
on 18 June 2012:

> Whatever we do, we must uphold and strengthen the spirit of self-reliance that
> has enabled us to succeed. We will always give Singaporeans the means and the
> incentives to help themselves, for personal effort and achievement are essential
> to our sense of dignity and self-worth, and the means to achieve our vision of
> becoming a leading global city.

This basically consists of a plan where the state is involved only in providing
basic and emergency help for the most destitute, while directing and supporting
its larger populace towards what it sees as biopolitically productive activities,
or activities deemed as relevant for the maintenance of that productivity (caring
for the aged in the family and community, physical exercise and friendship) and
keeping them away from the undesirable and unproductive ones (for example,
infidelity, excessive alcohol consumption and partying) (Chua, 2002; 2003; 2010;
Fernandez, 2004).

An organisation linked to the ruling political party (The People's Action Party)
has been instrumental for the implementation of such an inherently biopolitical
tactic in the form of tourism and leisure. Known succinctly as the "People's
Association", but also in its numerous sub-permutations such as the People's
Association Youth Movement and Teens Network, this organisation was created
in 1960 with the goal of fostering racial harmony and social cohesion (Chua,
2002; Fernandez, 2004). Some argue that the People's Association had its origins
as a national building programme designed to remove pro-Communist voters
away from the opposition (Kimball, 1993). One sub-component of the People's
Association Youth Movement is the Toa Payoh Adventure Club. The Toa Payoh
Adventure Club was the winner of a People's Association award in 1996 and is
now known for its commitment and excellence in conducting outdoor activities
for both novice and experienced adventurers (Figure 9.1). The Basic Outdoor
Adventure Training Programme, its flagship training course which was attended
by more than 400 adventurers since the start of the programme in 1985, provided
the kind of care and custody Prime Minister Lee and his party deliberately

champion. In its call for participants, the club outlines the possible motivations and goals to be achieved:

> Why should I join B.O.A.T. (The Basic Outdoor Adventure Training Programme)? Because ... You are sick of the concrete jungle and want to try something new. You get to know like-minded people and expand your social circle. You want to develop personal interests and learn basic outdoor skills. You get lots of fun and excitement you'll not forget for a long time. You get real fit and an improved body physique. You get to re-discover yourself and see things from a new perspective (16th B.O.A.T. Facebook page, accessed on 5 November 2013).

Indeed, ethnographic work and interviews with past participants of the programme revealed that "good health", "happiness" and "friendship" represented important aspects of their conduct of adventure during and after the training period. Physical preparation and healthy practices were important activities in the programme. So too were social gatherings aimed at fostering friendship and social bonds (Ong, 2004). Such an adventure course, however, is shaped by a broader discourse aligning adventure and the neoliberal "new economy" ideals. Adventure training was seen to be crucial in that most Singaporean adventure tourists had undergone at

Figure 9.1   Participants at the 2004 B.O.A.T. course
Source: authors

least one adventure course to provide them with the skills needed for "adventures" (Ong, 2004; 2005). Very often, these courses were conducted by "adventure experts" and consisted of real expeditions beyond the city-state's borders.

The Singapore state's interest in adventure training for its citizens somehow lied in the self-internalisation of state-endorsed workplace ideals. One of the authors, who was involved in the 2004 training session as an active participant – during the time in which the 'new economy' rhetoric reached its peak in Singapore – in his ethnographic work has observed that groups and collectives, but also individuals conducting their own adventure tours, practices of backpacking, climbing, scuba-diving and trekking and other similar activities, were often bound up with a conception of adventure tourism as a remedy for the supposedly socio-psychologically undesirable effects of living in a "sheltered" city like Singapore (see Ong, 2005). Climbing the peaks of the world was also seen as a cure for the "soft student-citizen" or "couch potato" youths formed by the air-conditioned comfort, exactly as observed earlier at the university mountaineering programme at the National University of Singapore. It was indeed implicitly conceived by the organizers as a practice of converting the participants into potentially adventurous citizens and leaders. Singaporean trainees who travelled to Peninsula Malaysia, for example, have been adopting workplace ethics by reconfiguring these tours into "scheduled workouts" performed in attractive and appealing "outdoor gymnasia" for the shaping of their minds and bodies. The adventurer-citizen minds and bodies envisioned were to be not merely rejuvenated and rested by this experience "out there", but also strengthened and made more "resilient". Ong's (2004; 2005) previous work has focused in particular on the presumed (or expected) economic resilience of the Singaporean "citizen-worker". Here it is instead argued that the Singapore state's intervention in adventure tourism is also the result of a broader interest in the biopolitical effects of tourism, particularly concerning the health, the happiness and the bodily pleasure of its citizen-workers (Chua, 2003; 2010). While Singapore adventure tourists can be hardly described as mindless and hedonistic pleasure-seekers, the state's interest in managing time and space of its worker-citizens stems from a view of them as being potentially vulnerable to such uses and temptations.

An emphasis on their potential abilities to handle "accidents", "crisis" and other situations one cannot "pre-plan" during expeditions clearly emerged in earlier fieldwork, but also from more recent observations in the cyberspace, where new participants reflected on how such a capacity was crucial in the terrains of contemporary economic and social life. In the words of adventure trainee Guo Yiling:

> One's true capabilities can only be tested and revealed in times of danger. It is only through coming face-to-face with danger can one understand one's own strength and weaknesses and character and I am glad that I am able to face risk and danger calmly. (OMY, 2013)

This arguably resonated with the existing tensions between the ruling Party's top-down policy described above and its promotion of autonomy and contingency in the desired adventurer-citizen subject. These real and perceived fast-changing adventure terrains, like the new capitalist workplace in 'soft' capitalism of the time of study (and still today reflected in the 2013 Prime Minister's speech mentioned above), were sites where disciplined but enterprising adventurer-citizens were wanted. Landscapes of adventures were seen and experienced as outdoor laboratories for Singaporean scuba divers and adventure trainees (Ong, 2005). These outdoor settings required not just a bodily and 'touristic' engagement with the landscapes of adventure, but also an alignment of workplace and adventure, consistent with the mainstream ideology of the political and business elites in Singapore. Thus, the adventurer-citizen bodies and minds envisioned by these training programmes were bodies and minds not merely rejuvenated and re-created, but also strengthened and made more resilient for the bourgeoning economy – a truly biopolitical operation.

The suspension of 'couch potato' norms and values for these Singapore residents indeed required a combination of segregation and real open adventure in place. From the isolated settings of the adventure camps to the entirely prescribed adventure and trekking routes in Malaysian forests, it could be argued that a sort of leisurely regime of exception was put in place, within which adventurers drank from murky river waters, were exposed to the natural elements and suspended themselves (literally) from heights (for example, abseiling). This was in stark contrast to the normal social codes back at home prescribing a 'safety first approach'. The vacuum left behind by the suspension of external rules, however, were quickly replaced by norms dictated by the 'adventuring regime', for instance those related to a scuba diving adventure tourist demanding that she 'eat, sleep and dive! (only)'. Smart phones and non-adventure related items were shunned and one had to be fully immersed, metaphorically and physically, in the adventure biopolitical machinery. Like Chua's (2003) discussion of 'structured' shopping and consumerism in Singapore, such a form of regimentation was directly supported and endorsed by the Singapore state through its sponsorship of the adventure club and its activities, since it promised to re-create 'healthy bodies and minds' for the capitalist economy, while discretely minimising the subjects' political awareness and assertiveness.

Further interviews conducted in 2013 via social media with graduates of the adventure training programmes revealed that, besides the key (biopolitical) concerns recently outlined by Prime Minister Lee, playfulness, pleasure seeking and risk taking in sublime natural settings still dominate Singapore adventure tourists' conduct and practice:

> I enjoy the time I spend out in nature. It is really nice and serene here, unlike the city. Sometimes a bit wild and primitive. You cannot do things the way you do in Singapore (city). You have to go back to the basics to have real fun you know?
> (Yee Hong, graduate of the 2009 Adventure Training Programme)

Conversations and interactions in cyberspace with adventure tourists involved in the programme, revealed that adventure training and travels have indeed helped them to become more 'resilient' people. This explains why many of them have gone on to take up more adventures. In the words of Teck Seng, a graduate of an adventure training programme in 2009:

> I think if you have been an adventurer once, you are always an adventurer. You cannot see things the way you see it in the past and it is not just when we are out here. It affects us even when we are in Singapore and at home. You learn some things and you see the world differently. And you always want to return to adventure (places) and *you never really go away* (italics added).

Yet, returning to the Hotel California metaphor, the sublime environments that were so enticing for some were perceived by others as having somehow subtle constraining effects. As observed in the aftermath of the 2004–5 study, friendship and social bonding may have created the peer and social pressure shaping and at the same time limiting the adventure tourists' imaginations and practices. Many had stayed on in the club after the adventure course as trainers and leaders, or simply as seniors, even though they may not love doing adventures as much as to warrant the time and energy spent running and managing the club's activities. In that sense, the deep social bonding of participants in the adventure training programme and the adventure club have prolonged and perhaps even intensified the inherently biopolitical effects of adventure landscapes.

Interviews with these participants have showed how some of them felt constantly drawn back into these landscapes in order to "realise themselves" in line with the cultural climate of the state-endorsed "New Economy". What is more, even when these tourists did actually 'check out', from their accounts it appears as if they never did actually leave "Hotel California", as if they were constantly locked into these sublime nature-related discourses and ideals, which they also helped perpetuating. We are not suggesting here any form of environmental determinism or disputing the agency of adventure trainees and tourists. Rather, our argument is that for those who chose to continue to pursue adventure tourism, their freedom and agency were somehow manifested within the overall state discourses that gave shape to those very programmes, and that for these newly established explorers, adventure tourism landscapes, while engaged under the agenda of freedom and a deliberate regime of exception, may have had constraining effects, in line with the biopolitics of care and custody announced and enacted by the government in the last decades.

The Singapore's state's (in)direct intervention in adventure tourism and training may also be interpreted as an attempt at managing the potentially hedonistic tourist experience and encounters of its citizenry and populace. Care for its subjects' free time, leisure and travel therefore resulted in an indirect although substantial custodian approach to this segment of travel and recreation. As such, rather than allowing tourism spaces to operate freely, the Singapore state decided to co-opt some of them into its manifestos and goals. In choosing to "realise themselves" in this way, Singapore adventure tourists somehow are governed through their own agency (Rose, 1999) and, at least according to their accounts of the training camps, the impression is that they rarely achieve the pursuit of escape they aspire to, since potentially turned into 'prisoners of our [their] own devices' (Lyrics, Hotel California).

9.3 Biopowering Leisurely Consumption: Chinese Casino-based Tourism in Macao

The second case that we report as an example of controversy in tourism biopolitical interventions is framed within the contest of an ongoing, expanding and diversifying Chinese outbound tourism. Chinese outbound tourism has been an area of academic focus for more than a decade by now (see for example, Arlt, 2008; Cai, Boger and O'Leary, 1999; Cai, O'Leary and Boger, 2000; Chan, 2009; Cheng, 2007; Huang and Hsu, 2005; Lim, Guo and Agrusa, 2005; Nyiri, 2009; Ong and du Cros, 2012a; Ryan and Mo, 2002; Zhang and Heung, 2002). While there has been some investigation of the role of nationality in shaping travel and tourist motivations in general (see Maoz, 2007; Pizam and Sussmann, 1995) and Chinese outbound tourism has been argued to have reached a third stage of increased diversification in terms of motivations and practices, the biopolitical elements of such a phenomenon continue to be almost entirely unexplored. Building on Chan's (2009, p.67) assertion that Chinese outbound tourism is constituted in a 'disorganised tourism space', this section thus discusses one of the Chinese state's strategies of "care and custody" of its citizens via tourism, in what has been defined as a "post-Mao" period of rapid and sweeping socio-cultural transformation (Halliday, 1980; Lee, 1999; Oakes, 1998; Smith, 1993; Wang, 2003; Zhang, 1999). Specifically, the post-Mao period is described by this literature as a time of rising capitalism and related retreat of socialism, after political power shifted from Mao Zedong to Deng Xiaoping with the death of the former in 1979 (Halliday, 1980; Lee, 1999; Smith, 1993; Wang, 2003; Zhang, 1999).

China has two Special Administrative Regions – Macao and Hong Kong. These are formerly ceded territories which are now granted fifty years of internal self-governance by the Chinese Central Government within the "One Country, Two Systems" framework (Vong, 2007). Formerly a colony of Portugal, Macao borders the southern city of Zhuhai. Under the "One-Country-Two Systems" framework, Macao operates as an autonomous internal governing state, with its own power to negotiate international trade quotas and agreements. According to the Statistics and Census Service Macao SAR Government, tourist arrivals from Mainland China, Taiwan and Hong Kong are not considered as domestic arrivals. Instead, Mainland China and Hong Kong are classified as "places of residence". Arrivals from other Chinese territories are therefore technically "international arrivals". Nevertheless, Macao does grant Chinese tourists more privileges than they would receive in many other tourist destinations under the Individual Visit Scheme. Tourist arrivals in Macao under the Individual Visit Scheme (IVS) are quantitatively and qualitatively important – making up more than 20% of the total arrivals since 2008 and totalling over 800,000 in the month of February 2014 (total visitor arrival is around 29 million for 2013) (Macao Statistics and Census Service, 2014). Currently, there is no existing study examining the exact range of motivations and activities of tourists visiting Macao under the IVS (also known as the Facilitated Independent Travel). However, the scheme allowed for mass Chinese travels at a time when Chinese citizens were (and still in part are) subjected to demanding visa-requirements or were denied access by many countries. According to Vong (2007), a significant portion of these tourists visiting Macao on the IVS were indeed "gaming tourists". A series of foreign-owned new generation mega casinos integrating large gaming floors with luxury shopping, adult and family entertainment, together with high end restaurants, pubs and convention spaces, mushroomed in the territory as a result of an effort at opening up the gaming sector in the early part of the new millennium and in light of increasing IVS arrivals.

Casino-based tourism in Macao commonly includes soft-gaming in the main halls of casinos, more hedonistic 'VIP' gaming in special all-inclusive clubs, luxury brand shopping, high-end dining, spa and medical tourism and, in some cases, sex tourism in the brothels and sex clubs or what is locally known as "saunas". Originally crafted for residents from affluent coastal cities only, the scheme has been described as a policy aimed at rejuvenating tired urbanites at a time when Chinese citizen's well-being were and still are pursued aggressively through mass consumption and material means (Pow, 2009). Together with the increase in the consumption of 'Western' imported goods such as wine, coffee and chocolates, a new Chinese middle class consumer has been said to have taken shape in the last decades (Pow and Kong, 2007). While nationalistic forms of domestic tourism have also been a key feature of post-Mao Chinese travels such as what has been termed 'Red Tourism' (Li and Hu, 2008), 'Nongjiale Tourism' (Li, 2012) and various shades of cultural and heritage tourism, more consumerist and hedonistic forms of travels to China's reclaimed territories of Macao and Hong Kong may also be argued to have become important to contemporary middle-class Chinese identities.

The sheer number of new luxury brand shops, mega casinos and resorts suggests that these identity formation practices have been incorporated also as pleasure seeking, consumption excitement and hedonistic activities. Such hyper consumerism affects ordinary and 'on-the-ground' individuals such as sale assistants Xiaoli and Xiaoyu:

> I do not like to come to Macao because I always overspend when I am here.
> However, it is hard to say no when your friends want you to come along ... some
> of them go for the casinos and gambling ... some just tag along like me ... I do

not gamble much but my weakness is in shopping. There are many beautiful clothes, branded handbags and nice accessories in the shopping malls of casinos such as Venetian and Wynn (Xiaoli, 6 April 2011).

In the mainland (China), you are always unsure of whether what you bought is fake. But in Macao and Hong Kong, it is different. You can buy a Gucci and a LV and not worry (about these being imitations) (Xiaoyu, 12 June 2012).

The above quotes are the result of a set of interviews conducted between 2011 and 2013 in Macao and its neighbouring Zhuhai city, and of more recent 'virtual ethnography' cyberspace interviews.[3] In order to analyse this case, we also confronted these interviews with interactions developed in 2013 on social media platforms including Facebook, WhatsApp, Wechat, Line and Momo with informants from one of our previous studies and with the textual analysis of related newspaper articles on the same topic.

Returning to our interviewees, given the significant difference between the cost of imported goods sold in these Macao luxury shops and the average household income of the Chinese population, for Xiaoli and Xiaoyu, sales assistants at small fashion boutiques in Zhuhai, such spending sprees in Macao may often exhaust months of savings. However, not all Chinese tourist-citizen-consumers feel the pinch. While her husband spends his time in one of the 'VIP rooms' – specialised high stake private gambling halls – Tiffany (another interviewee) spends her time shopping in the luxury boutiques and stores within the casino resort complexes (Figure 9.2). Tiffany sees luxury shopping as a life style and a form of expression of class and status:

Times have changed. It is very common now (to buy luxury goods). We need to pay attention to our image so people will pay us the respect. In China today, if you do not have money to spend on these things, and do not have the right image, nobody cares about you (Interview, 23 December 2012)

Instead of religion, nation or other sources of moral or cultural authority, Chinese citizens who choose to realise themselves via consumption seem to see wealth and the display of wealth as paramount goals in life (Garner, et al., 2006; Klingberg and Oakes, 2012; Oakes, 2012; Wang, 2003).

Such a "rich-is-king" mentality is even more pronounced among the gamblers. While some regard gambling as a "soft" entertainment game played occasionally (usually the popular local game baccarat or poker), a significant portion of gamblers from China play to "get rich" or for the thrills of possibly getting rich. This can be observed on the gaming floors and beyond. During our participant observation in one Macao casino, we have reported several occasions in which Chinese gamblers

---

3   On 'virtual ethnography' see, among others, Hine, 2000, 2005; Rybas and Gajjala, 2007.

Figure 9.2   Shopping in Macao's casino resorts
Source: authors

placed bets to their last Yuan/Reminbi and ended up spending the night in the street (and/or on the beach). Casino croupiers interviewed confirmed to have been witnessing the same. Such thrills often bring about gambling addiction. Yu, a businessman in the property field, admitted that:

> It is not about how much we bet. It is this inability to stop. You just feel this thrill when you are winning and you want that feeling to go on and on. It is the reverse when we lose. You feel angry but you always feel like you can ride out the bad luck if you just push on a bit longer (Interview, 20 December 2012).

Yu lost a sum equivalent to the cost of a luxury condominium at the time of the interview. He only stopped gambling that time when his elder brother travelled over and pulled him out from the gaming hall. Yatou, instead spoke about the peer pressure:

> I lost a lot in the past and I learned my lesson. However, my friends all wanted to go to Macao and I had no choice but to go with them. Then, I went into the casino again. I really regret this (Interview, 13 June 2012).

Like the Hotel California of the song, Macao seems to be conceived as a tourist site where one can never entirely check out from, for example, but not exclusively, as gambling addictions lock gamblers such as Yu and Yatou in. In other cases, in fact, gamblers also seek the services of sex workers. Solicitation can be done on the gaming floor or on the social media. Gamblers can also explore the numerous saunas that operate as fronts for the provision of sex services or brothels located in the casino areas. Like in Diken and Lausten's (2004) holiday camp, the rules are suspended rather than destroyed (see also Minca, 2009). The transgressions of the holidaymaker do not, in this sense, perform a "back-to-nature movement"; transgression does not suppress but except the rule (Bataille, 2001, p.36). Technically, prostitution occupies a grey area of the Macao juridical system – it is neither legal nor illegal. However, it is illegal in mainland China, and hence what is happening reflects what Diken and Lausten (2004, p.205) describe as a situation where:

> The identity of the tourist is stripped of its public connotations and his desire is moved by the promise of an eroticized, corporeal, 'animal' world experienced as freedom from the 'city': the dark, routinized, disciplinary 'iron cage' of the citizen.

In this case, Chinese citizens take on the identity of an eroticised and corporeal gambler-subject as they enter the casino spaces of Macao – away from communist spatialities from where they come from, and the disciplinary machineries those spaces weld. The Chinese state in this case is rather explicit in defining the spaces it wants its citizens to be cared for and to achieve happiness and wellness, unlike the case of Singapore and its adventure tourists discussed above, in which the state tends rather to define the practices the citizens should not over-indulge – heavy-drinking till the early morning and conducting acts of infidelity and threatening what it deems as brittle social and community structures. The Chinese state, instead, is both explicit in the activities the citizens ought to conduct and the spaces where these are allowed. In this specific case, activities that do not conform to the communist ethics are dispatched to the postcolonial spaces of its two Special Administrative Regions, and in particular Macao, which is deemed as China's contemporary hub for tourism, entertainment and leisure. Thus, the Chinese state's tactics at dealing with the potential hedonistic tendencies of its citizens lie in containment and custody – that casino gambling and prostitution happen only in Macao, while "soft"-gaming practices of horse racing, lotteries, sports betting, mah-jong are allowed to happen in Hong Kong and barring the recently created "charity tickets" (a lottery), gambling in all forms is illegal in the rest of China. Macao is thus in many ways China's Hotel California – a hyper-consumerist hedonistic enclave that locks some of its visitors into its arsenal of casinos, luxury shopping malls and other spaces of indulgence. A soft biopolitical enclave to contain and set free, precisely in order to somehow keep under control bodily and behavioural excesses of mainland citizens who can afford them, and the related economies of allowed exception to the rule.

9.4   Conclusion

In this chapter, we have tried to make the controversial argument that some tourist encounters, in cases in which tourism is indirectly involved in state biopolitics, may be provocatively described like a visit to the song's Hotel California, and that the Singapore and Chinese authorities have variously co-opted such encounters and their related spatialities. Such an argument has led us to reflect on how states may proactively intervene to biopolitically support the care and custody of its populace and citizenry, to produce certain supposedly docile subjectivities, by means of their leisurely and travel experiences (see Minca, 2012).

However, the biopowering of tourism in the two exemplary cases here discussed is at work rather differently. In Singapore, the People's Action Party led government has sought to actively promote, amongst other activities, one that it deemed beneficial for the health, happiness and well-being of its citizens, that is, adventure tourism. In particular, we looked at the ways in which care and custody were implemented through a state-based interpretation and construction of tourism, and at the implications of these for understanding Singapore adventure tourism inherent biopolitical dimension. The ways in which the Singapore state has been endorsing adventure has been relatively indirect, with no big official slogans, since slogans have largely been rejected by Singaporeans post-90s. It has been done rather through the sponsorship of a very popular adventure club and the co-opting of the adventure club leaders into the dominant political party's youth movement, since the club falls under its umbrella. Through the past decade, repeated ethnographic observations showed that many 2004 participants (the year in which the first research on this form of adventure tourism was conducted) have remained linked to the adventure club and have been taking up leadership positions and contributing to organizing events despite many of them holding very demanding professional jobs.

The Macao case, however, presents a different situation. Chinese casino-based mass tourism may in fact be interpreted as an attempt by the state at regulating and controlling hedonistic tendencies within a very special enclavic space, like the one that emerged in Macao in the last decade or so. As aspirations have risen due to societal changes during the post-Mao years, the state first allowed mass middle class consumption to happen at a controlled pace and in a regulated fashion in its own territories. Tourism, itself a form of mass consumption to which the growing Chinese middle classes aspire, was then incentivised in the two formerly ceded territories of Macao and Hong Kong, today functioning as internally-autonomous Special Administrative Regions. One of these Special Administrative Regions, Macao, has been in recent years increasingly designated as an entertainment hub for these same middle-classes coming from mainland China. It was to be the place that Chinese citizens may use for the achievement and maintenance of a certain kind of "leisure" and "well-being" (see also, Klingberg and Oakes, 2012; Oakes, 2012). However, while Macao offers also entertainment and personal services well aligned with the official communist ethos, such as medical and cultural tourism, it is better known for its massive casino and gaming based entertainment. Associated with this is the presence of a longstanding sex work sector. Although the latter services are illegal in mainland China, they are somewhat passively tolerated in Macao. As such, the Chinese state seems to be involved in the care and custody of its citizens by promoting certain forms of entertainment and activities compatible to their ethos, but also in the containment and regulation of those deemed less appropriate.

Our argument is thus controversial insofar as Hotel California is both enticing and custodian in nature. From the intense-internalisation of adventure ideals and the perpetual need for adventure spaces in Singapore adventure tourists, to the addiction to luxury goods, gambling and excessive consumption in the Chinese casino tourists in Macao, we would in fact like to argue that, for some, the state's attempts at co-opting pleasure, travel and leisure, as efforts at controlling, stewarding and managing tourist experiences and encounters, may indeed result in the creation of alluring *and* somehow addictive "Hotel Californias" of sorts, sites of pleasure that many find indeed difficult to leave.

References

Agamben, G., 2005. *State of exception.* Chicago: University of Chicago Press.

Arlt, W., 2008. Chinese tourists in 'elsewhereland'. In: J. Cochrane, ed. *Asian tourism.* London: Elsevier. pp.135–145.

AsiaOne, 2008. Macao beefs up visa restrictions on mainland visitors [Electronic Version]. AsiaOne. Available at:<http://www.asiaone.com/News/Latest%2BNews/Asia/Story/A1Story20080717-77259.html> [Accessed on 18 May 2009]

Baranowski, S, 2004. *Strength through joy.* Cambridge: Cambridge University Press.

Baranowski, S., 2005. Radical nationalism in an international context: Strength through joy and the paradoxes of Nazi tourism. In: J. Walton, ed. *Histories of tourism.* Clevedon: Channel View Publications, pp.126–143.

Bataille, G., 2001. *Eroticism.* London. Penguin.

Bianchi, R.V., 2004. Tourism restructuring and the politics of sustainability. *Journal of Sustainable Tourism,* 12(6), pp.495–529.

Bochaton, A. and Lefebvre, B., 2009. The rebirth of the hospital. In: T. Winter, P. Teo and T.C. Chang, eds. *Asia on tour: Exploring the rise of Asian tourism.* London: Routledge, pp.97–109.

Britton, S., 1991. Tourism, capital and place. *Environment and Planning D: Society and Space,* 9(4), pp.451–478.

Bruner, E., 1989. Of cannibals, tourists and ethnographers. Cannibal Tours. *Cultural Anthropology,* 4(4), pp.438–445.

Bruner, E., 1991. Transformation of self in tourism. *Annals of Tourism Research,* 18, pp. 238–250.

Cai, L., Boger, C. and O'Leary, J., 1999. The Chinese travellers to Singapore, Malaysia and Thailand. *Asia Pacific Journal of Tourism Research*, 3(2), pp.2–13.

Cai, L., O'Leary, J. and Boger, C., 2000. Chinese travellers to the United States. *Journal of Vacation Marketing*, 6(2), pp.131–144.

Chan, Y.W., 2009. Disorganised tourism space. In: T. Winter, P. Teo and T.C. Chang, eds. *Asia on tour: Exploring the rise of Asian tourism*. London: Routledge, pp.67–77.

Channelnewsasia, 2013. National day rally: New MediShield life for universal coverage, *Channelnewsasia*, 18 August. Available at: <http://www.channelnewsasia.com/news/specialreports/nd2013/news/nd-rally-new-medishield/781478.html> [Accessed on 4 January 2014].

Cheng, I.M., 2007. A comparative study of travel behaviour of single and multi-destination travellers from mainland China in Macao. *China Tourism Research*, 3(4), pp.449–477.

Chua, B.H., 2002. *Communitarian ideology and democracy in Singapore*. London: Routledge.

Chua, B.H.,2003. *Life is not complete without shopping*. Singapore: NUS Press.

Chua, B.H., 2010. The cultural logic of a single-party state, Singapore. *Postcolonial Studies*, 13(4), pp.335–350.

Cohen, E., 1979. A phenomenology of tourist experiences. *Sociology*, 13, pp.179–202.

Diken, B. and Laustsen, C.B., 2004. Sea, sun, sex and the discontents of pleasure. *Tourist Studies*, 4(2), pp.99–114.

Edensor, T., 2000. Staging tourism: Tourists as performers. *Annals of Tourism Research*, 27, pp.322–344.

Elsrud, T., 2001. Risk creation in travelling. *Annals of Tourism Research*, 28, pp.597–617.

Fernandez, W., 2004. *Thinking allowed?: Politics, fear and change in Singapore*. Singapore: SNP Editions.

Foucault, M., 1986. Of other spaces. *Diacritics*, 16(1), pp.22–27.

Foucault, M., 1990a. *The history of sexuality (Vol. 2)*. New York: Vintage.

Foucault, M., 1990b. *The history of sexuality (Vol. 1)*. New York: Vintage.

Foucault, M., 1990c. *The history of sexuality (Vol. 3)*. New York: Vintage.

Franklin, A., 2004. Tourism as ordering. *Tourist Studies*, 4(3), pp.277–301.

Galani-Moutafi, V., 2000. The self and the other. *Annals of Tourism Research*, 27(1), pp.203–224.

Garner, J., Chan, V., Ho, M. and Tao, D., 2006. *The rise of the Chinese consumer*. Singapore: Wiley.

George, C., 2000. *Singapore: The air-conditioned nation*, 1990–2000. Singapore: Landmark.

Grandits, H. and Taylor, K., eds., 2010. *Yugoslavia's sunny side: A history of tourism in socialism*. Budapest: Central European University Press.

Halliday, J., 1980. Capitalism and socialism in East Asia. *New Left Review*, I/124, pp.3–24.

Hine, C., 2000. *Virtual ethnography*. London: Sage.

Hine, C., ed., 2005. *Virtual methods: Issues in social research on the internet*. Oxford: Berg.

Hing, L.S., 2005. Casino politics, organized crime and the post-colonial state in Macao. *Journal of Contemporary China*, 14(43), pp.207–224.

Huang, S.S. and Hsu, C., 2005. Mainland Chinese residents: Perceptions and motivations of visiting Hong Kong. *Asia Pacific Journal of Tourism Research*, 10(2), pp.191–205.

Kimball, W.B., 1993. Singapore's People's Association. *CIA Historical Review Programme*, 22 September.

Kirshenblatt-Gimblett, B., 1998. *Destination culture*. Berkeley, CA: University of California Press.

Klingberg, T. and Oakes, T., 2012. Producing exemplary consumers: Tourism and leisure culture in China's nation-building project. In: L. Jensen and T. Weston, eds.*China in and beyond the headlines*. Lanham, MD: Rowman & Littlefield, pp.195–213.

Lall, S. and Albaladejo, M., 2004. China's competitive performance. *World Development,* 32(9), pp.1441–1466.

Law, L., Bunnell, T.G. and Ong, C.E., 2007. The beach, the gaze and film tourism. *Tourist Studies*, 7(2), pp.141–164.

Lee, H.L., 2012. Speech at the Economics Society of Singapore's annual dinner, 18 June, 2012. Prime Minister's Office. Available at: <http://www.pmo.gov.sg/content/pmosite/mediacentre/speechesninterviews/primeminister/2012/June/speech_by_prime_ministerleehsienloongateconomicsocietyofsingapor.html#. Usgk_9IW2uk> [Accessed on 4 January 2014].

Lee, O., 1999. A dialogue on the future of China. *New Left Review*, I/235, pp.62–106.

Li, Y.P. and Hu, Z., 2008. Red tourism in China. *Journal of China Tourism Research*, 4(2), pp.156–171.

Li, Y.P., 2012. Impacts and challenges in agritourism development in Yunnan, China. *Tourism Planning and Development*, 9(4), pp.369–381.

Lim, S.S., Guo, Y. and Agrusa, J., 2005. Preference and positioning analyses of overseas destination by mainland Chinese outbound pleasure tourists. *Journal of Travel Research*, 44(2), pp.212–220.

Loker-Murphy, L. and Pearce, P.L., 1995. Young budget travellers. *Annals of Tourism Research*, 22(4), pp.819–843.

Macao Statistics and Census Service, 2014. Visitor arrivals. Available at: <www.dsec.mo> [Accessed on 17 March 2014].

MacCannell, D., 1976. *The tourist*. New York: Schocken.

Maoz, D., 2004. The conquerors and the settlers: Two groups of young Israeli backpackers in India. In: G. Richards and J. Wilson, eds. *Global nomad*. Clevedon: Channelview, pp.109–122.

Maoz, D., 2007. Backpackers' motivations: The role of culture and nationality. *Annals of Tourism Research*, 34(1), pp.122–140.

Minca, C., 2009. The island: Work, tourism and the biopolitical. *Tourist Studies*, 9(2), pp.88–108.

Minca, C., 2007. The tourist landscape paradox. *Social and Cultural Geography*, 8(3), pp.433–453.

Minca, C., 2012. No country for old men. In: C. Minca and T. Oakes, eds. *Real tourism*. London: Routledge, pp.12–38.

Minca, C. and Oakes, T., 2006a. *Travels in paradox: Remapping tourism*. Lanham, MD: Rowman and Littlefield.

Minca, C. and Oakes, T., 2006b. Introduction. In: C. Minca and T. Oakes, eds. *Travels in paradox: Remapping tourism*. Lanham, MD: Rowman and Littlefield, pp.1–23.

Minca, C. and Oakes, T., eds., 2012. *Real Tourism*. London: Routledge.

Minca, C. and Oakes, T., 2014. Tourism after the postmodern turn. In: A. Lew, M. Hall and M. Williams, eds. *The Wiley Blackwell companion to tourism*. London: Wiley Blackwell, pp.294–303.

Noy, C. and Cohen, E., eds. 2005. *Israeli backpackers: From rites of passage to tourism*. Albany: State University of New York Press.

Nyiri, P., 2009. Between encouragement and control: Tourism, modernity and discipline in China. In: T. Winter, P. Teo and T. Chang, eds. *Asia on tour*. London and New York: Routledge, pp.153–170.

Oakes, T., 1998. *Tourism and modernity in China*. London: Routledge.

Oakes, T., 2006. Get real! On being yourself and being a tourist. In: C. Minca, and T. Oakes, eds. *Travels in paradox: Remapping tourism*. Lanham: Rowman & Littlefield, pp.229–251.

Oakes, T., 2012. Heritage as improvement. *Modern China*. (Published online first 12/7/12. doi: 10.1177/0097700412467011)

OMY, 2013. *You too can be an adventurer*. OMY Online Newspaper, 14 January 2013. Available at: <http://yzone.omy.sg/index.php?articleID=21881&option=com_article&cid=144&task=detail#prettyPhoto> [Accessed 4 January 2014].

Ong, C.E., 2004. *Adventurism: Singapore adventure tourists in the New Economy*. Msc thesis National University of Singapore.

Ong, C.E., 2005. Adventurism: Singapore adventure tourists in New Economy. In: C. Ryan and M. Aicken, eds. *Taking tourism to the limits*. London: Elsevier, pp.173–183.

Ong, C.E., 2011. *Guiding cultural utopia*. Ph.D Dissertation, The University of Waikato.

Ong, C.E. and du Cros, H., 2012a. The post-Mao gazes: Chinese backpackers in Macao. *Annals of Tourism Research*, 39(2), pp.735–754.

Ong, C.E. and du Cros, H., 2012b. Projecting post-colonial conditions at Shanghai Expo 2010, China. *Urban Studies*, 49(13), pp.2937–2953.

Ong, C. E., Minca, C. and Felder, M. (2014) Disciplined Mobility and the Emotional Subject in Royal Dutch Lloyd's Early Twentieth Century Passenger

Shipping Network, *Antipode: A Radical Journal of Geography*, 46(5): 1323–1345. doi: 10.1111/anti.12091

Ong, C. E., Ryan, C. and McIntosh, A. (2014) Power-Knowledge and Tour-Guide Training: Capitalistic Domination, Utopian Visions and the Creation of UNESCO's *Homo-Turismos* in Macao, *Annals of Tourism Research*, 48: 221–234.

Philo, C., 2001. Accumulating populations: Bodies, institutions and space. *International Journal of Population Geography*, 7, pp.473–490.

Philo, C., 2005. Sex, life, death, geography: Fragmentary remarks inspired by 'Foucault's Population Geographies'. *Population, Space and Place*, 11, pp.325–333.

Pizam, A. and Sussmann, S., 1995. Does nationality affect tourist behaviour? *Annals of Tourism Research*, 22, pp.901–917.

Pow, C.P. and Kong, L., 2007. Marketing the Chinese dream home. *Urban Geography*, 28(2), pp.129–159.

Pow, C.P., 2009. Neoliberalism and the aestheticization of new middle-class landscapes. *Antipode*, 41(2), pp.371–390.

Rose, N., 1999. *Powers of freedom*. Cambridge: Cambridge University Press.

Ryan, C. and Mo, X., 2002. Chinese visitors to New Zealand. *Journal of Vacation Marketing*, 8(1), pp.13–27.

Rybas, N. and Gajjala, R., 2007. Developing cyberethnographic research methods for understanding digitally mediated identities. *Forum: Qualitative Social Research* 8(3), Art. 35. Salanha, A., 2008. Heterotopia and structuralism. *Environment and Planning A*, 40, pp.2080–2096.

Semmens, K., 2005 *Seeing Hitler's Germany: Tourism in the Third Reich*. Houndmills: Palgrave Macmillan.

Shackley, M., 2002. Space, sanctity and service: The English Cathedral as heterotopia. *International Journal of Tourism Research*, 4(5), pp.345–352.

Sin, H.L. and Minca, C., 2014. Touring responsibility. *Geoforum*, 51, pp. 96–106.

Smith, R., 1993. The Chinese road to capitalism. *New Left Review*, I/199, pp.55–99.

Suntikul, W., 2013. War as a foundation of tourism: A case of Pattaya. In: R. Butler and W. Suntikul, eds. *Tourism and war.* London: Routledge.

Teo, P. and Leong, S., 2006. A postcolonial analysis of backpacking. *Annals of Tourism Research*, 33(1), pp.109–131.

Van der Duim, R., Ren, C.B. and Jóhannesson, G.T, eds., 2012. *Actor-Network Theory and tourism: Ordering, materiality and multiplicity*. London: Routledge.

Van der Duim, R., Ren, C.B. and Jóhannesson, G.T, 2013. Ordering, materiality and multiplicity: Enacting Actor–Network Theory in tourism. *Tourist Studies*, 13(1), pp.3–20.

Veijola, S., 2009. Gender as Work in the Tourism Industry. *Tourist Studies,* 9(2), pp.109–126.

Veijola, S. and Jokinen, E., 1994. The body in tourism. *Theory, Culture & Society,*
    11(3), pp.125–151.
Vong, F., 2007. The psychology of risk-taking in gambling among Chinese visitors
    to Macao. *International Gambling Studies,* 7(1), pp.29–42.
Wang, H., 2003. *China's new order: Society, politics and economy in transition.*
    Cambridge, MA: Harvard University Press.
Wilson, J. and Richards, G., 2008. Suspending reality. *Current Issues in Tourism,*
    11(2), pp.187–202.
Zhang, H.-Q. and Heung, V.C.S., 2002. The emergence of the mainland Chinese
    outbound travel market and its implications for tourism. *Journal of Vacation
    Marketing,* 8(1), pp.7–12.
Zhang, X., 1999. Postmodernism and post-socialist society. *New Left Review,*
    I/237, pp.77–105.

Chapter 10

A Fish Called Tourism: Emergent Realities of Tourism Policy in Iceland

Gunnar Thór Jóhannesson

10.1 Introduction

On a grey and windy Tuesday morning, 10 September 2013, a crowd of a few hundred people gathered for a half day conference in Iceland's most high profile conference facility, The Harpa, to learn about *The Future of Tourism in Iceland*. The conference was initiated by some of the largest tourism firms in Iceland in order to present a new report on the opportunities and challenges of Icelandic tourism, prepared by the international consultancy firm Boston Consulting Group (BCG) (The Boston Consulting Group, 2013). The Harpa provided a welcoming shelter for attending guests that were reminded of forces of nature as they almost blew through the door this autumn morning. They were welcomed by the Icelandic Prime Minister as well as the Minister of Industry and Tourism who opened the conference.

This event is interesting in many aspects. In basic terms, the conference is one of the latest efforts to carve out a tourism policy in Iceland and to shape an agenda for the future. The report by BCG is one in a series of similar reports that have recently been published, commissioned both by public institutes and private firms (Arion banki, 2013; Landsbanki Íslands, 2013b; PKF, 2013). Perhaps more importantly, the fact that the event attracted so many participants, is also a clear example of the mounting interest in tourism by people in Iceland as well as by private firms and public institutes. The sector has begun to attract the interest of investors while concerns of negative environmental and socio-cultural impacts of tourism development are repeatedly voiced in the media and by stakeholders that have warned against a gold-rush mentality in the sector (Eyjan.is, 2013; RÚV, 2013a). Last but not least, the event also shows that tourism is gaining in prominence as a sector that is crucial for the national economy and one that demands attention from the central government's key posts. Taken together, the event is a sign of how tourism, defined as an economic activity, recently reached momentum in Iceland.

Although tourism has been a significant source of currency revenues the last two to three decades, it has been struggling to gain recognition as a 'real' industry or occupation, both in general discourses by central authorities and policy makers (Jóhannesson and Huijbens, 2010). At present, tourism exports provide around

26% of foreign currency receipts and provides jobs for about 7,000 people or about 5% of the workforce (Arion banki, 2013; Ferðamálastofa, 2014b). Thus, there is no doubt about the status of tourism anymore; nowadays tourism in Iceland is 'real'. Its presence and impact on the economy has become undisputed.

In this chapter I deal with some of the ways in which the present tourism realities have emerged by following relational encounters between tourism policy, flows of tourists and nature. The chapter approaches Icelandic tourism policy as a space of encounters and potential controversy, materialized by heterogeneous assemblages of a wide array of actors. The aim is not to draw up a holistic picture of the development of Icelandic tourism policy but to follow some of the ways in which tourism policy as a practice enacts tourism. This is thus a study of realities in the making. Special attention will be given to the relationality of tourism policy and how it can be seen as performative and entangled with society and nature. It is argued that it is imperative to attend to the more-than-human or earthly connections of ordering attempts such as tourism policies in order to grasp the generative capacities of the Earth (Huijbens and Gren, 2012) and how tourism is an effect of relations that cut across the spheres of nature and culture as traditionally defined.

The chapter sets off by discussing the concepts of policy and tourism policy making and links it to ideas of relational ontology. It then proceeds with an account of tourism encounters and policy efforts in Iceland. It is recounted how tourism and in some sense tourists, have been translated into fish in an effort to conceive tourism as a real sector and eventually a subject of policy making on par with other key industries of the country. At present the tourism sector has gained an uncontroversial reckoning as a real business, which depends on and iterates a particular relationship to its main resource, namely nature. The chapter traces some of those relations as manifested in a recent policy tool in a form of multi-site access charge called the Environment Card. It is argued that policy making may usefully be analysed as a process of improvisation that continually encompasses the entanglement of human and more-than-human encounters and which has ontological repercussions. Hence, what seems at present to be an uncontroversial framing of tourism in Iceland as an industry may create serious challenges for sustainable development of tourism in the near future.

10.2   On Policy and Earthly Connections

10.2.1   *Policy and Policy Making*

In its broadest sense, policy and policy making is about ordering. Policy may be understood as a roadmap, drawn up through a planning work, representing present conditions as well as future directions ideally to be pursued. According to Hall, public policy is primarily a political affair and is as such 'influenced by the economic, social, and cultural characteristics of society, as well as by the formal structures of government and other features of the political system' (2000, p.8). It thus reflects the values, ideologies, set of principles or broad goals of governments or central authorities holding the power to issue a public policy. In the case of tourism, public policy making reflects how tourism is understood by policy makers, what its capacities and dynamics are thought to be and how it relates to and affects other phenomena in the world such as the economy and environment.

Tourism has increasingly become subject to policy making, both due to the continuing use of tourism as tool for economic development and concerns that some sort of policy is needed as corrective for market failure that threatens sustainable development of the sector (Dredge, Jenkins and Whitford, 2011; Hall, 2000). This has not however, necessarily resulted in more direct engagement by state authorities in tourism development. Together with the rising influence of neo-liberal ideologies during the last three decades the space of policy making has been opened up in the sense that it is no longer solely under the control of a central government but should rather be perceived as an interactive process of governance (Bramwell, 2011; Sørensen and Torfing, 2005). More diverse actors are being integrated into the policy making process such as private companies, public agencies, NGOs and/or user organizations. Ideally, the opening up of the policy making process should make it more responsive to diverse interests. However, the move from government to governance does not guarantee the equal opportunity of all to have a say in the process (Dredge, Jenkins and Whitford, 2011; Sørensen and Torfing, 2005). Dredge and Jenkins (2011) point to the increasing influence private companies seem to have on policy making and the possible effect of that. These include the privatization of the public sphere, which can lead to a situation where it is no longer clear who is responsible to the public for the policy (Hall, Müller and Saarinen, 2009) and the corporatisation of government agencies that has resulted in more focus on marketing and promotion rather than policy making and implementation (Hall and Zapata, 2014).

Studies of tourism policy have increasingly engaged critically with these and similar questions about the policy making process, touching on unequal distribution of power and how certain interests are silenced or othered, while some get voiced (Pforr, 2006; Thomas and Thomas, 2005; Wray, 2009). According to Dredge, Jenkins and Whitford (2011), policy and planning theory has however historically been based on rational and technical approaches. One of the implications of this trend has been that a gap has appeared between policy making and practice which is imbued with politics and its power relations. As Hall (2000, p.40) notes, one 'of the main reasons for this is that they [the policies] represent "rational" planning approaches which fail to consider the world in which the plans will operate'.

10.2.2 *Earthly Connections*

So what is the world for policy making like? As noted by Hall, one of the problems with policy making has been the image of the world as being apt for rational planning, not taking politics and cultural values into account that continuously alter the preconditions and contexts of policies. Furthermore, policy making practice has predominantly been based on the assumption that tourism is an industry and thus could be subject to general industrial policies that have had mixed success (Hjalager, 2002; Warwick, 2013). As such, policy making practice has not taken the movement or becoming of the social world sufficiently into account and neither the complexity of the sector although research on policy has increasingly grappled with such complexities. The basic premises of policy research has rested on the view that the world is social in the traditional meaning of the term as referring strictly to human associations through which the world is constructed (Latour, 2005). In the case of tourism, the challenge has been to manage a socio-cultural practice (tourism) and its resources, usually defined broadly as nature and culture. This is based on the common assumption in Western thought that humans stand somewhat apart from the earth, are able to look at it from afar and contemplate rational solutions to problems of society and nature (Ingold, 2000a; Pálsson, 1996). From this approach, nature or the more-than-human entities of the environment is a passive background or stage for the performances of human (social) actors, be it as resources to be exploited or conserved. It is the modernist dream (Latour, 1993) depicting human society on the one hand and nature on the other, that implicitly or explicitly has created the idea that humans are capable of ordering nature, by exerting their organizing powers upon it.

This stance is increasingly problematic as it does not recognize the generative capacities of more-than-human actors or the Earth, and how humans and more-than-humans are mutually constituted. In the face of a global environmental crisis and the recognition that the Earth and its inhabitants have entered the era of the Anthropocene, it is imperative to rethink the ontologies and methods which we use to think about our status and roles as humans in the world (Lorimer, 2012; Pálsson, et al., 2013). According to Pálsson, et al. (2013, p.8):

> [A]nthropocene societies could thus be characterized as involving humans being
> basically in conflict with themselves through the structures and systems that they
> have themselves created in order to improve their lifestyles and well-being).

Hence, the concept of the Anthropocene not only captures how humans have become a geological force, but also how they are increasingly becoming aware of their role in shaping the Earth, for instance how the climate is changing due to their activities such as travelling, and that they need to deal with it (Pálsson, et al., 2013).

A current of alternative approaches to describe the entanglement of nature and society have become increasingly prominent in the social sciences in the last three decades, including Actor-Network Theory and its later versions (Latour, 1986; 1993; 2007; Law, 1999; 2007; Law and Singleton, 2013; Lien and Law, 2013), feminist research (Braidotti, 2002; Haraway, 1991) and material phenomenology (Ingold, 2000b; 2011; McLean, 2009). They advocate relational ontologies that describe Nature and Society as relational effects, emergent through heterogeneous assemblages (Lorimer, 2012). Importantly, it is not relations between separate points that produce the world, humans and more-than-humans as well as our environment. Relations create points but not vice versa. Relations should then be thought of as 'lines of growth' (Ingold, 2006, p.6) and the environment then appears as field 'of interwoven lines, not a network but a *meshwork*' (Ingold, 2006, p.6, original italics). This implies that the environment is not out there for us humans to decide if we want to connect to it or not, or order it or not. In fact there is no outside or inside, only continuous becoming of heterogeneous beings, the Earth included.

It can be argued that the Anthropocene society is a topological society where 'we no longer live in or experience "movement" or transformation as the transmission of fixed forms in space and time but rather movement – as the ordering of continuity – composes the forms of social and cultural life themselves' (Lury, Parisi and Terranova, 2012, p.6). We might then usefully think about the space of policy making in topological terms (See Chapter 11 this volume). According to Harvey (2012, p. 78):

> The topological approach thus draws attention to the spatial figures where insides and outsides are continuous, where borders of inclusion and exclusion do not coincide with the edges of a demarcated territory, and where it is the mutable quality of relations that determines distance and proximity, rather than a singular and absolute measure.

From this approach, tourism can be described as growing out of heterogeneous relations or entangled with various issues, agendas and processes that cross the domains of nature and society as usually defined. At the same time it is an ordering that shapes those very same relations (Franklin, 2012). In terms of tourism policy making it becomes crucial to explore how it relates and enacts the spheres of nature and society and to recognize the heterogeinity of the world it is supposed to order.

This implies that it is not a straightforward and purely human exercise to construct a tourism policy. From this approach, policy making is a space of encounters and controversy, where inclusion and exclusion is constantly negotiated and thus, emerges through heterogeneous assemblages of a wide array of actors. Policy making practice is thus not a question of imposing a social order on the surface of more or less material environment. What we are used to think about as nature or natural environment is permanently entangled with our cultural practice and associated in the meshwork of life.

This understanding has implications for policy making. First, it underlines that policy making has to grasp continuous movement and becoming of the world and has to order continuity. The ordering of continuity grasps 'a world that is crescent rather than created' (Ingold and Hallam, 2007, p.3). Second, this underlines that realities are done and enacted (Mol, 1999). Taken together this means that policy is performative and has ontological implications as its enactment carves out more or less stable realities. It is not an easy task to order a continuously moving world, or a world 'where it is the mutable quality of relations that determines distance and proximity rather than a singular and absolute measure' (Harvey, 2012, p.78). The concept of improvisation may aptly describe policy making under these conditions. As Ingold and Hallam (2007, p.7) point out, improvisation is relational as it 'goes on along "ways of life"' that are entangled and mutually responsive. It is to respond to life's contingencies and to recognize that there is no script; 'no system of codes, rules and norms that can anticipate every possible circumstance' (Ingold and Hallam, 2007, p.2).

I will now turn to tourism encounters in Iceland and the story of policy making for the sector that illustrates the conceptual discussion above. An emphasis is put on the relationality of tourism policy making and how tourism has struggled to become recognized as a real industry.

10.3   Tourism Encounters and Tourism Policy Making in Iceland

The brief story of tourism development and tourism policy making as presented here can be read as an account of tourism encounters in the most general sense and how tourism has been framed as a real industry or occupation by Icelandic authorities and the private sector. The account is based on two kinds of data: 1) semi structured interviews with former ministers of tourism in Iceland, present and former public officials working at the Ministry of Tourism and the Icelandic Tourism Board and the Icelandic Tourism Industry Association all conducted in the period 2009–2011, 2) documentary analysis of policy documents from 1988 to the present, parliamentarian reports, laws and resolutions on tourism and other textual material on tourism affairs published by the Ministry of Tourism.

10.3.1   Controversial Realities of Tourism

Tourism has increased rapidly in Iceland. From the second half of the twentieth century, tourism in Iceland has experienced a steady and almost continuous growth in terms of tourist arrivals (Ferðamálastofa, 2013b). Since 2000, the number of tourist arrivals has doubled to 670 thousand in 2012. The Icelandic Tourist Board records data on tourist arrivals and issues news releases every month with staggering figures of increase. From year 2012 to 2013 the growth is measured as being 20% (Ferðamálastofa, 2014a). This makes the sector one of three key sectors of the national economy together with fisheries and heavy industries, especially aluminium smelting. In many ways, this signals a bright future for the sector and many actors are looking forward to take part in that future. However, alarm bells are ringing. Tourism stakeholders such as the Icelandic Tourist Industry Association and the Icelandic Tourism Association have voiced concerns over what they call the 'Gold-rush mentality' in tourism, which is manifested for instance in hundreds of rooms for rent for tourists on the black market (Eyjan.is, 2013; Viðskiptablaðið, 2013a; Visir.is, 2012; 2013). Furthermore, many actors, individuals, NGOs, public institutes and private firms as well as academics have voiced their concerns over the impact of the rapid increase in tourism, especially in regard to the fragile environment of the most visited sites (Alþingi, 2011; Jóhannesson, Huijbens and Sharpley, 2010; Landsbanki Íslands, 2013a; Ólafsdóttir and Runnström, 2013; Umhverfisstofnun, 2012). The reality of tourism in Iceland has, for better or worse, become undisputed. In some ways it even seems like tourism is spinning out of control. At least, the need for stronger policy and an action plan for the future is repeatedly being identified as crucial for the long-term viability of tourism (The Boston Consulting Group, 2013).

Not that long ago tourism had a quite different position in Icelandic society, and its real impact was doubted or in any case, there was no need to worry about its transformative powers. Iceland has for a long time been on the itinerary of explorers and adventurous travellers and has had an image of being a land of natural extremes (Gössling, 2006; Ísleifsson, 1996; 2011). The first origins of modern tourism can be found in late nineteenth century, but soon after the World War II Iceland began to emerge as a destination not least due to strong flight connections to both Europe and North America (Benediktsson, 1896; Jóhannesson, Huijbens and Sharpley, 2010). In 1964, the Icelandic Tourism Board was established and about ten years later the first attempt to create a formal tourism policy was initiated. It was carried out in 1973–1975 by a US based consultancy company, Checchi and Co. (Checchi and co., 1975). This work was paid by the UN development fund and aimed to provide viable ideas and plans for tourism development in Iceland. Many of the central themes that have since then run through tourism policy discourses in Iceland were already issued by Checchi and Co. Those include the idea that tourism is a tool for development, the necessity to invest in infrastructure, the need to boost marketing, the need to protect the environment and the need to enhance research and education in tourism. However, this report, detailing the current affairs of tourism on the island and pointing at future directions was never presented publicly. It disappeared within the Ministry of Industry and for the most part for the next twenty years, tourism remained absent in any discussion about economic development.

According to people working at the Icelandic Tourism Board during the 1980s and 90s, as well as former ministers of tourism, the weak position of tourism mainly stemmed from a lack of interest and understanding of the potentialities of the sector. Steingrímur J. Sigfússon, Minister of agriculture, communication and tourism in 1988–1991 recalls that when he came to the post 'tourism was not defined as an occupation and actually perhaps not recognized [as such]'. It was, in other words, largely absent in its own ministry. The general director of the Icelandic Tourist Board (1990–1991 and 1993–2007), Magnús Oddson, describes the attitude by the central administration and the members of parliament toward tourism in similar ways: 'It has always been possible to gain an understanding from the current minister of tourism each time, through discussions and so on. But it has always been difficult to translate that understanding further'.

Translation is difficult but not impossible, as we will see. In the early 1990s Magnús happened to play a decisive part in creating an understanding of tourism as a 'real job'. The key to that was fish, or actually the absence of fish, in the waters around Iceland.

10.3.2   On Understanding Cod

Throughout the history, Iceland, situated in the middle of the North Atlantic, has been highly dependent on fisheries. At the turn of the twentieth century Iceland was among the poorest nations of Europe (Ólafsson, 2005). Industrialisation of the fisheries in the first half of the twentieth century was a key to the modernization of the country. Fish, it seemed, was in abundance. Herring fisheries blossomed in the 1930s and 40s with state of the art processing factories being built in numerous places along the coastline (Sigurðsson, et al., 2007). During the World War II the national economy boomed due to construction work issued by the allied forces that occupied the country and the immediate post-war period was a time of upturn as well due to inflow of foreign currency from fish sales during the war and Marshall Aid. This was the precondition for building the necessary infrastructure for the development of heavy industries, later to become a highly significant source of foreign currency. Currently, fisheries rank number two in terms of foreign currency earnings behind tourism (Figure 10.1).

Throughout the twentieth century cod (*Gadus morhua*) has been the most important fish in Icelandic waters. Its proportional share in the total catch has decreased in recent years but it still is by far the most valuable fish comprising 30% of the total value in 2012 (Hagstofa Íslands, 2014a). The need for managing

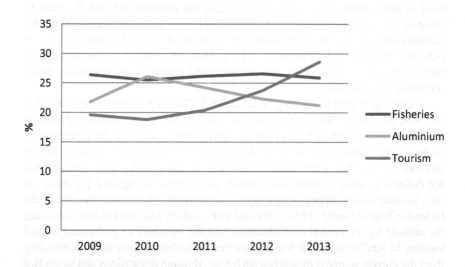

Figure 10.1   Proportional share of fisheries, aluminium production and tourism of total export from Iceland

Source: Hagstofa Íslands, 2014b

the fisheries was relatively soon realised by Icelandic authorities. The Marine Research Institute was formally established in 1965 and from the mid-1980s it has focused on studies of stock size and potential yields with the objective of securing long term viability of the fishing industry (Hafrannsóknarstofnun, 2014). Another important measure to manage and rationalize the fisheries was the introduction of the Individual Transferable Quota system in the mid-1980s. The Marine Research Institute annually recommends the total catch for different types of fish. In the beginning of the 1990s, the institute brought devastating news. Series of sub-average age cohorts of cod, that were to become the bulk of the cod stock, were measured in the waters around Iceland (Hafrannsóknarstofnun, 1995). In spring 1993, the Marine Research Institute thus recommended that only 150 thousand tons of fishing quota for cod would be allocated for the year 1994/5. This was dramatic by all standards, because in 1990 the fleet had landed more than double this catch (Hafrannsóknarstofnun, 1993). At the same time, prices went down on all fishery exports which meant a diminishing supply of foreign currency and a general struggle for the national economy.

At the time, Magnús Oddson, the general director of the Icelandic Tourist Board, wrote weekly columns on tourism in Morgunblaðið, by then one of the leading newspapers. On 4 June 1993, in his column titled, 'Foreign currency by each tourist the same as by one ton of cod', he convincingly argued that the export value of each tourist was similar to each ton of cod. In doing so he transferred important vocabulary of fishery management to tourism. He talked about the 'tourist stock' (ferðamannastofn), depicted the airplanes of the Icelandic airline Icelandair as 'trawlers' and argued that the stock would enable increased 'fisheries' in the years to come.

Magnús's argument attracted huge attention and in hindsight it is at about this time that the tide turned and tourism slowly began to make its way into the discourse of the national economy. He recalls:

> ... all of a sudden ... one afternoon, this just became the hot stuff in the debate. All of a sudden this was put in a context that people understood. [...] [...] this was the only way to get people to realize [the economic significance of tourism]. To try to connect it to something ... because people understood cod.

No doubt, other things also mattered. For one thing, ever more tourists arrived to the country, which gave a material presence to the phenomena. An important reason for that was the fact that Icelandair established a hub and spoke system in 1988 using the Keflavík International Airport as a hub on the route between North America and Europe. At the same time it renewed its fleet of airplanes offering larger capacity and better connections across the North Atlantic. Furthermore, tourism had already been taken up as one solution to the continual crisis in the agricultural sector with farmers being offered financial support to turn from farming sheep and cows to "herding" tourists. Tourism seemed to offer a "light of hope", as Magnús said, as the traditional stables of the economy were in crisis. However, no sudden change in the formal status of tourism took place and it was only in 1996 that the first tourism policy was installed by the Ministry of Communication and Tourism, followed by policies issued in 2005 and 2011 respectively (Alþingi, 2011; Samgönguráðuneytið, 2005).

In the following years, the interest in tourism waxed and waned in tandem with up- and downturns in the primary industries in Iceland, namely fisheries, agriculture and heavy industries (Jóhannesson and Huijbens, 2010). The connection to fish stocks, especially cod, in carving out a reality of tourism in the context of economic development and agendas has often been repeated and leaves its marks on present discourses on tourism and its future potentials[1]. This was for instance the case in the aftermath of the financial meltdown of the Icelandic economy in the fall of 2008. Approximately 80% of the banking sector collapsed in a matter of three weeks and the small island state was among the first to experience the international financial crisis (Matthiasson, 2008). The national currency devalued by 100% with the effect that exports created more value than before while imports increased in price accordingly. Tourism entered the limelight as an important part of the solution to the economic hardship and still it was tightly connected to and compared with heavy industries and fisheries as 'the third pillar' of the national economy (Össur Skarphéðinsson, 2008). An emphasis was put on raising numbers and diverse marketing schemes financed by the state (See e.g. Chapter 11). Stakeholders in tourism, be it central authorities or private firms, had once again 'gone fishing', framing tourism in the form of primary production industries.

10.3.3 Shaping the Future

What are the emergent trends in tourism policy making in Iceland? It is evident that tourism is accounted as a 'real business' judged by a recent interest in the sector by the banks and financial institutions. Furthermore, the fact that private firms are beginning to take active part in tourism policy making by commissioning policy reports, manifests a growing concern they have about the possible value of the core resources of tourism. It also sends a message about who they are and what the tourism sector in Iceland is supposedly about.

This brings us back to the morning conference in Harpa, September 2013. The report presented there, titled *Northern Sights: The Future of Tourism in Iceland*, provides one of the clearest examples of possible future policy realities of tourism in Iceland. The company issuing it, The Boston Consulting Group (BCG), is a global management consulting firm that specializes in business strategies. Its motto 'Shaping the Future Together' fittingly grasps its role in the current tourism policy making in Iceland (The Boston Consulting Group, 2014). Although it is only one in line of a number of policy papers recently published, it is one of the most important

---

1 For an account of the history of tourism policy making in Iceland see (Jóhannesson and Huijbens, 2010; 2013; Jóhannesson, Huijbens and Sharpley, 2010)

in the present context. The reasons are twofold. First, this report represents the first example of a policy report written by a private firm for a group of private and public stakeholders without a clear link to the central authorities. As such it represents an unprecedented opening up of the space of policy making where private actors have much to say about priorities and the scope of the work. Second, this report and its central suggestions have already, to a certain extent, been ratified by the central authorities. Apart from both attending the aforementioned conference, the current minister of tourism, Ragnheiður Elín Árnadóttir and the Prime Minister, Sigmundur Davíð Gunnlaugsson wrote forewords to the report where they welcome its valuable contribution to the debate on tourism development in the country. Furthermore, Ragnheiður Elín decided to start a work by the Ministry on one of the core ideas put forward in the report (Viðskiptablaðið, 2013b); the idea of the so-called Environment Card. It is a form of a multi-site access card, which is intended to provide access to approximately 30 of the key natural tourist attractions in Iceland and create revenues that will enable more sustainable management of those places and the development of new attractions.

The whole report revolves around the vision to:

> Maximise tourism's contribution to the whole of Iceland via managed, sustainable, year-round growth of visitors inspired by Iceland's distinctive nature, unique culture and warmhearted welcome. (The Boston Consulting Group, 2013, p.19)

In order to realize this vision the authors of the report stressed three themes: a) building the destination, b) funding of the vision and c) organisation of the sector. When the report was presented, emphasis was put on the second category, i.e. to raise funds for building up the destination. There, three kinds of funding mechanisms were discussed: 1) A flat charge on all visitors, 2) A multi-site access charge or Environment Card and 3) A single-site access charge (The Boston Consulting Group, 2013). These different options were assessed in relation to four criteria: to maximise revenues; to minimise the impact on visitor demand; to ensure distribution of resources among sites, and; to ensure feasibility and implementation at low cost (The Boston Consulting Group, 2013, p.44). The Environment Card was presented in detail as the solution that met best with these criteria. The report details a possible strategy for the implementation of the card as well as how the revenues should be redistributed or channelled to the sector. According to BCG, the strengths of the Environment Card are for instance that it 'allows tourism authorities to bundle the most popular sites with less well-visited attractions under one charging scheme' (The Boston Consulting Group, 2013, p.46). Furthermore, the Card is expected to become a product in itself while individual sites could develop secondary products to supplement their incomes on top of the charges for the Card. Also, an extensive enforcement scheme is not considered necessary. One of its primary strengths however is its 'ability to balance the need for a link between usage of sites and revenues with the requirement to be able to use some of the funds for investments in new or less-developed attractions' (The Boston Consulting Group, 2013, p.47).

It should be underlined that the design of the Environment Card is under construction by a taskforce initiated by the Ministry of Tourism and the minister has claimed that it is still uncertain if it will go through in the form the Boston Consulting Group recommended (RÚV, 2013b). What is however already evident is that the principle of the 'user pays' guides the minister's actions with support from some of the central stakeholders of the sector such as the Icelandic Tourist Industry Association and Icelandair Group (Ferðamálastofa, 2013a; MBL.is, 2012; Viðskiptablaðið, 2013b). It is therefore highly likely that some sort of user fee will be implemented in near future.

What is especially interesting in the present context is that the, by now, uncontroversial framing of tourism being 'real' business creates multiple controversies in relation to nature and nature experiences. Some issues are technical such as pricing and how to collect the fee and ensure compliance to the scheme. Others are more fundamental such as about who should pay. Should Icelandic citizens for instance pay the same fee as foreign tourists? Questions of equal access to common resources and criticism of the "user pays" principle have also been voiced (RÚV, 2014a; RÚV, 2014b; RÚV, 2014c).

The above discussion describes how tourism was metaphorically framed as fisheries, with tourists translated into fish stocks, which means that natural attractions can be seen as their feeding grounds. This translation exercise has meant that authorities and private firms have been busy fishing, focusing on the volume rather than value of tourists. The principle of the aforementioned "Gold-rush-mentality" is to harness as much revenue as possible with minimum effort. The Environment Card is presented as a change of course but it also has particular implications that have ontological repercussions.

First, the Environment Card is a means to cement the sector as an economic activity with untapped possibilities for growth in the future. Emphasis is put on optimising the revenues of tourism based on sound economic rationality. This however, hides away the organizational diversity of the sector itself, which includes small and micro sized companies that often adhere to different kinds of economic rationalities related to life-style (Gunnarsdóttir and Jóhannesson, 2014). Tourism business activities relate to multiple motives and rationalities that do not easily lend themselves to one encompassing definition of what is economic.

Second, as presented by the BCG, the Environment Card is framed on the basis of economic rationality while sustainable resource management is deemed necessary for long-term generation of revenues. However, as a policy tool, the Environment Card reduces nature to approximately 30 attractions (The Boston Consulting Group, 2013). Visitors to urban areas such as the capital Reykjavík, will for example not have to pay any fee. The Environment Card thus reproduces a traditional distinction between nature and culture where the former is a passive surface or stage for cultural schemes. Nature as a resource for tourism is to become clearly demarcated as sorts of stabilized islands of natural attractions, or unspoiled environment, in a sea of cultural practice. Tourism is seen and enacted as a purely cultural activity to be played out on natural stages of particular attractions that are defined by, again, a purely cultural scheme. This both reduces nature to the confines of particular enclavic spaces (Edensor, 2001) and dismisses how tourism and tourist experiences grow out of relational encounters between heterogeneous actors.

An interesting point regarding the parallel between fisheries and 'tourism-as-fisheries' is that the former has been tightly regulated for decades based on scientific knowledge produced by the Marine Research Institute. A long-term research strategy is probably not the only option but one of the most effective ones to engage with and account for the agency of nature. When tourism was translated into a fishery it only triggered the ideology of industrial production. The establishment of infrastructure to monitor and manage the key resource of the sector was not included and even though research has been identified as an important issue in policy papers limited investment has been made in it by public or private actors (Jóhannesson, Huijbens and Sharpley, 2010). Nature, as a resource for tourism was thereby left without 'spokesman', which could serve a similar role as the Marine Research Institute did for cod. At present, nature still remains mute and the Environment Card defines it as particular spots on a map of attractions. It thus hides away intrinsic nature connections through which valuable tourism experiences grow.

10.4 Ordering Continuity

This chapter has described some of the ways through which tourism has become a 'real' economic activity in Iceland. By focusing on tourism policy making it has concentrated on practices that have contributed to the present momentum of tourism on the island. By following policy making, the aim was not to write a full account of the status of tourism within the administrative system of Icelandic authorities, but to provide a partial description of the enactment of tourism in Iceland and the potential controversies involved in that enactment. They show how realities in practice are emergent, materially complex and multiple (Lien and Law, 2013). The idea is not to argue against the fact that tourism is to a large extent a business activity, but rather to interfere in what has become an uncontroversial claim in Iceland that tourism is more or less similar to fisheries.

We have seen how the reality of tourism in Iceland, defined as business, depends on a natural or earthly connection to fish in the form of cod. The absence of cod from Icelandic waters at this particular time strengthened the case that many were arguing for, namely that tourism could and would be an important economic pillar for the national economy. This connection hinted at what came to be the position of tourism in the discourse on the national economy, being described as similar to and on par with fisheries and heavy industries. As stated above, the aim is not to deny the economic importance of tourism, nor to defy the description of tourism as economic activity. The problem is that a overarching narrative of the sort that frames the whole tourism sector in terms of fisheries hides the complexities and multiplicity of tourism realities. In the context of tourism policy making it is important to be sensitive to the diversity of tourism activities, and the different kinds of businesses included.

The chapter also argued that policy research has been overtly social in the sense of not taking into account how nature and society are entangled in a continuous movement of life. But why is it important to take the Earth into account or the activities of more-than-human actors such as fish? The reason is that by failing to grasp the material heterogeneity and distributed agencies of diverse actors we miss out on the generative capacities of the Earth and their effects on our relations, agendas and orderings. No plan or order is perfect in the sense of being final. Every order has a capacity to change and this capacity lies at root of the continuous becoming of the world (Law, 2004). Earthly connections play a vital part in the continuous movement of the world as illustrated by the example of the cod. This is what the annual measurements by the Marine Research Institute helped to mediate in the case of fisheries.

In the case of tourism, the way in which people in Iceland 'understand cod' was translated to tourism. In the absence of any kind of 'spokesman' that could fulfil a similar role to the Marine Research Institute for tourism development, this translation reproduced a typical distinction between humans and their natural environment, with the former being dominant, and the latter, passive. The Environment Card partly represents a change in attitude towards the "feeding grounds" of tourists. It has dawned on central stakeholders that it is economically profitable to manage and regulate the resource, namely natural attractions. However, the principle of the connection between the tourism sector and nature remains intact. Nature has been reduced to particular attractions distinct from cultural attractions such as the Capital area and tourism is enacted as cultural practice to be performed on the passive stage or surface of nature. Hence, as a policy tool, the Environment Card implies that the Earth and nature are distinct from society. As the notion of the Anthropocene underlines, this distinction is increasingly difficult to sustain. It is not like (cultural) humans are able to order the (natural) environment. Rather, these two spheres are entangled and emergent through relational practices. It is therefore crucial to come to grips with how society and nature is one and many at the same time; how relational enactments such as tourism policy making have ontological repercussions or how our activities *do* nature and society.

If we are to by-pass the divide between nature and society in tourism policy making the challenge is to think about policy making in topological ways, admitting that there is no outside or inside given in the order of things but a meshwork of interwoven lines or relations. In short, if we are to order continuity we have to move, accept and grasp disturbance and stay with the non-coherent or the uncertain (Law and Singleton, 2013). To think about policy making as an effect of relational improvisation dependant on heterogeneous relations might sound as a weak suggestion to policy makers. However, the concept of improvisation underlines that policy making is a space of politically charged encounters and controversies. The concept of improvisation furthermore highlights the need of sensing as we go along and brings forth the importance of information, knowledge and active dialogue for policy to be responsive to the realities it is supposed to order. What is certain is that nature as the Earth itself, will not rest still and thus to improvise tourism policy without taking its earthly connections or more-than-human politics into account, is futile. The Marine Research Institute has served this role for fisheries while investment in research infrastructure in tourism has been miniscule, which has led to a weak knowledge base for policy making. Last but not least, the concept of improvisation sensitizes us as researchers and policy practitioners to the multiple realities of the subject matter of policy making, the contingent power relations involved in such practice and the ontological politics of every ordering attempt. The concept of improvisation does not free us from engaging in political struggles but rather underscores that such controversies may be necessary steps of 'slow motion' in carving ways forward, which different stakeholders can agree upon. In terms of research of tourism policy this implies that one should also be aware of the absences of controversies and seek to disturb what seems to be the usual order of things (Law and Singleton, 2013) while following realities in their making.

Acknowledgement

The research for this chapter was financially supported by the Icelandic Research Council through a post-doctoral project titled *Tourism in the periphery: The emergence and shaping of tourism in Iceland*. I would like to thank my co-editors and Dianne Dredge for valuable comments on an earlier version of this chapter.

References

Alþingi, 2011. Tillaga til þingsályktunar um ferðamálaáætlun 2011–2020 pp.758–467. mál. [online] Available at: <http://www.althingi.is/dba-bin/ferill. pl?ltg=139&mnr=467> [Accessed on March 20 2011].

Arion banki, 2013. Ferðaþjónustan: Atvinnugrein á unglingsaldri [Tourism: sector in its youth]. Reykjavík: Arion banki.

Benediktsson, E., 1896. Útlendingar á Íslandi [Foreigners in Iceland], *Dagskrá*, 1 July.

Braidotti, R., 2002. *Metamorphoses: Towards a materialist theory of becoming*. Cambridge: Polity Press.

Bramwell, B., 2011. Governance, the state and sustainable tourism: A political economy approach. *Journal of Sustainable Tourism*, 19(4–5), pp.459–477. doi: 10.1080/09669582.2011.576765

Checchi & Co., 1975. *Tourism in Iceland: Phase 2*. Washington, D.C.: Checchi & co.

Dredge, D. and Jenkins, J., 2011. New spaces of tourism planning and policy. In: D. Dredge and J. Jenkins, eds. 2011. *Stories of practice: Tourism policy and planning*. Aldershot: Ashgate. pp.1–12.

Dredge, D., Jenkins, J. and Whitford, M., 2011. Tourism planning and policy: Historical development and contemporary challenges. In: D. Dredge and J. Jenkins, eds. 2011. *Stories of practice: Tourism policy and planning*. Aldershot: Ashgate. pp.13–35.

Edensor, T., 2001. Performing tourism, staging tourism: (Re)producing tourist space and practice. *Tourist Studies*, 1(1), pp. 59–81.

Eyjan.is, 2013. Hafa áhyggjur af gullgrafaraæði í ferðaþjónustu – Allt of mörg hótel í pípunum [Concerns over gold rush mentality in tourism – Way too many hotels in the pipelines]. [online] Available at: <http://eyjan.pressan.is/ frettir/2013/03/13/hafa-ahyggjur-af-gullgrafaraaedi-i-ferdathjonustu-allt-of-morg-hotel-i-pipunum/> [Accessed September 25 2013].

Ferðamálastofa, 2013a. Fjármögnun uppbyggingar og viðhalds ferðamannastaða: Yfirlit yfir gjaldtökuleiðir [The financing of development of tourist attractions: Overview of possible ways to collect user fees]. Reykjavík: Ferðamálastofa.

Ferðamálastofa, 2013b. Heildarfjöldi erlendra gesta 1949–2012 [Total number of foreign visitors 1949–2012]. [online] Available at: <http://www.ferdamalastofa. is/is/tolur-og-utgafur/fjoldi-ferdamanna> [Accessed September 25 2013].

Ferðamálastofa, 2014a, 14.01. *Ferðafréttir: Fréttir frá Ferðamálastofu* [News on tourism: News from the Icelandic Tourism Board]. Reykjavík: Ferðamálastofa.

Ferðamálastofa, 2014b. Ferðaþjónusta á Íslandi í tölum: Apríl 2014 [Tourism in Iceland in numbers: April 2014]. [online] Available at: <http://www. ferdamalastofa.is/static/files/ferdamalastofa/Frettamyndir/2014/april/ ferdatjonusta_itolum_april14.pdf> [Accessed May 12 2014].

Franklin, A., 2012. The choreography of a mobile world: Tourism orderings. In: V.R. Van der Duim, C. Ren and G. T. Jóhannesson, eds. 2012. *Actor-Network Theory and tourism: Ordering, materiality and multiplicity*. London and New York: Routledge. pp.43–58.

Gunnarsdóttir, G.Þ. and Jóhannesson, G.T., 2014. Weaving with witchcraft: Tourism and entrepreneurship in Strandir, Iceland. In: A. Viken and B. Granås, eds. 2014. *Destination development in tourism: Turns and tactics*. Farnham: Ashgate. pp.95–112.

Gössling, S., 2006. Iceland. In: G. Baldacchino, ed. 2006. *Exrtreme tourism: Lessons from the world's cold water islands*. Oxford: Elsevier. pp.115–127.

Hafrannsóknarstofnun [The Marine Research Institute], 1993. *Nytjastofnar sjávar og umhverfisþættir 1992/93 – Aflahorfur fiskveiðiárið 1993/4*. Reykjavík: Hafrannsóknarstofnun.

Hafrannsóknarstofnun [The Marine Research Institute], 1995. *Nytjastofnar sjávar 1994/95 – Aflahorfur fiskveiðiárið 1995/96*. Reykjavík: Hafrannsóknarstofnun.

Hafrannsóknarstofnun [The Marine Research Institute], 2014. *Saga* [History]. [online] Available at: <http://www.hafro.is/undir.php?ID=2&REF=1> [Accessed February 18 2014].

Hagstofa Íslands [Statistics Iceland], 2014a. *Afli og verðmæti eftir tegundum og veiðisvæðum 1993–2012* [Catch and value by species and fishing ground].

[online] Available at: <http://www.hagstofa.is/Hagtolur/Sjavarutvegur-og-landbunadur/Afli-og-verdmaeti> [Accessed January 8 2014].

Hagstofa Íslands [Statistics Iceland], 2014b. *Vöruútflutningur* [Export of goods and services]. [online] Available at: <http://www.hagstofa.is/Hagtolur/Utanrikisverslun> [Accessed January 8 2014].

Hall, C.M., 2000. *Tourism planning: Policies, processes and relationships.* Harlow: Pearson Education Limited.

Hall, C.M., Zapata, M.J.C., 2014. Public administration and tourism – International and Nordic perspectives. *Scandinavian Journal of Public Administration,* 18(1), pp.3–17.

Hall, C.M., Müller, D. and Saarinen, J. eds., 2009. *Nordic tourism: Issues and cases.* Bristol: Channel View Publications.

Haraway, D., 1991. *Simians, cyborgs and women: The reinvention of nature.* London: Free Association Books.

Harvey, P., 2012. The topological quality of infrastructural relation: An ethnographic approach. *Theory, Culture & Society,* 29(4/5), pp.76–92. doi: 10.1177/0263276412448827.

Hjalager, A.-M., 2002. Repairing innovation defectiveness in tourism. *Tourism Management,* 23, pp.465–474.

Huijbens, E. and Gren, M., 2012. Tourism, ANT and the earth. In: V.R. Van der Duim, C. Ren and G.T. Jóhannesson, eds. 2012. *Actor-Network Theory and tourism: Ordering, materiality and multiplicity.* London and New York: Routledge. pp.146–163.

Ingold, T., 2000a. Globes and spheres: The topology of environmentalism. *The perception of the environment: Essays in livelihood, dwelling and skill.* London and New York: Routledge. pp.209–218.

Ingold, T., 2000b. *The perception of the environment: Essays in livelihood, dwelling and skill.* London and New York: Routledge.

Ingold, T., 2006. Rethinking the animate, re-animating thought. *Ethnos, 71*(1), pp.9–20. doi: 10.1080/00141840600603111.

Ingold, T., 2011. *Being alive: Essays on movement, knowledge and description.* London and New York: Routledge.

Ingold, T. and Hallam, E., 2007. Creativity and cultural improvisation: An introduction. In: T. Ingold and E. Hallam, eds. 2007. *Creativity and Cultural Improvisation.* Oxford: Berg. pp.1–24.

Ísleifsson, S., 1996. *Ísland framandi land [Iceland exotic country].* Reykjavík: Mál og menning.

Ísleifsson, S., 2011. Introduction: Imaginations of national identity and the north. In: S. Ísleifsson and D. Chartier, eds. 2011. *Iceland and images of the north.* Québec: Presses de l'Université du Québec. pp.3–22.

Jóhannesson, G.T. and Huijbens, E., 2010. Tourism in times of crisis: Exploring the discourse of tourism development in Iceland. *Current Issues in Tourism,* 13(5), pp.419–434.

Jóhannesson, G.T. and Huijbens, E., 2013. Tourism resolving crisis? Exploring tourism development in Iceland in the wake of economic recession. In: D. Müller, L. Lundmark and R.H. Lemelin, eds. 2013. *New issues in polar tourism: Communities, environments, politics.* New York: Springer. pp.133–147.

Jóhannesson, G.T., Huijbens, E. and Sharpley, R., 2010. Icelandic tourism: Past directions – future challenges. *Tourism Geographies,* 12(2), pp.278–301.

Landsbanki Íslands, 2013a. *Ferðaþjónusta. Tímarit Landsbanka Íslands.* Reykjavík: Landsbanki Íslands.

Landsbanki Íslands, 2013b. *Ferðaþjónusta á Íslandi: Greining Landsbanka Íslands.* Reykjavík: Landsbanki Íslands.

Latour, B., 1986. The powers of association. In: J. Law, ed. 1986. *Power, action and belief: A new sociology of knowledge.* London, Boston and Henley: Routledge and Kegan Paul. pp.264–280.

Latour, B., 1993. *We have never been modern.* Translated by C. Porter. Cambridge: Harvard University Press.

Latour, B., 2005. *Reassembling the social: An introduction to Actor-Network-Theory.* Oxford: Oxford University Press.

Latour, B., 2007. *A plea for earthly sciences.* [online] Available at: <http://www. bruno-latour.fr/articles/article/102-BSA-GB.pdf> [Accessed September 1 2010].

Law, J., 1999. After ANT: Complexity, naming and topology. In: J. Law and J. Hassard, eds. 1999. *Actor Network Theory and after.* Oxford: Blackwell. pp.1–14.

Law, J., 2004. *After method: Mess in social science research.* London and New York: Routledge.

Law, J., 2007. *Actor-Network Theory and material semiotics.* [online] Available at: <http://heterogeneities.net/publications/Law2007ANTandMaterialSemiotics. pdf> [Accessed November 17 2011].

Law, J. and Singleton, V., 2013. ANT and politics: Working in and on the world. *Qualitative Sociology,* 36, pp.485–502. doi: 10.1007/s11133–013–9263–7.

Lien, M.E. and Law, J., 2013. Emergent aliens: On salmon, nature and their enactment. *Ethnos,* 76(1), pp.65–87. doi: 10.1080/00144844.2010.549946.

Lorimer, J., 2012. Multinatural geographies for the Anthropocene. *Progress in Human Geography,* 36(5), pp.593–612. doi: 10.1177/0309132511435352.

Lury, C., Parisi, L. and Terranova, T., 2012. Introduction: The becoming topological of culture. *Theory, Culture & Society,* 29(4/5), pp.3–35. doi: 10.1177/0263276412454552.

Matthiasson, T., 2008. Spinning out of control, Iceland in crisis. *Nordic Journal of Political Economy,* 34(3), pp.1–19.

MBL.is, 2012. Þeir borga sem njóta [Users pay]. *Morgunblaðið,* 25 Sep. [online] Available at: <http://www.mbl.is/vidskipti/frettir/2012/09/25/eir_borga_sem_ njota/> [Accessed January 21 2014].

McLean, S., 2009. Stories and cosmogonies: Imagining creativity beyond nature and culture. *Cultural Anthropology,* 24(2), pp 213–245. doi: 10.1111/j.1548–1360.2009.01130.x.

Mol, A., 1999. Ontological politics. A word and some questions. In: J. Law and J. Hassard, eds. 1999. *Actor-Network Theory and after*. Oxford: Blackwell. pp.74–89.

Ólafsdóttir, R. and Runnström, M.C., 2013. Assessing hiking trails condition in two popular tourist destinations in the Icelandic highlands. *Journal of Outdoor Recreation and Tourism*, 3–4, pp.57–67. doi: http://dx.doi.org/10.1016/j. jort.2013.09.004.

Ólafsson, S., 2005. Normative foundations of the Icelandic welfare state: On the gradual erosion of citizenship-based welfare rights. In: N. Kildal and S. Kuhnle, eds. 2005. *Normative foundations of the welfare state: The Nordic experience*. London and New York: Routledge. pp.214–236.

Pálsson, G., 1996. Human-environmental relations: Orientalism, paternalism and communalism. In: P. Descola and G. Pálsson, eds. 1996. *Nature and society: Anthropological perspectives*. London: Routledge. pp.63–81.

Pálsson, G., Szerszynski, B., Sörlin, S., Marks, J., Avril, B., Crumley, C. and Weehuize, R., 2013. Reconceptualizing the 'Anthropos' in the Anthropocene: Integrating the social sciences and humanities in global environmental change research. *Environmental Science and Policy*, 28, pp.3–13. doi: http://dx.doi. org/10.1016/j.envsci.2012.11.004.

Pforr, C., 2006. Tourism policy in the making: An Australian network study. *Annals of Tourism Research*, 33(1), pp.87–108. doi: 10.1016/j.annals.2005.04.004.

PKF, 2013. *Promote Iceland: Long-term strategy for the Icelandic tourism industry*. Reykjavík: PKF accountants and business advisors.

RÚV [The Icelandic National Broadcasting Service], 2013a. Gullgrafaraæði í ferðaþjónustu [Gold rush in tourism]. [online] Available at: <http://www.ruv. is/frett/gullgrafaraaedi-i-ferdathjonustu> [Accessed January 21 2014].

RÚV [The Icelandic National Broadcasting Service], 2013b. Samráðsfundur um náttúrupassa á mánudag [Joint meeting on the Environment Card on monday]. [online] Available at: <http://www.ruv.is/frett/samradsfundur-um-natturupassa-a-manudag> [Accessed January 21 2014].

RÚV [The Icelandic National Broadcasting Service], 2014a. Kastljós: Kallað eftir stefnumótun í ferðaþjónustu [Spotlight: Call for tourism policy]. [online]11 February. Available at: <http://www.ruv.is/sarpurinn/kastljos/13022014/efast-um-natturupassann> [Accessed February 17 2014].

RÚV [The Icelandic National Broadcasting Service], 2014b. Kastljós: Ferðamálastjóri: Vörumst fótanuddtækjasyndrómið [Spotlight: The general director of the Icelandic Tourist Board: Beware of the foot-massage-machines-syndrome]. [online]12 February. Available at: <http://www.ruv.is/ sarpurinn/kastljos/13022014/efast-um-natturupassann> [Accessed February 17 2014].

RÚV [The Icelandic National Broadcasting Service], 2014c. Kastljós: Efast um náttúrupassann [Spotlight: Doubting the Environment Card]. [online]13 February. Available at: <http://www.ruv.is/sarpurinn/kastljos/13022014/efast-um-natturupassann> [Accessed February 17 2014].

Samgönguráðuneytið, 2005. *Ferðamálaáætlun 2006–2015.* Reykjavík: Samgönguráðuneytið.

Sigurðsson, B., Sigurðsson, B., Jóhannesson, G.T., Gíslason, H., Ragnarsson, H., Jakobsson, J. and Lúðvíksson, S.J., 2007. *Silfur hafsins – Gull Íslands: Síldarsaga Íslendinga.* Reykjavík: Nesútgáfan.

Sørensen, E. and Torfing, J., 2005. The democratic anchorage of governance networks. *Scandinavian Political Studies,* 28(3), pp.195–218.

The Boston Consulting Group, 2013. *Northern sights: The future of tourism in Iceland.* [online] Available at: <http://www.icelandictourism.is/> [Accessed September 25 2013].

The Boston Consulting Group, 2014. *Vision.* [online] Available at <http://www.bcg.com/about_bcg/vision/mission.aspx> [Accessed January 21 2014].

Thomas, R. and Thomas, H., 2005. Understanding tourism policy-making in urban areas, with particular reference to small firms. *Tourism Geographies,* 7(2), pp.121–137. doi: 10.1080/14616680500072323.

Umhverfisstofnun [The Environment Agency of Iceland], 2012. *Náttúruvernd og ósnortin landsvæði* [Nature conservation and wilderness]. [online] Available at: <http://www.umhverfisstofnun.is/umhverfisstofnun/utgefid-efni/pistlar-og-greinar/grein/2012/08/24/Natturuvernd/> [Accessed September 27 2013].

Viðskiptablaðið, 2013a. Hundruð ólöglegra gistiplássa í ferðaþjónustu [Hundreds of illegal rooms in tourism]. <http://www.vb.is/frettir/82018/> [Accessed September 27 2013].

Viðskiptablaðið, 2013b. Náttúrupassar verða að veruleika [The Environment Card will be reality]. [online] Available at: <http://www.vb.is/frettir/97447/> [Accessed January 21 2014].

Visir.is, 2012. *Segir gullgrafaraæði í ferðaþjónustu* [Says tourism is characterized by gold-rush mentality]. [online] Available at: <http://www.visir.is/segir-gullgrafaraaedi-i-ferdathjonustu/article/2012120729391> [Accessed September 27 2013].

Visir.is, 2013. *Gullgrafaraæði á gistimarkaði* [Gold-rush mentality in accommodation]. [online] Available at: <http://www.visir.is/gullgrafaraaedi-a-gistimarkadi/article/2013701109883> [Accessed September 27 2013]

Warwick, K., 2013. *Beyond industrial policy: Emerging issues and new trends.* Paris: OECD.

Wray, M., 2009. Policy communities, networks and issue cycles in tourism destination systems. *Journal of Sustainable Tourism,* 17(6), pp.673–690.

Össur Skarphéðinsson, 2008. *Ræða ráðherra á ferðamálaþingi 2008* [Minister's speech at the annual tourism industry conference]. [online] Available at: <http://idnnadarraduneyti.is/radherra/raedur-greinar/nr/2661> [Accessed January 22 2009].

Chapter 11
Topological Encounters:
Marketing Landscapes for Tourists

Edward H. Huijbens

11.1 Introduction

This chapter deals with landscapes and the ways in which they are presented to and encountered by tourists visiting Iceland, and in land-use controversies surrounding tourism development. The aim of the chapter is to show how wilderness and natural landscapes in Iceland are given voice and agency, enabling them encounters with the visiting tourist. However, the work that goes into giving wilderness landscapes a voice in marketing and promotion entails the exertion of force upon the earth, moulding its surface into marketable form. In order to make sense of this force this chapter draws conceptually on topological imaginaries as presented in literature on cultural topologies and vitalist geo-philosophy as outlined in the work of Gilles Deleuze and those who have elaborated thereupon (see Protevi and Bonta, 2004). With concepts and tools developed through these two theoretical strands landscapes emerge as a malleable continuous surface at one with us and the earth, taking on different forms as it enters e.g. marketing media. The forces exerted to produce the different forms of landscapes become the focus of the analysis as it is through these forces that a malleable continuous surface takes shape. The wellspring of this force is the demand for marketability and the generation of surplus in modern capitalist experience economy. This charges a potential landscape encounter with controversies that the chapter seeks to unravel through two examples provided.

The chapter proceeds in three parts. First, topologies will be introduced and how these are dealt with in recent literature in terms of culture. The inroad to the topological theorising is through mathematics and arts. Relating this understanding to culture is premised upon our modern day culture being a specific logic of late capitalism (Jameson, 1991, p.ix), which today has morphed into catering to ever more closely defined 'niches' of individual needs under the terms of the experience economy (Pine and Gilmore, 2011). This particular morphing 'bale[s] free flowing ideas into marketable commodities', such as freedom, individuality and experiences (Smith, 2005, p.891). Making commodities out of these is the mainstay of modern day tourism and for its products to emerge, landscapes, peoples and places need to be reshaped and fitted to purpose. What emerges are cultural topologies upon which the chapter will move to a second part which outlines two distinct forces at play in moulding the wilderness landscapes of Iceland into their marketable form, i.e. that of perceived wilderness and nature and the practices of marketing. Through unravelling these two examples controversies emerge, not least through the realisation that the force exerted to mould landscapes is not at the beckon call of all. 'The world may be flat for those who can afford a business class ticket to fly around it ... while for those gazing up at passing airplanes in Sub-Saharan Africa or the Indian countryside, the opportunity represented by London or Bombay or New York is an impossible climb ...' (Smith, 2005, p.894). In recognition of this uneven geography of tourism this chapter concludes with explaining the central tenants of the politics of cultural topology.

11.2 Cultural Topology

Topology is derived from the mathematical theorization of sets, or so-called set theory and entails '... the study of collections of objects with certain prescribed structures' (Mendelson, 1975, p.2). In topology, this structure does not prescribe a one-to-one correspondence between points in a given set. Rather, the correspondence is prescribed by functions that define transformations (Mendelson, 1975, p.128). A set of points, e.g. on the Earth's surface, are defined by the relations (functions) that exist between them, that in turn define the space provided for by a given set of points. Through emphasis on functions and thus relationality, a key feature of this topological space is its continuous nature. Well-known mathematically demonstrated topological spaces include the Klein bottle, the Möbius strip and the Torus (figure 11.1). All share the distinguishing characteristic of one being unable to tell the outside from the inside as they appear infinite or continuous.

More complicated shapes and forms are difficult to establish mathematically. However, the artist M.C. Escher has provided 'intriguing visual metaphors for abstract mathematical concepts' such as topological change which was one of his key devices in prints (Schattschneider, 2010, p.715–716). In Escher's work topological change manifests in figures of landscapes and phenomena where one is unable to pinpoint the beginning or the end of a particular shape. As the mathematician Bert Mendelson (1975, p.49) explains: 'We may therefore describe a continuous function as one that commutes with the operation of taking limits'. Meaning that through continually defining outsides and insides or the limits to any relation, spaces unfold.

Putting this topological understanding of space to use in people's spatial registers has some limitations. Both Escher's artwork and the mathematically demonstrated shapes remain observable only online or in printed form. The inherent detachment of viewing these shapes on a sheet of paper or computer screen makes the viewer unaware of how the universe, the Earth's surface and us, are exactly such a continually unfolding space. The Cambridge mathematician Ian Stewart (2001) outlines what a topological world would look like through the words of his story's protagonist, a space hopper:

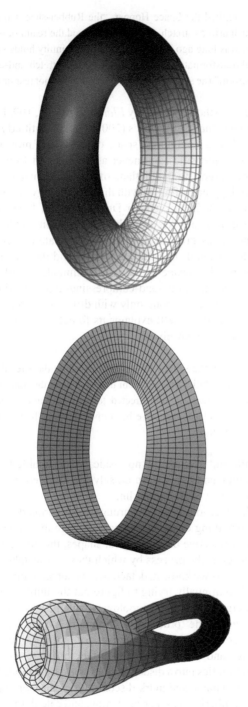

Figure 11.1 The Klein bottle, the Möbius strip and the Torus.
Source: Wikipedia Commons

> "Topologica", replied the Space Hopper, "the Rubber-sheet Continent, which
> doesn't so much drift as stretch ... We have entered the realm of topology, from
> which rigidity was long ago banished and only continuity holds sway. The land
> of topological transformations, which can bend-and-stretch-and-compress-and-
> distort-and-deform" (he said this all in one breath) "but not tear or break" (p.89).

As a deliberate reply to the 19th Century *Flatland* (Abbott, 1992[1884]) explaining
geometry and dimensionality, Stewart's (2001) book is entitled *Flatterland*. In the
book, "Topologica" is a continuous space of flows and movements that are of
differing speeds and intensities, but never as such depart from a singular plane.
Hence the Flatterland reply to the Flatland of classic geometry.

Intuitively topology has affinities with the flat ontology arguably underpinning
ANT theorising (Latour, 2005; Van der Duim, Ren and Jóhannesson, 2012) and
ideas of ordering in tourism. Accordingly, we are at one with the world and all
that is. Our agency is as great as any of the inanimate objects we deploy, that
which presumably surrounds us is at one with us and there is no higher order or
lower order to being. The shape of the world, immediate and at large, depends
on the bending-and-stretching-and-compressing-and-distorting-and-deforming
anyone or anything can bring about, only with different degrees of force. In terms
of tourism Franklin (2004, p.280) explains its forcefulness as composed of sites,
mobility and the tourists themselves:

> Tourism orders both the spaces of tourism, including the sites that are visited
> and the spaces of mobility that get them there but also, the tourists themselves.
> They become self-ordering, self-directed tourists constantly interpellated by,
> and curious for the places that have been opened up in their name and which
> become relevant to them.

There is no outside and presumably no inside, one is unable to tell where things
begin and where they end and we are ourselves embroiled in this Flatterland, or
interpellated to use the words of Franklin.

Ordering is the exertion of force. Through force forms deform, change shape
and morph into something different and parts change their relation to the whole.
From a detached perspective on topological shapes, the operation of defining the
inside and the outside is the process by which these forms take shape as in figure
11.1. Yet in the world as we know it, detachment is not an option. We are embroiled
in this Flatterland, continually trying to figure out the limits of what we perceive
and do. What emerges are cultural topologies which Lury, Parisi and Terranova
(2012, p.4) argue entail the 'ordering of continuity [which] emerges, sometimes
without explicit coordination, in practices of sorting, naming, numbering,
comparing, listing, and calculating. The effect of these practices is both to
introduce new continuities into a discontinuous world by establishing equivalences
or similitudes, and to make and mark discontinuities through repeated contrasts'.
Sorting, naming, numbering, comparing, listing, and calculating are the operations

of defining limits. These are the methods by which we bound spaces to make them comprehendible (Perec, 2003). These methods cannot be detached from the world in which we find ourselves. With tourist spaces and landscapes being undissected topologies of movements, changing shape through intensities or the forces of us and the Earth, an inventory establishes equivalences or similitudes, and marks discontinuities through repeated contrasts.

The key word here is 'repeated'. Discontinuities emerge only through repeated contrasts as an inventory cannot ever be complete or exhaustive. 'Everything is connected and contained within everything else' (Law, 2004, p.22), spaces and places are continuous and any discontinuities or apparent boundedness can only be marked through contrast. Spaces and places only emerge through their relations and this unfolding within the context of that relationality means that 'circumstance gives the relation its sufficient reason' (Deleuze, 1991, p.103). It is the circumstance that forms the context for the emergence but it is at the same time that very same context we can inventory. The context is about the relations forged and the focus should be on the relation's 'contingency, difference and incommensurability, and a resistance to universalising abstractions through emphasis on the particularity of situated, historical practices' (Bough, 1993, p.15). Indeed 'the global is situated, specific, and materially constructed in the practices that make each specificity' (Law, 2004, p.24). The situated, material and specific ways of ordering relations and introducing 'new continuities into a discontinuous world' is highly significant 'for to know is by definition to say that something is something else and be believed when one says it; since every understanding by necessity is an act of interpretation, it follows that knowledge is always an exercise in translation' (Olsson, 2007, p.93). The question is: Who translates and thus wields this knowledge under which circumstances?

To sum through some recognised geographical theorising. The space of 'topologica' is the 'smooth space' of Deleuze and Guattari (1987), i.e. that of continuous variation that affects and provides for intensities that continually deform and destabilise any 'striated space' of fixity, order and established 'lines of power' (Olsson, 1991; 1992). These 'lines of power' prop up the power geometries of any space (Massey, 1993) and it is these that need to be unravelled if we are to understand the emergent properties and implications of cultural topologies. Space maybe flat and non-hierarchical, but the world is not as Smith (2005) reminded us of in the introduction and key to having effect resides in the plausibility of your concerns.

11.3   Topological Encounters

'Are you dressed in the road map of your travels? says the perfidious wit' (Serres, 1997, p.xiv). The context is what matters as therein lies the sufficient reason of any relation as Deleuze stated above. The cultural topologies to emerge through 'sorting, naming, numbering, comparing, listing, and calculating' (Lury, Parisi and Terranova,

2012, p.4) will be outlined through the way in which discourses on wilderness and nature conservation and marketing practices has unfolded in relation to tourism in Iceland in the last years. Through unravelling these practices of translation and knowledge exertion, the wellspring of the prevailing rhetoric in each case can be identified. In this way the dominating practices in these two examples emerge in their topological and controversial guise and can then be contrasted with alternatives.

11.3.1   Wilderness Topologies

Icelandic wilderness landscapes are key to the marketing and promotion to foreign tourists as for many of the Nordic countries more generally (Hall, Müller and Saarinen, 2009, pp.17–21). Among the natural features that constitute Iceland as a destination are the country's geothermal, volcanic and glacial landscapes, and vast tracts of land void of signs of human habitation or what has been termed 'wilderness' (Sæþórsdóttir, Hall and Saarinen, 2011). Most people come to Iceland to experience nature (Icelandic Tourist Board, 2013) and varying degrees of wilderness (Ólafsdóttir, 2007; 2008; 2011; Sæþórsdóttir, 2010; 2013) and these tourist desires are reflected and featured in Icelandic tourism marketing and promotion (Gunnarsdóttir, 2011; Huijbens, 2011; Huijbens and Benediktsson, 2013).

Landscapes are spaces and as such without fixed points, a mere continuous surface that never tears or breaks. The point of analysis is the context as each landscape at each moment in time has its time and a place, its own space and time. The perennial question remains however as to the ultimate reference point '… writing-earth-writing-earth-writing … which came first: this earth or this writing, this map or this territory, this (social) space or this perspective?' (Doel, 1999, p.104). Arguably it is the earth that is the ultimate reference point (Gren and Huijbens, 2012). With emerging topics of anthropogenic climate change, environmental concern and the newly proclaimed geological era of the Anthropocene (Crutzen, 2002), what is perceived as wild, natural and pristine, however misguided, provides a particularly intriguing entry point into the situated politics of moulding landscapes.

When the wilderness landscapes of Iceland are promoted it is put to work for a very specific audience, one that can afford to fly and is accustomed to mediated images and their deciphering under the terms of the cultural logic of late capitalism (Smith, 2005). Sought after landscapes for tourists in Iceland are glacier landscapes, but 10% of the island is covered with ice. Ice sheets and glaciers provide a much used tool in environmental rhetoric. The very glacier a potential visitor might come to stand on is a signifier for natural scientists and the public at large of the changes being brought about by the current institutional conditions and international political decisions. In the tourist news monthly *The Reykjavík Grapewine,* under the headline 'The Glaciers Are Melting' (Fontaine, 2012), the well-known fact of anthropogenic climate change warming the North and leaving polar bears stranded on ever smaller iceberg, fires the public imaginary and leads some to advocate the glaciers' voice in 'communicating the message of change' (Vox Naturae, 2012, p.2).

The glacier as avatar of change stands in stark contrast with the mode of getting to Iceland. Those who visit Iceland, or come to be inspired by the 'land of ice and fire', conflating two promotion tag lines, arrive mostly by air, leaving behind them not only the mundane but also ripples in the sky as visible traces of their emission of greenhouse-gases. But, of course, also those who travel by cruise ships or ferries emit their shares that are hidden behind the numbers presented in Table 11.1.

Table 11.1   Means of transport for those visiting Iceland and total number of Visitors in 2012

Entry point	Keflavík International	Other airports	Reykjavík harbour in Cruise Ships	Seyðifjörður harbour with Smyril line	Total
Number	646.921	13.072	91.954	12.780	**764.727**
% of total in 2012	84,5	2	12	1,5	**100**

Source: Icelandic Tourist Board, 2013

These particular lines of flight sustain tourism in Iceland, but at the same time run headways onto its main attractive feature, characterised by the glacier. It is obvious that Icelandic tourism rests in the realm of aviation and this rest with Icelandair, responsible for 85% of all passengers passing through Keflavík airport (in 2012). Aviation is also a significant contributor to the Icelandic economy, topping the worldwide country listing charts when it comes to air connectivity per GDP and providing for 6,6% of GDP in 2010 (Oxford Economics, 2011, p.12 and 4). Indeed certain lines of power prevail, certain structures seem more prominent than others and it is from these that the power to define, order and shape flows, and the airline, Icelandair sits at the helm.

The environmental impact of global aviation comes mainly through radiative forcing, which entails the multiplied impact of CO_2 and other greenhouse gasses as they are released in the stratosphere. The Intergovernmental Panel on Climate Change (IPCC) estimates that aviation is responsible for 3,5% of anthropogenic climate change and set to increase if nothing is done with increased air travel this century (Lee, et al., 2009). The share of international aviation in Icelandic national totals in the National Inventory Report, following IPCC guidelines (Hallsdóttir, et al., 2011, p.55 and 71), is 7% in 2009. As for the interpretation of the data:

> It is likely that the economic crisis had led to fewer air flights abroad and therefore more travel within Iceland during summer vacation. This would explain why emissions from road transport have not decreased more during 2008 and 2009 despite significantly higher fuel prices, owing to the depreciation of the Icelandic

króna during the year, thus can also be seen in decreased international aviation in
2008 and 2009 (Hallsdóttir, et al., 2011, p.31).

Interestingly enough, at the same time as aviation grows, emissions are decreasing.
Icelandair's environmental strategies (Icelandair, 2012) may thus be regarded as
adequate and ambitious, also regarding an aim of carbon neutral growth by 2020.
However, climate change is unrecognizable in the company's environmental policy,
and it is therefore not possible to investigate 'whether and how the recognition of
climate change in strategy papers also become visible in practice' (Reddy and
Wilkes, 2012, p.229). On a company level this may all be fine and legitimate, but
in the context of global climate change and warming the environmental policy
might just be understood as an illustration of a green-washing in the service of
perceived market demand. Irrespective of the environmental policy, their aim
and strategy is growth and they are succeeding. Evident from the policy is that
technology is to take care of other concerns.

   In terms of climate change, one would suspect that melting glaciers would be
a cause for concern in Iceland. The key controversies in Icelandic tourism politics
however revolve around the perception of landscapes as malleable for hydro- and/
or geopower development for the benefit of multinational aluminium companies,
or if these should be preserved for visitors (Sæþórsdóttir, 2012). Climate change
debates and possible melting of glaciers and landscape transformations come a far
second behind the controversies surrounding the melting of aluminium.

   The raging land-use debates in Iceland animate environmental discourse and
tourism development, but they also hint at climate change issues. The proponents
of heavy industry argue that if aluminium production is developed in Iceland, by
using green energy, the country is in effect contributing to the overall reduction
of greenhouse gasses. That Iceland appears to be able to save the world gets an
interesting twist in the debate when the same energy is arguably to be sold via a
submarine cable to Europe. The flip side of this world redemption rhetoric is to be
found in another issue of contestation in Icelandic environmental politics; if the
potential oil reserves of Drekasvæði ('the Dragon fields') in the ocean northeast
of the coast of Iceland should be tapped. In 2012 the presidential candidate Ari
Trausti Guðmundsson, a geophysics expert, argued that short sightedness and
zealotry beliefs in quick profits are steering the course of that particular debate. He
explains how 'Politics play a crucial role in these matters … Icelanders have the
opportunity to emerge as a brave and strong voice amongst nations of the world'
(Guðmundsson, 2012, p.34) if they choose not to tap this oil.

   The possible emergence of this sturdy Icelandic voice is rather meek given
that Iceland in the end of 2012 contributed less than half of the funds pledged at
COP15 in 2009 for the following three years in order to tackle climate change
(Goswami, 2012). The country has also far exceeded its Kyoto 10% increase in
carbon emission allowance, and today with the new Doha negotiation rounds
complete (COP 18), Iceland's heavy industry and aviation are made exempt as
they will be subject to EU's carbon trading scheme.

With consumption and growth being religiously indoctrinated in Western societies, lately disguised as reason, it is nigh on impossible to promote responsible climate policies in the 'Land of Ice and Fire'. At least that is what Elísson (2011b) believes. He illustrates this by outlining how a vociferous opponent of the harnessing of the oilfields lost her seat in the Icelandic parliament, crossed out by her own party members in Iceland's only environmental party the Left Green. The event might, however, partly represent a shift back to the days when environmental policies were being hotly debated in Iceland. That was before the collapse of the financial system and the ensuing recession, when becoming 'green' had become somewhat of an obsession in corporate policy and public planning (Elísson, 2007). The financial collapse seems to have quelled all concerns for the environment, further underlining Elísson's (2011b) arguments about consumption and growth.

According to Elísson (2011a, p.130, see also 2008), with growing information about global warming, its denial among Icelanders will become more deep-seated. Ultimately, it is unlikely that people will change their ways, especially when consequences of inaction are deferred to future generations. Drawing on works by Thomas (2007), Elísson proposes that the denial mechanism behind the climate change debate is on a par with that of alcoholism and drug abuse. For Elísson, a clear manifestation of the state of denial is tourism, whereby 'newspapers publish editorials and columns on the trouble with climate change whilst the advert space is filled with offers to travel to exotic places around the globe' (Elísson, 2011a, p.93).

In this example Icelandic tourism has emerged as heavily imbricated in the geography of high-carbon path-dependent system of international aviation and growth oriented capitalism led by Icelandair, thoroughly imbricated in anthropogenic climate change. The cultural topology thereby outlined is set askew recent marketing efforts of the Icelandic Promotion authority. In videos and through social media campaigns promises of the pristine are marketed. The next example will pick up on these voices and their context.

11.3.2   Marketing Topologies

The current marketing drive of Icelandic tourism dates back to a campaign launched by the Icelandic tourism authorities in response to the eruption of Eyjafjallajökull in spring 2010. Promote Iceland is the executive arm of the public sector responsible for the campaign, although it is a public/private partnership in nature. At the time of the eruption they had just received a new mandate (law 38/2010) taking over marketing responsibilities from the Icelandic Tourist Board. This is to be coupled with attracting foreign direct investment (FDI) to the country and enhancing Iceland's reputation generally to ease exports of goods and services. The campaign Promote Iceland launched is called *Inspired by Iceland* and originally featured video commentaries and online chat forums where various celebrities share their experience of Iceland (http://www.inspiredbyiceland.com). The campaign was launched with what the marketers termed 'the Iceland hour' 5 May 2010, with a nationwide media synchronized launching of a Facebook page that all Icelanders were encouraged to share with friends worldwide.

The rationale for launching the project in the first place was to convey the message of Iceland as a safe destination to visit in the wake of the eruption that caused immense disruptions to air travel in Europe. The main ideology of the marketing campaign, as stated in a report by the project's executive committee, was:

> [T]hat people would speak directly to each other about why they should visit the country through using the new communication networks people have set up via social media and encourage people to use these to deliver messages on Iceland, in addition to using the attention Iceland has had in worldwide media to introduce the power of Icelandic spectacular nature and put right wrong ideas people might have had (Pálsdóttir and Haraldsson, 2011, p.6).

The aims and ambitions of Promote Iceland in terms of tourism development are outlined in their vision for tourism's goals. In general the aim is:

1. That tourism consumption in Iceland is not under a fixed rate five year average growth,
2. That tourism foreign revenue grows in tandem with growing numbers of inbound tourists,
3. That tourism bed nights will grow on average by 6% annually, and proportionally more in the off-season (outside June-August),
4. That inbound tourist numbers will grow on average 6% annually, and proportionally more in the off-season (outside June-August).

More specifically in terms of promotion and marketing:

1. That the promotional website 'visiticeland' maintains its position on search engines, coming up in 1st-5th place when you search for 'Iceland' and that hits on the website increase on average 5% annually,
2. That published promotional material meets market needs,
3. That trade fairs and travel related events have maximum results,
4. That marketing and promotion reflects the expectations and experiences of tourists in Iceland and the knowledge of the country in foreign source markets,
5. That a better overview is developed over foreign requests in order to evaluate marketing success,
6. That an overview of the number and results of foreign press visits to Iceland is provided and to maximise media exposure surrounding press visits,
7. That Iceland competes and compares favourably in terms of the country's marketing and promotion.

As can be seen from the seven points above, and when compared with the four preceding ones, Icelandic marketing inspirations are to be delivered by word of mouth for the purposes of increasing business in the Icelandic tourism industry. The marketing campaign is very clear about its aspirations. Social media is the channel for communicating marketing messages and through this, people would 'see the truth through different eyes' (Pálsdóttir and Haraldsson, 2011, p.7) ultimately to be translated into tourism revenue and a favourable reputation facilitating exports and FDI as per the mandate of Promote Iceland.

Serres' (1997) perfidious wit asks us if we are conceptually equipped for our travels? When we conceptualize landscapes as a continuous surface, where we are one with it, surely it must take shape as it enters marketing media. Under these circumstances we need to ask who is doing the moulding, what exerts the force, whence are the intensities derived? The Eyjafjallajökull eruption in April 2010 was a pivotal event for the newly established tourism marketing authority of Promote Iceland. The staff was most certainly plunged in at the deep end when the Eyjafjallajökull started erupting. However, inspiration for this strategy was not far-fetched and luckily for the new marketing authority the tools to battle this crisis in inbound tourism caused by the eruption were ready at hand.

In March 2010 Peter Dennis, CEO of the Time Communications Group, had been invited by the Icelandic Travel Industry Association to deliver a keynote address to the association's annual meeting. His agenda entailed an outline of the 'social media revolution' (SAF, 2012). With an attendance of 150 people from the industry and public sector stakeholders in tourism, his extremely well-choreographed performance at the Hilton Reykjavík Nordica lodged social media potential squarely in the minds of those present. Emphasising that electronic distribution and communications is the front door to Iceland, Mr Dennis made it abundantly clear that the 'unprecedented change in communication, commerce and entertainment' (own notes from presentation slides) was the gateway to added value for tourism. Once Eyjafjallajökull started belching ash frantic senior executives at Promote Iceland, along with the dominant private sector tourism firm Icelandair, proposed a joint public/private sector marketing campaign. Partly inspired by Mr Dennis' talk and partly by the burgeoning marketing hype on social media, their ideas, albeit unformed, veered towards that particular marketing strategy.

As Mr Dennis emphasised, the 'social media revolution' and society's digitization, have indeed brought a new understanding of the World Wide Web, named Web 2.0 (or even 3.0). The proliferation of web-applications that facilitate participatory information sharing, collaboration, user-centred design and any kind of interactivity animates this web (Parra-López, et al., 2011). The degree of self-presentation and disclosure varies with 'media impressions created by consumers, typically informed by relevant experience, and archived or shared online for easy access by other impressionable consumers' (Xiang and Gretzel, 2010, p.180, quoting Blackshaw, 2006). Social media websites help users to share their travel-related comments, recommendations, opinions and personal experiences, which serve as source of information for others. It can therefore be argued that consumers of tourist products gain more power in determining, generating and distributing tourism-related information on the Internet, using this so-called 'electronic word-of-mouth', sometimes referred to as 'word of mouse' (Riedl and Konstan, 2002).

What is particularly intriguing in terms of landscapes is a recent addition to the Inspired by Iceland web domain. As of 2012 people were able to upload their pictures from their visit to Iceland and name the country anew under the campaign heading: *Iceland by another Name*. In the spirit of user generated content of social media, those visiting the site could then vote on their favourite picture and name. By summer 2013 results were in. 'We had a brilliant response to our final names but the beautiful landscapes and magical nature really caught your imagination, making Isle of Awe Land the world's favourite name for Iceland!' (Promote Iceland, 2013).

Iceland's new name with reference to landscapes and nature, is *Isle of Awe Land*, topping others in that realm such as *Extreme Land, Fall in Love Land, Niceland, Lifeland, Snowspinland, Waterland, Lets get lost Land, Beauty Land* and *Wonderland*. Looking at the pictures uploaded and names given to the country allow for an affirmation of the country's main allure, that is nature and its wilderness landscapes. However their affirmation or reification is a function of a very specific set up, i.e. tourism commodification in the times of social media.

As shown in the Land of Awe example, social media and Web 2.0 technologies represent a break away from the producer/consumer individual, or "producer-consumer" dichotomy and allows for the establishment of a virtual community of prosumers (Toffler, 1980) manifest in, e.g. information that informs travel plans or the naming of a destination. Word of mouse thus changes the very relations we have to places on the Earth's surface and allows us to recast their image and perception through naming and relating information about the place from a particular perspective. The specific function defining the point to point relations is thus set under the terms of prosumptive social media practices, representing a disruptive revolution.

One of the most obvious consequences of the technological disruption in spatial and topological ordering is a disruption in our sense of location – "our sense of place" – a disruption that occurs through new technological devices such as the computer, internet, aircraft, automobile, and telephone ... constitute changes in the modes by which our own being is disclosed – changes in the ways in which we encounter ourselves and others, and in the character of such encounter (Malpas, 2006, p.296).

Ritzer and Jurgenson (2010) argue that the way in which we encounter places and others through social media 'is the emergence of what may be a new form of capitalism' (p.31). The avatar of this new capitalism is the prosumer, i.e. one that is '… expected to make more and more extravagant investments in the act of consumption itself' (Thrift, 2005, p.7). The expectation leads capitalism to intervene and make a business out of thinking, feeling and being in the everyday (Thrift, 2005, p.1). As a consequence the 'market is no longer outside the value chain, acting as a point of interchange between producer and consumer' (Thrift, 2008, p.42), but has become part of the everyday as it indeed always was on the most general level. This time round though, individual experiences, feelings, affects and perceptions become a consumer's experience and become key to marketing value. In terms of tourism in Iceland, experiencing the country's landscape is what sustains value, immersing yourself in a sensual encounter has become part of the marketing strategy.

The prosumers of the Icelandic marketing authorities are people in Icelandic source markets, who have become 'enlightened travellers' and to which the marketing and promotion of Promote Iceland is to be directed (Morgunblaðið, 2011). These prosumers embed foreign cultures, practices, tastes and fashions into their daily lives through wielding a mouse (Williams, 2009). Contrary to Uriely's (2005, p.209) conclusion that 'the availability of various aspects of the tourist experience in the routine of everyday life seems to threaten future demands', tourist marketers target online chat forums, inspiring people online in order to develop profit from travel experiences embedded in online everyday life. Indeed '... finance and information technology and regulation have interwoven with new developments to produce new possibilities for profit' (Thrift, 2005, p.5).

The cultural topologies to emerge from the marketing efforts of the Icelandic marketing authorities entail the 'prosumerisation' of the modern day experience economy. Drawing on the trust we have in the contribution of others when using social media, altruism and a desire for recognition creates value for the destination (Parra-López, et al., 2011); seemingly not amenable to the values dictated by the commercial exchange. This sustains the allure of social media for tourism marketers and at the same time makes it amenable to current capitalist practices '... each "person" will cut their substantial link to their individual body and conceive themselves as part of the new holistic Mind which lives and acts through him or her' (Žižek, 1997, p.157). However '... what is obfuscated in such direct "naturalization" of the World Wide Web or market is the set of power relations – political decisions, institutional conditions – within which 'organisms' like internet (or market capitalism ...) can only thrive' (Žižek, 1997, p.157). Are the efforts of those who name Iceland by another name indeed "business as usual", holding no particular emancipatory potential? Is our trust, altruism and desire for recognition being merely manipulated for profit? Herein lie politically charged controversies which can be understood more comprehensively if we draw us, landscapes, capitalism, aviation, social media and melting glaciers into one topological realm.

11.4   Controversial Topologies

Do the voices of those who have encountered Icelandic wilderness landscapes during their visits have an effect in bringing about change in the topology of Icelandic landscapes? Can those who come and show concern for the attractions they come to visit through naming and even proclaiming, e.g. what needs to be protected, put a dent in on-going landscape transformations? Can they exert a force upon these transformations wrought by e.g. anthropogenic climate change, exemplified in vanishing glaciers, through the lens provided by Promote Iceland. The very entity embroiled in fuelling tourism's geography of high-carbon path-dependent system of international aviation?

The central tenants of the cultural topology of Icelandic tourism landscapes have been identified and arguably represent the wellspring of forces affecting the landscape and its perceptions. These forces are key to understanding what a landscape is and can be. Icelandic wilderness landscapes are transforming through climate forcing, a climate that is changing due to anthropogenic forcing, a factor in which is radiative forcing from international aviation, which in turn props up tourism and its potential for national revenue in Iceland and sustain its marketing efforts. People and their experiences of wilderness landscapes are ripe for reaping surplus value in late capitalism's quest for creative destruction and Icelandair along with Promote Iceland play to this. 'Creating a sense of place and telling a story' is a slogan invariably cited by the promoter of the Inspired campaign at Promote Iceland. Arguably this sense of place has no intrinsic value that can be established apart from relating to it and thus becoming part of it. Thus, it cannot be pitched in the right or wrong way to the right or wrong group of people. Marketers seem confident that if the trip was enjoyable this will be reflected in online commentaries, the particular type that visits Iceland will automatically profile the country for others. From the veritable smorgasbord of marketed and promoted individual experiences, each can find expressions of their individuality and be catered to. Seemingly simple, and a convincing rational for the uses of social media, surfing the endless diversity of the human condition, yet the enlightened prosumer is a fantasy of the experience economy.

The particular method of disseminating marketing message, through sharing via social media, is only seemingly open for plurality and diversification, pays mere lip-service to catering to the aware prosumer and will invariably run up against the conditions of excess which defines capitalism.

> We are our technologies, our tastes, our lifestyles and brands, our literal spaces. These are constantly under deformation, always a different figure showing, yet having their topological equivalent the structures of meaning comprise us as singular 'rings of string'. Further, like foam, these are fragile and always threatening to burst ... This is an imaginary in excess of function that drives media culture, consumer culture, and the knowledge and information society (Lash, 2012, p.271).

This is indeed an imaginary in excess of function, playing into the hands of those who established the lines of communication and transportation and hold the reigns to power. As Žižek (2004, p.186) sees it fit to warn: '... the falsity of multiplication resides in the fact that it frees the universal notion of modernity of its antagonism, of the way in which it is embedded in the capitalist system, by relegating this aspect just to one of its historical subspecies ...' Our everyday activities of continually defining limits in order to make sense of our surroundings can hardly find novel expressions in predefined pathways. The prosumer has become co-opted or interpellated into this particular ordering of tourism and the Icelandic landscape. The cultural topology to emerge is one dominated by market led interests and this has a very tangible effect on the physical topology of the Icelandic wilderness landscape through defining the pristine and sought after.

Yet there is an avenue forward and alternatives can be forged. As Amin and Thrift (2007, p.114) explain, 'Of course, we do not reject the analysis of centred power, but we would also wish to defend (even celebrate) practices of alterity that do make a difference by bringing about transitional changes that ultimately might help to change the world and its ways'. Space is indeed in a perpetual state of movement and essentially at one with us, a continuous surface without breaks or tears, but with ruptures of novelty and sinkholes of stability. The inventory exercise of gauging the context of Icelandic tourism marketing is revealed as politically charged in its aims and ambitions buying into the brave new world of IT, interpellated with finance to produce new possibilities for profit. Making explicit these dynamics of the prevailing cultural topology reveals the controversies that ensue from Iceland by another Name. The alternative resides within this controversy. Social media marketing in general and Iceland by another Name in particular hold a special allure of giving each a voice placing responsibility and care on each of our shoulders in each moment and every encounter. This responsibility can be talked of in terms of hospitality, generosity, openness or experimentation, but basically revolves around situations that do not lend themselves to straight forward rationalisations or scripted political projects. As a consequence, politics are everywhere in everything we do, with each and every moment there is 'an endless struggle with the difference of daily existence' (Caputo, 2003, p.171) engaging space in its own transformation.

Those who uploaded their pictures and renamed Iceland express '... their capacity to enlarge the universe by enabling its potential to be otherwise, to be framed through concepts and affects' (Grosz, 2008, p.24). In this sense it would seem that modern day capitalism is made up of innumerable and infinitely smaller ones generally comprehendible as everyday life. This leads to a different account of the locus of power, yet at the same time there are pervasive and dominant structures exerting force. This is the crux of the issue. 'We always need to be several steps ahead of the capitalist mulching machine, reinventing these struggles, devising new language, new political strategies, new ideas, new forms of activism' (Smith, 2005, p.891). These individual reinventions, manifest e.g. in uploaded pictures framing affects are only representable; 'in terms of our fragile fleeting life spans as mortal beings embedded in a living, flowing world, among an unfathomable myriad of comings-into-being, lingerings and passings-away' (Davies, 1999, p.196).

The social, hedonic and especially functional benefits from travel-related social media perchance allows us to be ahead, inventing new ways of being and doing, which potentially have the power to affect, producing a ripple effect through Topologica destabilising dominant sinkholes. However plausible one finds this scenario, the topological imaginary gives us all a place from which we have the power to affect. The inventory exercise of gauging the context is politically charged as it is imperative that one is believed when one sorts, names, numbers, compares, lists, and calculates. The plausibility of our matters of concern animate the politics of cultural topology. These are situated politics that lead up to an elaboration on 'non-representing' space (Thrift, 2008) and the 'art of the political' (Amin and Thrift, 2013) that can allow travel to become a responsible act of empowerment.

References

Abbot, E.A., 1992[1884]. *Flatland. A Romance of many dimensions*. New York: Dover.

Amin, A. and Thrift, N., 2007. Commentary. On being political. *Transactions of the Institute of British Geographers NS*, S32, pp.112–115.

Amin, A. and Thrift, N., 2013. *Arts of the political. New openings for the left*. Durham: Duke University Press.

Blackshaw, P., 2006. The consumer-generated surveillance culture. Available at: <http://www.clickz.com/showPage.html?page=3576076> [Accessed 14 May 2012].

Bough, B., 1993. Deleuze and Empiricism. *Journal of the British Society for Phenomenology*, 24(1), pp.15–31.

Caputo, J.D., 2003. Against principles: A sketch of an ethics without ethics. In: E. Wyschogrod and G.P. McKenny, eds. 2003. *The Ethical*. Oxford: Blackwell, pp.169–180.

Crutzen, P.J., 2002. Geology of mankind: The Anthropocene. *Nature*, 415, p.23.

Davies, C., 1999. Ephémère: Landscape, earth, body, and time in immersive virtual space. In: R. Ascott, ed. *1999. Reframing consciousness*. Exeter: Intellect books, pp.196–201.

Deleuze, G., 1991. *Empiricism and subjectivity. An essay on Hume's theory of human nature*. New York: Columbia University Press.

Deleuze, G. and Guattari, F., 1987. *A thousand plateaux, capitalism & schizophrenia*. Minneapolis: University of Minnesota Press.

Doel, M., 1999. *Poststructuralist geographies. The diabolical art of spatial science*. Edinburgh: Edinburgh University Press.

Elísson, G., 2007. Nú er úti veður vont: Gróðurhúsaáhrif og íslensk umræðuhefð [Outside the weather is raging: Greenhouse effects and Icelandic traditions of debating]. *Ritið*, 1/2007, pp.5–44.

Elísson, G., 2008. Efahyggja og afneitun [Doubt and denial]. *Ritið*, 2/2008, pp.77–114.

Elísson, G., 2011a. Dómsdagsklukkan tifar. Upplýsing og afneitun í umræðu um loftslagsbreytingar [The Doomsday Clock is ticking. Denial discourse in climate change debate]. *Ritið*, 1/2011, pp.91–136.

Elísson, G., 2011b. Vekjum ekki sofandi dreka. Loftslagsmál, pólitísk umræða og olíuleit á íslenska landgrunninu [Let us not wake a sleeping dragon. Climate issues, political debate and the search for oil on the Icelandic continental shelf]. *Tímarit Máls og Menningar*, 4, pp.10–25.

Fontaine, P., 2012. The glaciers are melting. *The Reykjavik Grapevine*. Available at: <http://www.grapevine.is/News/ReadArticle/The-Glaciers-Are-Melting> [Accessed 15 July 2013].

Franklin, A., 2004. Tourism as an ordering: Towards a new ontology of tourism. *Tourist Studies*, 4(3), pp.277–301.

Goswami, U.A., 2012. UN climate change negotiations 2012: Industrialised countries fail to provide $30 bn to tackle climate change in developing nations. *The Economic Times, [online]*. Available at: <http://articles.economictimes. indiatimes.com/2012-11-25/news/35346648_1_climate-finance-climate-change-fair-share> [Accessed 15 December 2013].

Gren, M. and Huijbens, E., 2012. Tourism theory and the earth. *Annals of Tourism Research*, 39(1), pp.155–170.

Grosz, E., 2008. *Chaos, territory, art. Deleuze and the framing of the earth*. New York: Columbia University Press.

Guðmundsson, A.T., 2012. Litla stúlkan með eldspýturnar? [The little match girl?] *Fréttablaðið*, 29 November, p.34.

Gunnarsdóttir, G., 2011. The front page of Icelandic tourism brochures. In: S.R. Ísleifsson, ed. 2011. *Iceland and images of the North*. Quebec: Presses de l'Université du Quebec, pp.531–553.

Hall, C.M., Müller, D.K. and Saarinen, J., 2009. *Nordic tourism: Issues and cases*. Bristol: Channel View Publications.

Hallsdóttir, B.S., Finnbjörnsdóttir, R.G., Guðmundsson, J., Snorrason, A. and Þórsson, J., 2011. *Emissions of greenhouse gases in Iceland from 1990 to 2009. National inventory report 2011*. Reykjavík: The Environmental Agency of Iceland.

Huijbens, E.H., 2011. Nation branding: A critical evaluation. Assessing the image building of Iceland. In: S.R. Ísleifsson, ed. 2011. *Iceland and images of the North*. Quebec: Presses de l'Université du Quebec, pp.553–583.

Huijbens, E. and Benediktsson, K., 2013. Inspiring the visitor? Landscapes and horizons of hospitality. *Tourist Studies*, 13(2), pp.189–208.

Icelandair, 2012. *Umhverfisstefna Icelandair* [Environmental policy of Icelandair]. Available at: <http://www.icelandair.is/information/green-icelandair/ environmental-policy/> [Accessed 14 July 2013].

Icelandic Tourist Board, 2013. *Tourism in Iceland in figures*. Reykjavík: Icelandic Tourist Board.

Jameson, F., 1991. *Postmodernism, or, the cultural logic of late capitalism*. Durham: Duke University Press.

Lash, S., 2012. Deforming the figure: Topology and the social imaginary. *Theory, Culture & Society*, 29(4–5), pp.261–287.

Latour, B., 2005. *Reassembling the social: An introduction to actor-network-theory*. Oxford: Oxford University Press.

Law, J., 2004. And if the global were small and noncoherent? Method, complexity, and the baroque. *Environment and Planning D: Society and Space*, 22, pp.13–26.

Lee, D.S., Fahey, D.W., Forster, P.M., Newton, P.J., Wit, R.C.N., Lima, L.L., Owen, B. and Sausen, R., 2009. Aviation and global climate change in the 21st century. *Atmospheric Environment*, 43(22–23), pp.3520–3537.

Lury, C., Parisi, L. and Terranova, T., 2012. Introduction: The becoming topological of culture. *Theory, Culture & Society*, 29(4–5), pp.3–35.

Malpas, J., 2006. *Heidegger's topology. Being, place, world*. Cambridge: MIT Press.

Massey, D., 1993. Power geometry and a progressive sense of place. In: J. Bird, B. Curtis, T. Putnam and G. Robertson, eds. 1993. *Mapping the future. Local cultures, global change*. London: Routledge, pp.59–69.

Mendelson, B., 1975. *Introduction to topology*. New York: Dover.

Morgunblaðið, 2011. Ísland allt árið – Bjóðum heim! [Iceland all year round – let's invite home]. *Morgunblaðið*, [online]. Available at: <http://www.mbl.is/vidskipti/pistlar/marketing/1206801/> [Accessed 15 July 2013].

Olsson, G., 1991. *Lines of power, limits to language*. Minneapolis: University of Minnesota Press.

Olsson, G., 1992. Lines of power. In: T.J. Barnes and J.S. Duncan, eds. 1992. *Discourse, text and metaphor in the representation of landscape*. London: Routledge, pp.86–96.

Olsson, G., 2007. *Abysmal*. Chicago: University of Chicago Press.

Ólafsdóttir, G., 2007. *Relating to nature: The performative spaces of Icelandic tourism*. Ph.D. University of Bristol.

Ólafsdóttir, G., 2008. Náttúrutengsl og upplifanir ferðamanna á Íslandi: Fjögur tengslamynstur vellíðunar [Nature connection and experiences of tourists in Iceland. Four relations to wellbeing]. *Landabréfið – Journal of the Association of Icelandic Geographers*, 22, pp.51–76.

Ólafsdóttir, G., 2011. Practicing (nature-based) tourism: Introduction. *Landabréfið – Journal of the Association of Icelandic Geographers*, 25, pp.3–14.

Oxford Economics, 2011. *Economic benefits from air transport in Iceland*. Oxford: Oxford Economics.

Pálsdóttir, I.H. and Haraldsson, E.K., 2011. *Inspired by Iceland. Skýrsla samstarfsaðila* [Inspired by Iceland. Report from participants]. Reykjavík: Promote Iceland.

Parra-López, E., Bulchand-Gidumal, J., Gutiérrez-Taño, D. and Díaz-Armas, R., 2011. Intentions to use social media in organizing and taking vacation trips. *Computers in Human Behavior*, 27, pp.640–654.

Perec, G., 2003. *Life: A user's manual*. London: Vintage.

Pine, B.J. II, and Gilmore, J.H., 2011. *The experience economy – Updated edition.* Boston: Harvard Business School Publishing.

Promote Iceland, 2013. *Inspired by Iceland.* Available at: <http://www.inspiredbyiceland.com/> [Accessed 15 July 2013].

Protevi, J. and Bonta, M., 2004. *Deleuze and geophilosophy: A guide and glossary.* Edinburgh: Edinburgh University Press.

Reddy, V.M. and Wilkes, K., 2012. *Tourism, climate change and sustainability.* London and New York: Earthscan from Routledge.

Riedl, J. and Konstan, J., 2002. *Word of mouse.* New York: Warner.

Ritzer, G. and Jurgenson, N., 2010. Production, consumption, prosumption: The nature of capitalism in the age of the digital 'prosumer'. *Journal of Consumer Culture,* 10(1), pp. 13–36.

SAF, 2012. *Aðalfundur 2010: Glærur Peter Dennis.* [online] Available at: <http://saf.is/saf/upload/files/a_dofinni/adalfundur_2010/iceland_pd_changing_dynamics_presentation.pptx> [Accessed 7 June 2012].

Schattschneider, D., 2010. The mathematical side of M.C. Escher. *Notices of the American Mathematical Society,* 57(6), pp.706–718.

Serres, M., 1997. *The troubadour of knowledge.* Minneapolis: University of Michigan Press.

Smith, N., 2005. What's left? Neo-critical geography, or, the flat pluralist world of business class. *Antipode,* 37, pp.887–897.

Stewart, I., 2001. *Flatterland. Like Flatland, only more so.* London: MacMillan.

Sæþórsdóttir, A.D., 2010. Planning nature tourism in Iceland based on tourist attitudes. *Tourism Geographies,* 12(1), pp.25–52.

Sæþórsdóttir, A.D., 2012. Tourism and power plant development: An attempt to solve land use conflicts. *Tourism Planning and Development,* 9(4), pp.339–353.

Sæþórsdóttir, A.D., 2013. Managing popularity: Changes in tourist attitudes in a wilderness destination. *Tourism Management Perspectives,* 7, pp.47–58.

Sæþórsdóttir, A.D., Hall, C.M. and Saarinen, J., 2011. Making wilderness: Tourism and the history of the wilderness idea in Iceland. *Polar Geography,* 34(4), pp.249–273.

Thomas, P., 2007. How to beat denial – A 12-step plan. *The Ecologist,* January, pp.26–29.

Thrift, N., 2005. *Knowing capitalism.* London: Sage.

Thrift, N., 2008. *Non-representational theory. Space, politics, affect.* Abingdon: Routledge.

Toffler, A., 1980. *The third wave.* New York: William Morrow.

Uriely, N., 2005. The tourist experience: Conceptual developments. *Annals of Tourism Research,* 32(1), pp.199–216.

Van der Duim, V.R., Ren, C. and Jóhannesson, G.T., 2012. *Actor Network Theory and tourism. Ontologies, methodologies and performances.* London: Taylor and Francis.

Vox Naturae, 2012. *Advocating and mobilizing for ice – Concept brochure.* Kópavogur: Vox Naturae.
Williams, S., 2009. *Tourism geography. A new synthesis.* London: Routledge.
Xiang, Zh. and Gretzel, U., 2010. Role of social media in online travel information search. *Tourism Management,* 31, pp.179–188.
Žižek, S., 1997. *The plague of fantasies.* London: Verso.
Žižek, S., 2004. *Organs without bodies. On Deleuze and consequences.* New York: Routledge.

Chapter 12
Possible Greenland:
On 'Futuring' in Nation Branding

Carina Ren

12.1 Introduction

Possible Greenland was the intriguing title of an exhibition held in 2012 in Venice at the Danish pavilion during the 13th International Architecture Exhibition, or *Biennale*, the most important of its kind. This chapter investigates the constitutive power of imagining the future by describing the stages of planning and holding the exhibition of Possible Greenland, Greenland's largest nation branding endeavor ever, seeing it as a future-generating device (Bruun Jensen, 2010). Along the way, the chapter will address how the future is enrolled as part of transforming the present by showing how the world, or in this case Greenland, is represented and enacted through visions of the future. As will be clear, this is not a simple procedure, but rather a cohort of complex and controversy-ridden "futuring acts".

According to Mike Michael, 'the present is managed by deploying representations of the past and the future' (2000, p.3). The case presented in this chapter substantiates this claim by showing how local and global Greenlandic agendas and discourses entangle with future scenarios at the exhibition. The case offers a semiotic study of nation branding, displaying Possible Greenland as a performative representation of the future. As such, the exhibition – and branding attempts at large – may be seen as tools to engage in the world but also as activities which actively shape places into becoming *visitable* (Dicks 2004). As a consequence, it is argued, the studying of place exhibitions and branding attempts shape and prepare places to be visited and consumed in certain ways rather than others.

In the following, I will show in more detail how this multi-faceted engagement was carried out, sketching out a relevant exhibition context, introducing actors that contributed to the exhibition in various ways and taking a closer look at the final exhibition parts and how their visions of the future connected to present agendas and debates. This will make clear that picturing the future is a way not only to represent, but also to strategically perform a nation and that envisioning the future is far from an innocent endeavor. It is one which involves – and impacts – a broad range of local and global actors in often far-reaching ways.

In order to substantiate this assertion, I first introduce the field of future research. I access this field using a performative approach, raising the question of how we may study things not only in the making, but in their becoming as they are imagined and enacted into being. I shortly sketch out my approach, which takes inspiration from ANT and from the rising interest in Science and Technology Studies of looking at controversy as an entry point into the study of the social. Also, praxiography is introduced as a suitable way to approach this type of study. Next, the exhibition of Possible Greenland is presented. A short introduction to Greenland, perhaps less known to most readers, is provided, outlining some of the current geo-political and socio-economic challenges facing the world's largest island, home ruled under the Danish Commonwealth. Drawing on conducted fieldwork, I then describe how the exhibition content was negotiated among stakeholders in the different stages of planning, developing and opening of the exhibition and display a number of outcomes in the following analysis by the use of illustrative examples from the exhibition.

As I show, the exhibition themes make use of very different strategies for envisioning the future. The exhibition may be used as a prism to illustrate how architectural fantasies, political visions and practical concerns get entangled and enrolled in scenarios building. Possible Greenland displays that not only the present or physically existing objects can become controversial or be turned into matters of concern (Latour, 2004). So can things and issues which are (still) only envisioned or "to be". I argue that the acknowledgement of how futuring is intrinsically connected to the present – and how it should be tended to accordingly – holds implication for tourism studies.

12.2 Researching Performative Futures

The exhibition of Possible Greenland is but one contribution to the 'crafting of the future' of an Arctic nation which is currently facing serious challenges while at the same time attracting vast global attention. Yet, as an exemplary study, it may be used to unravel some of the complex ways by which it – at least partially – connects to an even larger debate on the future of Greenland. As noted by Brown, Rappert and Webster, 'social actors, at individual, institutional or wider cosmopolitan levels construct future expectations which may run in parallel with and contest each other, occupying different time-frames and carrying different interests' (2000, p.6). Along this line of thought, the present chapter attempts to introduce the future as a performative representation; that is a representation which is enacted in certain, rather than other, ways as expectations are constructed in this case through the use of scenarios. As a consequence of seeing future management as performative, that is as creating effect through the way by which the activity is assembled and put into practice, we need to ask how some futures come to prevail over others. How are resources deployed, argument raised or in this case scenarios built to inspire, raise concern, convince or in other ways manage impressions, discourses and actions towards what is (made) to come?

The Possible Greenland exhibition, presented in further details below, is perceived as a conglomerate of heterogeneous and partially connected (Strathern, 1991) entities, narratives and performances, which are deployed as strategic resources in political and economic-developmental agenda-setting processes by different actors. The present focus on the socio-material setting of the exhibition, the exhibited objects and narratives, the building, the planning and work processes leading up to the final exhibition etc., that is *the practices of exhibiting and enacting the future through scenarios*, takes inspiration in particular from three interrelated strands of a larger body of Science and Technology Studies (STS).

The first is *actor-network theory* (ANT) in which the concept of "actors", usually connected to human agency, is spread out to include everything within a given practice or network which creates an effect and therein is accorded agency (Latour, 1993). Following ANT and the idea of distributed agency (Callon, 2008; Latour, 2010), the future is not just "there". Rather, and as this case shows, it is represented, acted upon and tinkered with through meticulous arrangements by human actors, organizations and political interest groups by drawing in various discourses, procedures and technologies. As a consequence of this, the future should not be seen as a passive noun, but as a verb and as a process, a process of *futuring*. This chapter will therefore explore how scenarios of Possible Greenland "future" Greenland, to the processes of distributed agency by which this is done, to detectable scenario effects and to the scenario constructing practices and connection which enabled them. I do so for instance in looking at what it means to portray Greenland as possible in one way rather than another and how this can raise controversy.

This brings me to my second strand of inspiration, namely the notion of *controversy* as a complex social phenomenon, where the disagreement in case has precluded any sort of stabilization. According to Venturini, the controversy, which has lately become an object of intense interrogation in STS (see Venturini 2010; 2012 and the introductory chapter of the present volume), begins 'when actors discover that they cannot ignore each other and controversies end when actors manage to work out a solid compromise to live together. Anything between these two extremes can be called a controversy' (2009, p.261). Hence, the study of controversy offers us 'the best available occasion to observe the social world in its *making*' (Venturini, 2010, p.263, emphasis in the original).

Venturini describes controversies as debates and conflicts containing features such as the involvement of many different actors, the displaying of the social in its most dynamic form and the resistance to reduction. As the introduction to Greenland will also show in the following, this description fits well with the current Greenlandic situation, where the country and government face a number of serious unresolved discussions and decisions on for instance uranium extraction, large scale aluminum production and the development of mass tourism, issues which are far from agreed upon. Hence, the future scenario building is, albeit somewhat implicitly, linked to larger questions of social, economic and political controversy, which I shall return to later on.

Question is how to study the performances or effects of an exhibited future, how to describe the ways by which the exhibition is enacted through practices of future building and how to merge the wishes to gain insight into complex and ongoing (re)configurations of actor-networks, to enactments of multiplicity and to controversies. The task is indeed insurmountable and I neither claim, nor wish, to depict the full picture of a future Greenland. Nor do I claim to possess a clear vision or singular, stable position from where to research it. As opposed to offering a smooth, ongoing narrative of how the exhibition showcases and brands Greenland as "possible", what I seek to bring forward is instead some Points of impact, which offer diverging, contested and controversial narratives of a Greenland in its becoming. I do so through the last bundle of resources which I draw from, namely *praxiography*. The term is introduced by Anne-Marie Mol and describes how knowledge is created and situated in and through specific socio-material settings, which should accordingly be studied. In The Body Multiple, Mol (2002) describes how the body becomes or rather is enacted into being as a multiple object through the practices by which it is represented, handled and researched.

Similarly, I address the future as a socio-material outcome of a number of practices, which I attempt to foreground in the analysis by displaying how the production of the future takes place in this particular setting. The scope of this chapter is not to conclude on the actual future-generating capacity of the exhibition or to evaluate its ability to "directly" induce some kind of change. Instead, it seeks to complement a purely discursive or narrative take on envisioning the future for instance in the sociology of expectation (see also Bruun Jensen, 2010), by insisting on the close connections between materiality, practice and discourse, something which is rendered visible through close descriptions of 'what happens' when something is played out. As stated by Mol (2002), reality multiplies through practices. By looking at how the future is not only represented but enacted through the scenarios, I also attempt to show how reality – or the future – can be seen as multiple and how some versions of the future seek to exclude or rule out others.

The partially overlapping concerns and sensitivities arising through the analytical resources of ANT, controversy and praxiography enable me to frame the future of Greenland as it is represented at the exhibition as an issue which has moved from a position of local concern to one of global controversy. As but one of the many socio-material actors which engage in the process of futuring, the exhibition of Possible Greenland provides a view into the presently ongoing, controversy-ridden collective building of a future Greenland, a future building *in action*, so to speak. In order to gain a better understanding of not only the initiators and contributors to the futuring taking place at Possible Greenland, but also the global and local context which enabled the exhibition to come together, I provide a more detailed case presentation below which also sheds a light on how I became involved in all of this activity.

12.3   Future Greenland: Who, Why and How?

The planning of a large exhibition on Greenlandic futures was made known to me in September 2011, when Hausenberg, a company providing ethnographically based urban planning counseling, announced over Facebook that they had been invited by DAC (Danish Architecture Centre) to participate in the exhibition of Possible Greenland (at that time entitled Future Greenland) in Venice in 2012. The DAC website further described the project which included Danish as well as Greenlandic architects as a presentation of visions of a Greenland of the future. The visions were ordered under the themes of *Connecting, Migrating, Cultivating* and *Inhabiting* Greenland. Along with the actual exhibition and the scenarios, the project was also to foster a publication, which was to 'document and supplement the vision projects in the exhibition with a broader and deeper illumination of the Greenlandic challenges and potential ' (DAC, 2011, my translation). Soon after, I could see on Facebook that Hausenberg had embarked on a trip to Greenland along with the other Danish partners for a workshop with all partners, Danish and Greenlandic.

During the months to come, my interest in the exhibition started to grow as I occasionally followed the early stages of the exhibition planning and workshops through Facebook and the DAC website. Although the project initially attracted my attention because of my research in nation branding, it became even more interesting due to media coverage that Greenland was attracting in Denmark at the time. Naturally, Greenland attracts attention in Danish media from time to time as a former colony now self-ruled since 2010 under the Danish commonwealth. Since COP15 in Copenhagen in 2010, where Greenland was used as a platform or "showroom" to display climate changes (Bjørst, 2012), the island was all over the place. News reports also differed from the usual "post-colonial" stories of economic difficulties and social distress. Instead, the interest and reports were connected mainly to two things: climate change, as mentioned, and furthermore, the rise of new global business opportunities.

Where Greenland had served as a showcase for climate change or as a 'climate witness' during COP-15, where many of the involved politicians had been invited to visit the melting ice fjord of Ilulissat, climate change discourses were now changing as the ensuing melting of ice was gradually being connected to potential new earnings for Greenland. The specific interest in Greenland was explained by a rising international interest in extracting oil, uranium and rare minerals, now more easily reached because of the melting ice. Also, the clearing of ice in the North-West passage during summer had created an attractive alternative for routes between America and Asia and hereby an increase in ship traffic in the Arctic Sea. A last economic prospect was the development of cruise tourism. In all of these cases, climate change and the view to new earnings seemed to intertwine, as less frost, cold weather and snow were seamlessly translated into future or present opportunities for easy mining access, increase in vessel traffic and more tourists during a longer summer season. Greenland was surfacing as a "climate winner"!

The rising interest in Greenland could also be seen as just one example of how, according to Avango, Nilsson and Roberts (2013) climate change is 'depicted as the hegemonic "driver" of Arctic change, with commercial, political and military consequences flowing from the ice′s rapid recession' (p.431). As a consequence, 'states, companies, scientists and any number of concerned individuals are actively seeking a stake in the future of the Arctic, and articulating visions of what that future ought to look like' (p.442). However, as they note, 'ranging from optimistic forecast of mineral-derived wealth to pessimistic assessment of environmental damage, the quantity and diversity of these futures is yet to be matched by a similar investment in critical reflection on how and why these visions are produced' (p.432). The present work represents such an attempt to further describe and reflect upon Arctic futuring.

In the present Greenlandic case, the *present* melting of ice is conjoined with *emerging* climate changes in the Arctic and *expected* oil drilling, mineral extraction, shipping and mass tourism development. This could be seen in reports with headings such as *Greenland – In the middle of the world* and *Greenland – The new Mediterranean* (Andersen, 2012a; 2012b), *Here you go, Greenland – The future is yours* (Ifversen, 2012) and *The future of Greenland* (Vahl, 2012). Articles such as these offered stories of hope, a new dawn and dynamic forces on the rise for this young nation and hereby challenged usual discourses on Greenland of a more gloomy kind, which in combination with accounts of wild Arctic nature and (vanishing) indigenous culture had so far dominated accounts on Greenland in the Danish media.

Having formerly lived in Greenland and now researching sustainable and 'climate' tourism, I was intrigued to see how tourism would be included in the work with projecting a future Greenlandic society. Also, my previous studies of nation branding through exhibitions and architectural contributions, such as the Danish Welfairytales pavilion at the Shanghai World expo in 2010 (Ren and Gyimóthy, 2013 Ren and Ooi, 2013), had familiarized me with the often complex – and therefore highly interesting – work processes and negotiations connected to the planning of such national endeavors. As a consequence, I decided to contact DAC to ask permission to participate in the working process while getting started with collecting material, such as press releases, blogs and newspaper articles in the subsequent months. As my ethnographic assemblage slowly came up to speed, my role was mostly to observe during workshops, meetings and the opening of the exhibition. I also took part in conversations and discussions with the various people engaged with the exhibition and contributed to the exhibition catalogue with a short article on Greenlandic nation branding (Ren, 2012).

Through conversations with participants and by taking part myself, I learned how many different ideas, models and scenarios had initially been presented at collective workshops in first Greenland and later Denmark before the scenarios were finalized and presented in their finished form at the exhibition. At these workshops, ideas and subsequent tentative scenarios were discussed, shot down or praised by the other participants. After feedback was given and received at these workshops, architects, planners, designers, ethnologist and engineers (because in fact, architects turned out to be more than just architects!) would return to their studios to continue the work on their projects.

At many stages during my engagement with this project, I found myself wondering why DAC had decided to embark on this project of envisioning a future for Greenland. As a former colonial power and having previously received much critique for its imperialist eagerness to modernize Greenland, for instance through the notorious G-50 and G-60 modernization plans (Adolphsen and Greiffenberg, 1997), it would seem that the Danish state had learned its lesson of not engaging itself, at least officially, in any public planning for its now former colony. Yet, as a state-sponsored event, the Danish participation at the Biennale could in fact be seen as an attempt to actively and overtly influence societal change in Greenland. This was perhaps why so much emphasis was put on the exhibition as a collaborative effort between equal partners, the Danish and Greenlandic architects and on a very open and processual working format which welcomed dialogue and feedback.

The following exempt from my field notes provides an example of how this feedback process would work. During a workshop which I attended, a Greenlandic architect criticized a much older, respected architect for placing what she described as a 'historic relic' in the shape of a fur clad kayaker in the prospect of a living room of a future Arctic home. The character was subsequently removed. To some, the exhibition never completely managed to cut away all the "Arctic décor". For instance, polar bears were placed on the runway of an airport planned to be built in a location with no polar bear population. In spite of this, the DAC received only little criticism on its role as future-maker and representative of a former colonial power, perhaps due to the explicit and often cited intentions of keeping the planning process as open, transparent and democratic as possible.

From DAC, some vigor was put into explaining how the participating Danish architects had been selected. According to DAC, selection had been made based on their 'understanding of and involvement in Greenland as well as their communicative qualities' (DAC, 2011, my translation). The website provided ample descriptions of the selection criteria and process of the Danish partners. The selection criteria were not clarified for the Greenlandic partners, all much smaller architect practices than their often very large Danish "counterparts". It would seem that engaging with future visions was only problematic or in need of further motivation when Danes were involved, although – as can be noted – many of the "Greenlandic" architects turned out to be of Danish origin. However, in spite of these difficulties in creating a non-hierarchical process and the clearly uneven distribution of power, prestige and resource, the collaboration was highlighted by participants and later on at the opening by politicians from both nations as exemplary[1].

The motivation provided by the exhibition initiators for getting engaged with the project was Greenland's growing global prominence. As stated by Minik Rosing, a renowned Danish Greenlandic professor of geology appointed head curator of

---

1   An exception was an architect who decided to leave the project and who later displayed what he saw as the project's problems in the largest newspaper of Greenland.

the exhibition, 'Greenland is moving from the periphery into the center of global attention' (Rosing, 2012:8). This entering upon an international 'center stage' due to climate change, the subsequent melting of ice and related opportunities for commercial development, was in many contexts used to justify the creation of the exhibition. According to Kent Martinussen, DAC's CEO, it was Greenland's current climatic (and subsequent geo-political) context combined with 'the relevance of testing architecture's capacity under the impact of the Anthropocene' which made DAC take initiative to the exhibition. To distance themselves from any claims of neo-colonialism, the attractive economic development opportunities for the Greenlandic society projected through climate change, itself presented as an unproblematic future to work on, were presented in the exhibition and during the preceding workshops as a way to help Greenland reach financial independence from Denmark, who currently contributes to the Greenlandic state budget with a yearly block grant (3.5 billion kroner (Euro 500 million in 2013- or over 62,000 kroner (Euro 8,000) per inhabitant). Hence, climatic and global changes and concerns as well as purely Greenlandic interests were given as an explanation for engaging into the discussion of Greenland's future as opposed to what could have been interpreted as national (Danish) interests.

Figure 12.1 Visualizing Greenland's central global position at the exhibition. A huge *Fuller projecting map* at the entrance of the Danish pavilion at the Biennale was used to illustrate Greenland's shift from global periphery to center.
Source: author

12.4   Presenting Exhibition Futures – and some Nature

Regardless of whose interest the exhibition was to further, the exhibition was clearly an important event for Denmark as well as for Greenland. This was reflected in the turn-out of officials at the exhibition opening in Venice at the end of August 2012, where politicians, notabilities, a good press line up and even royalty provided the opening with some panache. The vice-chair of the Greenlandic self-rule took part in the official exhibition opening as did the Danish Crown Prince and the Danish minister of culture. The exhibition was attended by the mayors of all four Greenlandic municipalities and officials from Denmark and Greenland alike. On both sides, the fruitful exhibition collaboration was brought forth and during the opening one sensed the feeling of a collective celebration of a harmonious relationship, something which was praised many times and pointed to as unusual between former colonies and colonial rulers. In the following, I will provide the reader with a further description of what the exhibition offered on display and also how the exhibition parts provided a much less smooth and seamless narrative of a Greenlandic future.

The exhibition was installed in the Danish pavilion at the Biennale and ran from early September to late November of 2012. Its most important features were the four thematic exhibition parts: Connecting, Migrating, Cultivating and Inhabiting Greenland. Where the Inhabiting theme displayed examples of a new Arctic building practice, Migrating provided a number of ideas of how to accommodate for tourism, mining and mineral exploration by exploring historic migrations and urban development as well as its potential future. Connecting Greenland presented the ambitious Air+Port project, the building of a combined transatlantic airport and container harbor while the Cultivating Greenland project displayed a different, more open layout, a number of questions on a wall on democracy and sustainable development under the theme of "How to swallow a whale" in an attempt to map current Greenlandic debate.

Apart from these themes, the pavilion also contained a number of loosely connected "add-ons" installed by the curators, for instance a wooden house. According to Minik Rosing, the house was an attempt to display the everyday life of ordinary Greenlanders, hence creating a contrast to the smooth, polished and futuristic surfaces and structures presented elsewhere in the exhibition. Textures, even smells (for instance of dried fish displayed on the outside of the wooden house) stands out. The house is staged as a meeting place between visitors and Greenlandic culture and present. Still, walking into the wooden house, one finds a deserted living room empty of people other than visitors taking a look at family pictures on the wall, listening to the choir music on the radio, browsing through coffee table books while resting in the sofa.

Another untraditional 'add-on' was a large million year old rock. Along with a rolling power point show set up next to the wooden house in a separate room displaying calving icebergs, other 'charismatical megafauna' (Michael, 2000, p.26) besides the before mentioned polar bears as well as many other fantastic

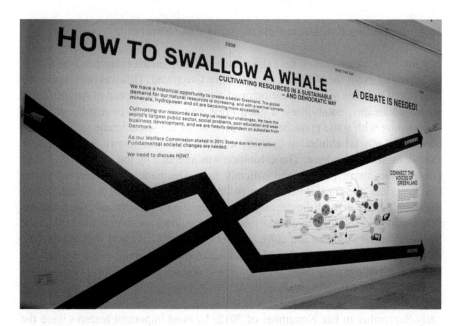

Figure 12.2   The wall "How to swallow a whale" at the Danish pavilion.
Source: author

natural wonders, the rock appointed a prominent role to nature at the exhibition. This impression was further supported by a centrally placed giant wooden table in the shape of Greenland, slightly rounded following the curve of the Earth to illustrate the size and magnitude of Greenland. This conspicuous position was no coincidence. As stated by head curator Minik Rosing: 'The land mass is of immense value, both for its mineral resources and potential for fresh ideas on the development of a sustainable society in a global world'. Unlike the wooden house, where culture and everyday life is displayed in a somewhat empty or passive fashion, the land and nature stand central as future change agents, constantly on the move (melting, calving) yet 'rock hard', resilient. Here was the future of Greenland: full of ideas, ready to welcome innovation and fulfill a potential, richly illustrated in the visions of the architects.

At least through the add-on themes of the exhibition, nature and culture are represented in quite diverse ways in which nature seems to play the part as a strong change agent. As we shall now see, the exhibition themes deploy yet other ways to engaging with and performing the future as will be exemplified through the Connecting and Cultivating scenarios. In the following, I conceptualize the Cultivating contribution as a *debating* approach to engaging with the future, while showing the Connecting scenario as a *building* approach. Based on this conceptualization, I discuss the performative potential of these opposing strategies of futuring.

12.4.1   Engaging with the Future: Building or Debating?

As described, the four separate themes of Connecting, Migrating, Cultivating and Inhabiting Greenland each provided suggestions as to how to engage with the future. According to Rosing, the themes served as "avenues" creating what he goes on to describe as 'a foundation on which the people of Greenland can make the choices that redeem and illuminate their hopes and dreams for the future' (2012, p.9). But how can we understand the role of the themes as "avenues" or as foundational for a future Greenland? In the exhibition part of Cultivating Greenland, the avenue is perhaps seen more as a winding road:

> There is no shortcut to a better future. There are a lot of choices to be made, a lot of barriers to be broken, a lot of dilemmas to be solved ... let the debate continue. (Exhibition wall)

This quote taken from a huge mural displayed on one of the pavilion walls is used by the group behind the Cultivating theme to describe the obstacles ahead. In its work with developing a future scenario on how to cultivate Greenland and its resource in the future, the Cultivating team had made use of in-depth interviews with many relevant social and political actors in Greenland and had deliberately drawn on local knowledge and controversial issues (personal communication). An example of this is their questioning the future of the *bygd*, the Greenlandic village which as a habitation form takes on very different meanings and values whether perceived from a socio-cultural or an economic perspective. In the Cultivating representation of the future, we are warned of the bumpy road leading us towards the future. No shortcuts, many choices, barriers and dilemmas. This rough journey awaiting the future adventurer is not to be made alone. For it should be one in which 'many people (get) involved in a broad and deep societal debate to gain the necessary insights, to make wise decisions and develop smart solutions' (Team Cultivating, 2012).

The cultivating project can be seen as a strategy which opens up and complicates the future. The aim is not to reach solutions, but rather to ask questions, to point at how things are unsettled and to show how 'a debate is needed'. The group is inviting people to 'define common values and visions' through the discussion of – or reflecting on – ten "simple" questions. These could be read on the wall and were further elaborated in the exhibition catalogue. The stated aim was to help 'shape a vision for the future of Greenland'. To broaden the debate, the group also sought to disseminate the questions by getting them printed in a special "exhibition section" of the newspaper of Sermitsiaq, Greenland's largest paper. Also, attempts were made to get them printed and sent out to schools or public spaces such as post offices.

In this example, we see how a strategy is deployed which opens up and complicates the future. In its work leading up to the final scenario, the team sought to assemble different opinions on how to cultivate future resources and how to value them. Through their representation of its theme, it further sought to democratically distribute the process of futuring. This enacts a vision of the future as unsettled, up for debate and as a cooperative effort. Such a strategy of futuring is contrasted by the Connecting Greenland theme as a radically different way to represent and engage with the future. As he introduces the project Air+Port of the Connecting Greenland theme, main architect Bjarke Ingels states: 'Since so far we are trying to inform the public and initiate a political debate we really don't want to get lost in very complex details. When you see the Air + Port, it seems almost self-evident and straightforward. This makes it less fragile to a controversial discussion' (Kaltenbach, 2012).

In this scenario, the foundational avenue which according to Rosing should serve as a tool to guide or lead Greenlanders to make choices, is no longer seen as a winding road as in the above. Rather, it is deliberately framed as a smooth ride – or in this case one could say, a runway. The Air+Port scenario makes use of a flattened and immanent scenario of what Lash, Quick and Roberts have coined 'connections, fluxes, and objective intensities' (1998, p.4), where a runway not only metaphorically, but very concretely – as an actual structure – is presented as a way for Greenlanders to take off towards a better (connected) future.

Figure 12.3   Ready for Take-off. The Air+port project
Source: author

This team replaces the debating strategy to engage with the future with an explicit wish to represent naturalized ease. Instead of mapping complexity, the project proposes simplicity: 'Our propositions as architects can become tools in the public debate about what to do and how to embrace the future. I think for that purpose, at an early stage, to make things very simple is important' (Kaltenbach, 2012). Although no claims are made as to the matter of air transportation being in itself a simple thing (in fact, the placement of a future transatlantic airport is a very complex, politicized and controversial thing in Greenland), the proposition as a debate tool is still presented in a simple and closed manner as a way, as stated in the above, to make it less fragile to controversial discussion.

According to Rosing, the avenues of the exhibition function as foundations for choice. When we consider the two strategies in the Cultivating and Connecting scenarios for engaging with and enacting the future exemplified, the avenue can be seen as a windy road, giving us time during the exhausting journey to think about our direction and to engage in conversation with fellow travelers. Or it may be seen as a broad, straight forward airstrip where we can take off towards the future in full speed. The foundation for choice also takes on different meanings. Where the Cultivating project offers a wobbly, complex and "debatable" foundation, Connecting Greenland's foundation is strong and pre-molded.

This was illustrated at the opening in Venice, where vice-premier Jens B. Frederiksen walked straight over to the Air+port model and exclaimed how this was something which was to be in 10–15 years' time. As he stated, not necessarily at its position in the scenario – where the architects had (controversially) located it right outside of the capital of Nuuk – but still 'this is what we want'. Later, he explained to a newspaper: 'There are divided opinions on whether a new airport should be built in Nuuk. Obviously, such a discussion should take place at home in a democratic fashion. It's not the architects that ought to decide. But their proposals can definitely inspire and give us politicians some tools to be able to make better decisions' (Duus, 2012, my translation). Next, I will explore a bit further how choice and change agents in regards to the future are represented in the exhibition.

12.5 Bringing it Back Home – to Whom?

As seen with Frederiksen, the actions of making better decisions over the future were 'delayed' or delegated to a later time and place through the concept of "bringing it back home". In that sense, the scenarios were not accorded any role or agency in actual futuring by Frederiksen. As with him, many Greenlandic politicians and representatives talked during interviews and speeches about bringing the exhibition 'back home', back to Greenland to inform a debate among Greenlanders about the future. As explained by vice-chair Jens B. Frederiksen: 'When the exhibition comes to Greenland next year, I hope that it can contribute to create extra debate on our society' (Duus, 2012). In the same vein, the mayor of Sermersooq county, Asii Chemnitz Narup explained how she was excited to welcome the exhibition to Nuuk in February 2013 (personal communication), when the exhibition was to open in relation with the holding of the biannual conference of Future Greenland organized by the employers' organization of Greenland.

However, in contrast to the Biennale exhibition which was given much attention in Danish and Greenlandic press, its Greenlandic opening did not generate much public debate in either place, although the exhibition ended up being seen by many people. As reported to me by a participating colleague in Nuuk present on the first days during the opening, the exhibition was addressed as a 'has been' having lost its interest soon after Venice. Furthermore, the English exhibition texts made the exhibition hard to access for most Greenlanders. This was especially the case for text-heavy parts such as the Cultivating wall full of open questions. This goes to show that scenarios – and the politicians which enter into discussion with them – are dependent of many other arrangements and attachments (Bruun Jensen, 2007), to future. In this case, the scenarios were unable to link to – or cut across – societal controversies, unable to raise concern.

As stated by Minik Rosing, the visions of the exhibition were to 'inspire and guide public debate and help identify the possible avenues of development to build a new viable nation' (Rosing, 2012, p.9). The above example shows how future scenarios impact or craft realities of the present in a very tangible way. In relation to tourism, future scenarios such as these can be seen as cultural probes which, according to Dicks (2004), help places "'make the most of themselves' – rather like the well-toned body promoted in healthy living magazines. In this way, they can find their niche in in the new cultural economy of visitability" (p.1). Exploring the exhibition as a performative tool of futuring and crafting visitability raises our attention to how the exhibition does more than just provide inspiration. Also, it creates Greenland as somewhere to go and somewhere to experience (Dicks 2004). Brown, Rappert and Webster (2000) warn the analyst to look for the location of future-oriented agency, whether 'in a future representation, in its authors or in agents who cannot properly be said to harbor expectations of any kind of all' (p.10). Following this, it is crucial to address how a public 'at home' whom the organizers were said to work for, are represented and subsequently appointed with agency.

As already touched upon in the above, the exhibition showed almost no 'real' people. This absence of people, of human life, was not only striking inside the wooden house. In the exhibition, a Greenlandic public is strangely absent. Even if one of the explicit aims of the project was to create a project aligned with Greenlanders and Greenlandic sovereignty, the Greenlandic public is invisible or indistinguishable in the exhibition, distant in time or in place. Although the planners sought to support better and more informed choices when the exhibition was to "come back home", the exhibition in Venice seemed to take place as a "rehearsal" for discussions, which were to take place at a later stage, in a different place, with people not present (or represented, some would argue) at the exhibition. And, as it turned out, when the time came for the "real" opening, only a few people showed up.

So where do we find this future-oriented Greenlandic actor in the scenarios, who is seen as able, willing – or at least just present to take future into her hands? How does the exhibition represent those who are asked by politicians to get engaged with the future? In the exhibition, these people are strangely absent as anything else but computer generated dots plotted into the scenarios. Instead, we are left with a claimed very entrepreneurial and knowledgeable agency in the shape of the Air+port, moving at high speed by use of engineering, infrastructure and transportation systems. 'This is the future'!

During the planning of the exhibition, a lot of work was put into emphasizing that this exhibition was to move beyond the 'stereotypes' and tell other stories rooted in the initial climatic and geo-political changes and point to other agential capacities such as innovation, entrepreneurship and mobility. As argued by Michael (2000), the subjects, or entities seen as experiencing the future, whether individual or collectives, each serve a rhetorical function. One of these functions is to create a sense of responsibility, which – as a downside – also works as a delimiter to those or that, which we do *not* take responsibility for. When the exhibition talks about Greenland as an innovation or educational hub, it neglects or others those 'unconnected' but statistically very 'present' Greenlanders without jobs or education. When constant reference is made to the future as a mobile space, those stuck in the bygd often without road connections to the exterior are left behind.

12.6   What the Future Might Build – Concluding Remarks

As the exhibition commissioner, DAC explicitly stated a wish to accommodate for new voices in the architectural envisioning of a Greenlandic future. They did so by inviting a number of architects, urban planners and engineers as well as students and teachers from an architect school and a technical university – even a researcher on branding and tourism was brought on board. However, in spite of the motivation for the exhibition being Greenland's new global importance or relevancy, the planning was still framed within a national or Commonwealth setting, where DAC, the Danish pavilion and Commonwealth planners discussed the future of Greenlanders. Even though actors such as Chinese investors or multinational enterprises were constantly mentioned or implicitly assumed, none were urged to enter into dialogue on Greenland's future.

What choices can or should be made with and about the future? In his work with climate related future scenarios, John Urry introduces the concept of the fitness landscape, which to him describes how 'any new physical-and-social technology has to find its place within the environment that is structured by the pre-existing patterning of that landscape' (Urry, 2008, p.264). So how did the proposed futures sketched by the two scenarios, loosely translatable as "new physical-and-social technologies" resonate with the present? This is still an open question since in the time of writing, the exhibition is still "touring". This does not however restrict us from addressing the performative powers of the scenarios and how they enable (or disable) choice and certain forms of accessibility, activity and visitability. As seen, the two scenarios frame the future and the way *towards* the future very differently. While the first deployed strategies of *complexification/inclusion* in order to allow many voices, controversies and insecurities to be heard, the second used a strategy of *simplification/exclusion* by not engaging in or even ignoring controversy. In doing so, they create different grounds for the future and for the ability to engage with it. Both ways can be seen as ways of futuring – however with different tools, means and outcomes.

The case shows how the actual materialization of the exhibited scenarios required shortcuts, reductions and othering displaying some futures rather than others. By interrogating the materialized representations of the future at the exhibition and the practices by which they came to matter, the analysis shows how a number of futures and related agencies were enacted into being and how they connected and conflicted, as is exemplified through the two scenarios. The Cultivating theme addressed the future as complex and unsettled, hence seeking to create what Whatmore terms a generative and disordering event (2009) in which, according to Stengers, reasoning is forced to slow down hereby creating 'an opportunity to arouse a slightly different awareness of the problems and situations mobilizing us' (Stengers 2005, p. 994). In the reverse manner, the Connecting team explicitly sought to cut across or erase complexity and controversy in their scenario, conveying a "speeding up" of the future.

According to Mol, 'the reality we live with is one performed in a variety of practices' (Mol, 1999, p.74). This performative understanding of reality as multiple also stipulates that we are not only *confronted* with different realities created through practices and objects, but are also (at least potentially) given the option and possibility to *choose* between them. It is therefore vital to acknowledge that the way that places are told, arranged and crafted – be it as future visions –impacts on how they are in fact made real, made livable in some ways rather than others. As a consequence, 'if actors are to secure successfully for themselves a specific kind of future then they must engage in a range of rhetorical, organizational and material activities through which the future might be able to be "colonized"' (Brown, Rappert and Webster, 2000, p.3).

As a rhetorical, organizational and material undertaking, the exhibition displays different futuring attempts which display that 'the voices which declare a right to speak to the future are arguably more numerous, drawing on much wider, more heterogeneous forms of social authority' (Brown, Rappert and Webster, p.5). However, as was also shown, the wish to include, disclose, engage and accord agency to an even broader range of actors, such as the Greenlandic public or international investors had its limitations. For instance, engaging the Greenlandic public seemed difficult. In spite of the inability to raise public debate on the spot, hope is that discussions and reflections first sparked at the exhibition in Venice may continue. Under a new title, *Greenland – heading for the global hub*, the exhibition on tour (still, increasingly) urges us to ask: a global hub *for whom*? By attuning to questions of how the future is made possible and how it may be studied in the present as exemplified here, the investigation of how Greenlandic – and other – futurings happen and are made possible continues.

References

Adolphsen, J. and Greiffenberg, T., 1997. Greenland and modernity. *Socio-economic Developments in Greenland and in Other Small Nordic Jurisdictions*, 27.

Andersen, M.K., 2012a. Grønland – I midten af verden (Greenland – In the middle of the world). *Weekendavisen*, 24 February.

Andersen, M.K., 2012b. Grønland – Det nye middelhav (Greenland – The new Mediterranean). *Weekendavisen*, 31 August.

Avango, D., Nilsson, D. E. and Roberts, P., 2013. Assessing Arctic futures: Voices, resources and governance. *The Polar Journal*, 3(2), p.431–446.

Bjørst, L.R., 2012. Climate testimonies and climate crisis narratives. Inuit delegated to speak on behalf of the climate. *Acta Borelia: A Nordic Journal of Circumpolar Societies*, 29(1), p.98–113.

Brown, N., Rappert, B. and Webster, A., eds., 2000. *Contested futures. A sociology of prospective techno-science*. Aldershot: Ashgate.

Bruun Jensen, C., 2007. Sorting attachments: Usefulness of STS in healthcare practice and policy. *Science as Culture*, 16(3), pp.237–251.

Bruun Jensen, C., 2010. *Ontologies for developing things: Making health care futures through technology*. Rotterdam: Sense Publishers.

Callon, M., 2008. Economic markets and the rise of interactive agencement. In: T. Pinch and R. Swedberg, eds. *Living in a material world: Economic sociology meets science and technology studies*. Cambridge: MIT Press. pp. 29–56.

DAC, 2011. *Greenlandic and Danish architects to develop future visions of Greenland*. [online] Available at: <http://www.dac.dk/da/service-sider/nyheder/2011/september/groenlandske-og-danske-arkitekter-skal-i-faellesskab-udvikle-visioner-for-fremtidens-groenland/> [Accessed 5 October 2012].

Dicks, B. (2004) Culture on Display. The Production of Contemporary Visitability. McGraw-Hill International.

Kaltenbach, F., 2012. Possible Greenland – The Earth as common ground. Interview with Bjarke Ingels. [online] Available at: <http://www.detail-online.com/architecture/news/possible-greenland-the-earth-as-common-ground-interview-with-bjarke-ingels-019886.html> [Accessed 5 October 2012].

Duus, S.D., 2012. Grønlandsk stolthed over eksponering (Greenlandic pride over exposure). *Sermitsiaq*, [online] 28 *August*. Available at: <http://sermitsiaq.ag/node/134649> [Accessed 5 October 2013].

Ifversen, K., 2012. Værsgo Grønland, fremtiden er jeres (Here you go, Greenland – The future is yours). *Politiken*, 1 September.

Latour, B., 1993. *We have never been modern*. Cambridge, MA: Harvard University Press.

Latour, B., 2004. Why has critique run out of steam? From matters of fact to matters of concern. *Critical Inquiry*, 30(2), pp.225–248.

Latour, B., 2010. *The making of law. An ethnography of the Conseil d'Etat*. Cambridge: Polity Press.

Lash, S., Quick, A. and Roberts, R., 1998. Introduction: Millenniums and catastrophic times. In: S. Lash, A. Quick and R. Roberts, eds. *Time and value*. Oxford: Blackwell, pp. 1–15.

Michael, M., 2000. Futures of the present. From performativity to prehension. In: N. Brown, B. Rappert and A. Webster, eds. *Contested futures. A sociology of prospective techno-science*. Aldershot: Ashgate, pp.21–43.

Mol, A.,1999. Ontological politics. A word and some questions. *The Sociological Review*, 47(S1), 74–89.

Mol, A., 2002. *The body multiple: Ontology in medical practice*. Duke University Press.

Ren, C.B. and Gyimóthy, S., 2013. Transforming and contesting nation branding strategies: Denmark at the Expo 2010. *Place Branding and Public Diplomacy*, 9(1), pp.17–29.

Ren, C.B., 2012. Envisioning Greenland: Contested naturecultures in the making. *Conditions*, 11/12, pp.154–155.

Ren, C.B. and Ooi, C-S., 2013. Auto-communicating micro-orientalism: Articulating 'Denmark' in China at the Shanghai Expo. *Asia Europe Journal*, 11(2), pp.129–145.

Rosing, M., 2012. Curator statement. Greenland belongs to all Greenlanders – all ground is common ground. *Conditions*, 11/12 (& Possible Greenland exhibition catalogue), pp.8–9.

Stengers, I. (2005) The cosmopolitical proposal. In Latour, B. and Weibel (eds.) *Making things public: Atmospheres of democracy*, pp. 994–1003.

Strathern, M., 1991. *Partial connections*. Savage: Rowan and Littlefield.

Team Cultivating, 2012. Educational material. *Sermitsiaq*, August 2012.

Urry, J., 2008. Climate change, travel and complex futures. *British Journal of Sociology*, 59(2), pp.261–279.

Vahl, K., 2012. Fremtidens Grønland (The future of Greenland). *Grønlandsposten*, 8 August.

Venturini, T., 2010. Diving in magma: how to explore controversies with actor-network theory. *Public Understanding of Science*, 19(3), pp. 258–273.

Venturini, T., 2012. Building on faults: how to represent controversies with digital methods. *Public Understanding of Science*, 21(7), pp. 796–812.

Whatmore, S. J., 2009. Mapping knowledge controversies: science, democracy and the redistribution of expertise. *Progress in Human Geography*, 33(5), pp. 587–598.

Chapter 13

Postscript: Making Headways, Expanding the Field and Slowing Down

Carina Ren, René van der Duim and Gunnar Thór Jóhannesson

In May 2014, Copenhagen was the host of the Eurovision song contest, an international singing competition held since 1956 with competitors from 37 countries and 170 million television viewers globally. To organise this mega event, a holding company was established by Wonderful Copenhagen, the destination marketing organization of Copenhagen, in order to pool resources with the Copenhagen Municipality, the capital region of Denmark and the real estate company owning the former shipyard, where Eurovision was set to take place.

A consortium, entitled Host City Copenhagen, was created for the purpose of organising event related activities. Among many other things, Host City Copenhagen was in charge of creating outreach through a week-long program of activities and events all over city. It included a Eurovision village in a central square in Copenhagen, a "Fan Mil" along the walking street of Strøget, a Fan café and a number of concerts, school contests etc. "Eurovision weddings" were offered by the municipality, a kissing chain down the Fan Mile was arranged by the AIDS-foundation, a Danish NGO, and a garden termed the "Green Room", referring to the place where Eurovision contestants sit while awaiting the results, was established in the Eurovillage. This organic herb garden was to connect the Eurovision in Copenhagen with its status as European Green Capital 2014[1], as was the "Water Bar", where by passers where served fresh tap water from the unpolluted undergrounds of the city.

Through these sub-events leading up to the actual song contest, Eurovision was turned into "more than a TV show", as several of the interviewed stakeholders explained. Their accounts as well as the organizational scheme and program sketched out in the above show how organizing large events often transcend the lines of public, civic and private sectors and illustrate the intricate and collaborative work which lies behind such endeavour. However, the crossing of established administrative, corporate, political or other boundaries in such cross-sectorial and innovative set-ups creates challenges, related to what we might see, in line with the themes of this book, as new and emerging encounters. With new

---

1   This description is drawn from fieldwork on the planning of Eurovision carried out by Carina Ren in January to May 2013 along with colleague Morten Krogh Petersen from Aalborg University.

bed fellows and new "co-creation settings" also followed a range of lurking and, at times, rising controversies. At the 2014 Eurovision especially discussions of costs and outcomes became controversial issues to hit the news headlines. Fieldwork, interviews and roundtables discussions with involved public and private event stakeholders made it clear that manoeuvring between different perceptions of value and determining a good outcome were complex challenges amongst and between the now collaborating entities.

We bring forward Eurovision as an example of how public/private collaboration and other types of partnerships and alliances are increasingly being accentuated for their ability to foster new kinds of inventions (Thrift, 2006) by bringing together different resources and types of knowledge and skill. Also in tourism, strategic alliances, co-creation, user involvement and public/private partnerships are increasingly heralded for their potential in fostering innovative tourism solutions (Hjalager and Nordin, 2011). This type of boundary crossing collaboration is just one, blatant, example of how tourism – as well as related activities or businesses (or what else we might choose to coin it) in the areas of hospitality, leisure, sports and events is increasingly developed in collaboration with or even seen as integrated into other parts of the social, such as city planning, cultural policy and regional development. We would take it even further by suggesting that tourism and the social are increasingly becoming co-constituted. However, while many have noted a rise of co-creation, the people, organizations and companies who engage in cross-cutting collaborations still have only few conceptual and analytical aids to grasp it with. In the following, we will depart from co-creation as a "social fact" in order to tease out how this book might be used to deal with and reflect upon this raising trend, but also more broadly with co-existence in tourism at a large.

We will do so by first highlighting two main points drawn from our engagement with encounters and controversies in tourism, that of *expanding the field* and of *slowing down*, after which we discuss how a new relationality allows us to see tourism as a 'knot in motion' (Haraway, 2003:6) and to think about tourism development as an exercise in co-existence.

13.1   Two Learnings: Expanding the Field and Slowing Down

In this book, we have proposed two central things. Our first proposition has been to *expand the field* of investigation when researching tourism in order not to limit our attention to an all too enclosed area of what might be termed "tourism proper". As illustrated through the Eurovision case, organisations, budgets and policies do not only stem from or direct themselves towards tourism related outcomes, but may also be about citizenship, national or local identity, values, pride, city or business development or other issues mentioned to us during our fieldwork. As the contributors and we have sought to argue throughout this present volume, tourism is not only about tourism, but also – and in some situations even *mostly* – about other aspects of the social. Tourism orderings (or ordering attempts) connect or disengage with other ordering attempts and enact different versions of these orders and their relations. Hence, there is no one tourism order as the common description of tourism as a homogeneous sector with relatively clear boundaries implies. Neither are there any stable set of types of tourism available of for instance, "nature tourism", "cultural tourism" etc. Rather there are multiple tourism related orderings that play part in the continuous becoming of society and space and which our research practice plays part in accomplishing. This multiplicity of tourism realities should, we believe, be reflected in our empirical data, our research methodologies, our readings and the ongoing dialogue with other research fields. Also, and importantly, our understanding of tourism realities as multiple should also, we believe, be distinguishable in our attempts of doing ontological politics, for instance in the scholarly or other engagement with tourism development.

We have attempted to show here how developing tourism is empirically related to other fields of activity – be it conservation, fisheries, cooking, arts, architecture or other. But why focus on controversy? And how is this new in tourism studies? As we proposed in the introduction and as also argued by Venturini (2010:262), the controversy is a resistance to reduction (see also Munk in this volume). Hence, the controversy invites us to make use of a number of procedures, through which tourism emerges as a complex and relational entity. Such procedures also lead us to the second proposition which involves the *slowing down of reasoning*. As proposed by Stengers (2005), the slowing down of reasoning entails the 'opportunity to arouse a slightly different awareness of the problems and situations mobilizing us' (p. 994). Slowing down, staying open, alert and attentive to the many intricate ways in which tourism attaches itself to an array of other orderings and attachments (Jensen, 2007) might prone us, sensitize us, to our field. By contemplating the controversial nature of things, we come to spend time in the field, with our data. As a way to depart from a view on controversies as "bad situations" in need of "fixing" (Petersen, 2014), offered in both critical and managerial tourism research, we abstain from seeing the controversy as a merely counterproductive social phenomenon. By attending to controversies, an alternative space for critique is opened up, one that does not depend on fixed forms or identities, but draws on the process of formation or orderings of those. As showcased in many of the present chapters, the controversies are also an opportunity, a fruitful way to studying the social in its making. In controversial encounters, parties take on new or more strongly defined roles and subject positions and construct or negotiate new realities.

Returning once again to the Eurovision case, a heated debate arose in national press of the municipality's decision to let some of its employees volunteer for Eurovision in their working time. While this issue certainly raised political, fiscal and administrative controversy (Could public workers really take part in this during working hours? Do they have time for it? What would such an engagement cost public taxpayers and how to create accountability?), the municipality saw it as a new opportunity to renegotiate the meaning and status of being a municipal employee. To the municipality, taking part in this event enabled them, or so they were hoping, to redefine the public opinion of the municipality as a work place.

Also, the event became an opportunity for them to upgrade the competencies of selected employees, for instance in project management and event planning. Traditionally, taking on event manager roles and skills have been uncalled for – or purely unwanted – in public administration, but in an increasingly competitive state (Cerny, 1997), the state – and hence public officers and administrators – are increasingly asked to enter a private market. In this light, "rehearsing" new roles in such a setting makes good sense in a competitive state logic and even though controversy was raised, the municipality did not perceive the "blurry" connection to the Eurovision event as negative, but rather as a new fact, which they were trying to handle as best as possible. In this case, the collaborative setup of the Eurovision worked as an experimental platform for the involved parties in which new roles and subject positioned were prompted and could be explored.

13.2   New Relationality?

Throughout the book, we argue for a relational approach to tracing the connections along which tourism and its necessary (but never predefined or presupposed) "others" emerge. In that we follow the insight provided especially by the mobilities paradigm that social theory and research needs to become mobile in order to respond to the post-modern condition (Urry, 2000; Hannam, Sheller and Urry, 2006: Büscher and Urry, 2009). Much talk has been about relational approaches and relational turns in the social sciences the last decade or so and the field of tourism research is no exception (Cohen and Cohen, 2012). Often this emphasis has focussed on relations between points, as in network topology evident for instance in many early ANT studies but less so on other kinds of relationality, which may be better described as fluid.

In the beginning of this book, we described how this entails not seeing tourism encounters as a potential clash between already created entities, but rather to look at how the entities and the boundaries between them are shaped in and *through* the encounter and thus to perceive tourism as a gathering of or a knot of intersecting and entangled "lines of becoming". In the words of Deleuze and Guattari: 'A becoming is neither one nor two, nor the relation of the two; it is the in-between' (2004, p. 323 in Ingold, 2011, p. 83). In the case of Eurovision, this means that we should not already expect or presuppose to find an "inherent" controversy between public and private stakeholders when researching Eurovision as a cross-sectorial innovation project. Rather, we should focus on how the encounter between new parties is part of shaping them, their roles and activities anew, hereby enacting new things into being. As an innovation project it might furthermore usefully be studied as a "knot in motion", in a forward mode, coming into being through process of improvisation (Ingold and Hallam, 2007). To read or research innovation or any other thing forward is to understand it as multiple "goings on" and to join in with its formative process instead of starting from the end product (Ingold, 2008).

We would like to end by urging tourism researchers to open up for multiple versions of relationality. Far from issuing a new turn or a paradigm shift then, together with the contributors of the present book, we claim the need for a stronger and more nuanced engagement with relationality of tourism. We need to critically question a common understanding of relationality as ordered into a network of nodes and 'lines of interaction' (Ingold, 2011, p. 63) and open actively for a more nuanced framing of relations as "lines of becoming" that may eventually be figured as a network. Approaching tourism as a bundle of threads or lines that may engage or disengage with co-existing trajectories of other things indeed blurs the figure of tourism as conventionally framed. It does also not meet the expectations of providing tourism research with a paradigm to follow. However, it highlights the ontological politics involved in tourism development as well as tourism research and opens up possibilities to interfere with alternative or already present tourism orderings.

References

Büscher, M., and Urry, J., 2009. Mobile Methods and the Empirical. *European Journal of Social Theory, 12*(1), pp. 99–116. doi: 10.1177/1368431008099642

Cerny, P. G., 1997. Paradoxes of the Competition State: The Dynamics of Political Globalization. *Government and Opposition, 32*(2), pp. 251–274. doi: 10.1111/j.1477–7053.1997.tb00161.x

Cohen, E., and Cohen, S. A., 2012. Current Sociological Theories and Issues in Tourism. *Annals of Tourism Research, 39*(4), pp. 2177–2202. doi: http://dx.doi.org/10.1016/j.annals.2012.07.009

Hannam, K., Sheller, M., and Urry, J., 2006. Editorial: Mobilities, Immobilites and Moorings. *Mobilities, 1*(1), pp.1–22.

Haraway, D., 2003. *The Companion Species Manifesto: Dogs, People, and Significant Otherness*. Chicago: Prickly Paradigm Press.

Hjalager, A. M., and Nordin, S., 2011. User-driven Innovation in Tourism – A Review of Methodologies. *Journal of Quality Assurance in Hospitality & Tourism, 12*(4), 289–315.

Ingold, T., 2008. *Bringing things to life: Creative entanglements in a world of materials*. [online] Available at: <http://www.reallifemethods.ac.uk/events/vitalsigns/programme/documents/vital-signs-ingold-bringing-things-to-life.pdf> [Accessed 19 February 2014].

Ingold, T., 2011. *Being Alive: Essays on movment, knowledge and description*. London and New York: Routledge.

Ingold, T., and Hallam, E., 2007. Creativity and Cultural Improvisation: An Introduction. In T. Ingold and E. Hallam (Eds.), *Creativity and Cultural Improvisation* (pp. 1–24). Oxford: Berg.

Jensen, C.B., 2007. Sorting Attachments: Usefulness of STS in Healthcare Practice and Policy. *Science as Culture* 16 (3), pp. 237–251

Petersen, M. K., 2014. Contributions from Techno-Anthropological Ethnography to Innovation and Design Projects. In Børsen, T. and L. Botin, eds. *What is techno-anthropology?* Aalborg: Aalborg University Press, pp. 365–384

Stengers, I., 2005. The cosmopolitical proposal. In Latour, B. and P. Weibel (eds.) *Making things public: Atmospheres of democracy*, pp. 994–1003.

Thrift, N., 2006. Re-inventing Invention: new tendencies in capitalist commodification. *Economy and Society* 35(2), pp.279–306

Urry, J., 2000. *Sociology Beyond Societies: Mobilities for the Twenty-first Century.* London: Routledge.

Venturini, T., 2010. Diving in magma: how explore controversies with actor-network theory, *Public Understanding of Science,* 19(3), pp. 258–273.

Index

Printed in Great Britain, Germany for distribution worldwide in same
EU representative: CPSR Compliance GmbH, Kaulbachstraße 22, 80539 München,
Verlag GmbH, Kaulbachstraße 22, 80539 München, Germany